The Embrace
Forty Days in the Desert

Bruce Benson

The Embrace
© 2012 Bruce Benson

Bruce Benson
103 Timber Creek Road
Hendersonville, North Carolina 28739
1-828-692-0370
bensonegypt@hotmail.com

ISBN 978-0-9738725-2-1

Printed in the USA

A Journal...

To the Embrace...
that binds us all in love and friendship

To the Embrace . . .
that binds us all in love and friendship

I drove my son Jake, to school this morning. I got him there before 6:30 so he could sign up for Driver's Education. The first 30 students get signed up, and at 15 years old, he's really keen. Then I went back and woke my wife Linda, and frantically searched for my wallet. I was approaching panic mode when I found it going through the clothes I had packed in my big suitcase. Heart-rate slowed . . . to miss my flight . . . ?

Linda woke my other son Tiberius, and daughter Ally, and I hugged them both.

"I love you, Dad," said Ti, 13 years old. Ally was a little whimpery.

On the way to the airport Linda said Ally had asked why I had to go.

"It's something he feels he has to do," she had answered.

Probably not understandable to an 11-year-old. Or would it be more understandable? Would a child get it better than an adult? Certainly Linda was a long time coming around on this. And I still doubt myself. *What the hell am I doing?*

But I do believe in the embrace. There is my rock.

Reading *the Economist* on the plane, I would vacillate between hope and despair—huge ups and downs. But I just have to think that I have a job to do, and go do it. Don't question it, just do it.

I am going to Egypt for forty days to pick up garbage near the Great Pyramids of Giza—my forty days in the desert.

There was a little child sucking on a soother across the aisle from me on the plane. She was actually in my seat, as the mother and daughter had been assigned aisle seats across from each other. They switched before I arrived, and I readily consented.

"I go to Grace Church," she said to me out of the blue. "What church do you go to?"

I hesitated.

Seeing my hesitation the mother began explaining to the girl, "Some people don't go . . . "

I gently interrupted her.

"I go to many churches," I said to the girl. "I believe in something called the embrace." Then I asked the engaging little girl if I could have one of the crackers she had in a plastic container. She eagerly pried the lid off and gave me one.

"I like to share," she said, smiling.

"See, you believe in the embrace too," I said.

February 3
"Ya big dummy!"

I'm in Egypt now, in my room at the Siag Pyramid Hotel. The room is somewhat shabby. It has three small beds in it and a view of the pyramids from the window. I had not realized Cairo is developed right up to the pyramids, a sprawling city on one side, the great Sahara desert on the other.

Everything in the hotel seems to be in a state of decay, and the noise of Cairo outside the window is almost deafening when the big glass door to the patio is open.

It looks like they're constructing a freeway above Sakkara Road, the very street the hotel is on. I wonder what that'll do to business.

I've got a tv, fridge, a phone, and a power source. I'm charging my cell phone now, then I'll do the camera, then this computer.

I was met outside Cairo Airport by Hamid Ahmed holding a piece of paper with my name on it. It made me feel like a rock star. He was friendly enough, but I think he was a little unsure of his English, as he rarely spoke to me and engaged in animated conversation with the driver in Arabic.

When I came to Egypt two years ago with my son, Jake, then 13, three people came to get us at the airport. As we got into a small van, one man sat beside the driver. Jake and I were in the seat behind them, and another man sat behind us. My imagination went wild. So much news about kidnaping and terrorist attacks in Muslim countries, particularly the Middle East, had me paranoid.

Why would three people come to pick us up? I thought. *There can only be one reason, they mean to take us hostage.*

Terrified for our safety, I looked at the door handle to the van door. It didn't look locked. I began to form a plan. If we slowed down, I could probably open the door with my right hand, grab the unsuspecting Jake blissfully staring out the window with my left, and use my right shoulder to push the door open. The momentum from shoulder-blocking the door should carry us out of the van and into the street. Traffic looked bad, but we would have to take our chances with other vehicles on the road.

The driver and the man beside him were looking forward, so they wouldn't be a problem. But I had to act when the man behind us wasn't looking. It was quite clever of them to have us surrounded.

The vehicle slowed as we rounded a corner, and I could see the traffic ahead was creeping along slowly. Carefully, so as not to alert our captors of my bold plan, I turned my head to my left, pretending to be looking out the window. I was hoping my peripheral vision would be enough to let me know what the man behind us was looking at. It wasn't. So, risking all, I slowly turned my head further, as if I was maintaining eye contact with something that interested me as we drove past it. I tensed up, now would be the moment. If he didn't have a gun on us, and didn't appear ready to pounce should we attempt an escape, we would make our move. I turned my head further.

The man was fast asleep, with his head tilted to the sky and bobbing up and down in synch with the bumps in the road, drool coming out of the right side of his mouth.

The driver today was crazy. I remember now the psychotic driving in Cairo. It's absolutely insane. I'm sure many people are killed every day. We narrowly missed at least twenty people and a hundred cars. The lines in the pavement marking the lanes are not even considered as mere suggestions, and bedlam rules. I have always felt there is a pattern to the flow of traffic that seems to mimic life itself. The speeding up, slowing down, getting on and off the freeway, all can be metaphors for what we do in our own lives. Here in Egypt, the pace is more frantic than in North America, and much more dangerous, as is life itself more frantic and dangerous in this country.

Despite the chaos, with horns honking and lights flashing, we made it to the hotel miraculously unscathed.

Hamid took my passport and asked me to wait around the corner as he checked me in. I couldn't see what was happening, and I was nervous paying $915 cash to Hamid for my stay. I had paid 25 per cent of my room fee upon booking, the remainder to be paid in cash upon my arrival. Since the deal was made with Hamid's company, they had to pay the hotel, taking their cut out of it. Hamid did not want me to know what that cut would be.

I had thoughts of Hamid shooting the breeze with the front-desk people.

"So, how ya doin'?" he'd say. "What about them Israelis invading Palestine, huh?" Then he'd book me in for one night and leave with his pockets full of cash *and* my passport, never to be seen again.

Fortunately, I had nothing to fear. He was as honest as most Egyptians, which in my experience is very honest.

But you do have to be careful. On the way from the airport we stopped at a small store for some Stella, a popular Egyptian beer, and I got ripped off big time. The store operator said ten Egyptian pounds per beer, or about US $2. The exchange rate is close to five pounds to a dollar. I said I wanted eight bottles of beer, he charged me for nine, and gave me six. Quite the feat. I didn't figure it out until I was in my room. Oh well, I am in Egypt, and Hamid was rushing me. The three guys in the beer shop are probably howling with laughter at the big dummy.

That's what my wife would call me as I was sorting out recyclables from garbage I had picked up in Hendersonville. She'd imitate Fred Sanford speaking to his son Lamont on the television sitcom, Sanford and Son.

"Ya big dummy."

Linda was never a fan of the Trashman.

I first picked trash in my hometown of Gimli, a small fishing village settled by Icelanders in 1875 in the province of Manitoba, Canada. In my youth I spent two summers working as a garbage man, Trash-man, a job I thoroughly enjoyed.

I remember running down the back lanes of Gimli's seven streets, me on one side of the gravel road, my partner Dave Debrecen on the other. We would compete to see who could throw more garbage into the hopper at the back of the garbage truck, stopping only to push the button to have the giant claw reach out and pull the refuse into the dark abyss behind it.

"You are the only one who can *almost* keep up to me," Dave would often say. "*Almost.*"

I thought I actually did keep up with him, but didn't push it.

A garbage man for six years, Dave had other plans.

"I won't be a garbage man all my life," he said often, shaking his head, or stroking his thin moustache. "I'm going to be a teacher. First I'll get my grade 12, then I'll go to university."

I really liked Dave, but doubted he would ever be able to realize his ambitions.

Rounding out our crew was Gordie Hussey, our chain-smoking driver who had only a few years to retirement. I discovered early that Gordie was a product of the Great Depression. Every opportunity he had to save a penny, he took.

"Don't hit the button!" he'd often yell out to us. Then he'd come out of the truck to the back to see what gems we had thrown into the hopper. At the pharmacy in town, there were magazines galore. The covers were ripped off and sent back to show they hadn't been sold, but the rest of the magazine was there in the trash bins. Gordie had a predilection for skin mags, and I imagine he had quite the collection.

"Why pay for them, when you can get them for free?" he would say out of the side of his mouth, a cigarette slowly burning.

Gordie rolled his own cigarettes, and he rolled them so tight it was impossible to get the smoke through the densely packed tobacco.

"I don't inhale," he told me.

"Then why do you smoke?"

When Gordie was working on a highway crew as a young man, his boss hollered at him for standing around when he should have been working.

"What about them?" Gordie said, pointing to his co-workers who seemed to be loafing as well.

"They're having a smoke break."

Gordie started smoking.

At the grocery store garbage bins he would pore over the discarded fruit, like a discerning crow looking for the juicy bits.

"They throw it out, but lots of it is still good."

Gordie took pains to show me just how clever he was.

"See this," he said to me once, holding up a sirloin steak he found in the garbage behind the local IGA grocery store.

"It's green!" I said to him.

"It's only green on this side," he said, pointing. "The other half is still good."

This was too much for me, and I looked at him to see if he was joking. For the first time I noticed a green pallor to his skin, a hue not unlike the meat he held in his hand. I vowed never to eat at his house.

Gordie retired a few years later, but I still see him from time to time, almost thirty years later. He's well into his eighties now, still drives, smokes cigarettes and drinks beer. Maybe he knew what he was talking about.

Dave, unlike my predictions, quit the garbage truck shortly after the end of that summer. He did get his grade 12, went to university and earned a Bachelor and Master's in Education. He taught up north for some 25 years, retiring as a principal at a young age. He now manages many residential properties he acquired along the way.

Last October, returning from a day of commercial fishing on Lake Winnipeg to my home on Fourth Avenue, I noticed a big trash can had been knocked over in the schoolyard. Garbage was spread out over the well-trimmed grass.

"Look at that, that's just terrible," I said to my brother-in-law Laurence sitting next to me.

"Why don't you go clean it up?" he asked. "You're going all the way to Egypt to pick up garbage, why not pick up some right here?"

The bellhop carried my suitcase up to my room. His name is Samir.

"Call me Sammy."

He might weigh a hundred pounds soaking wet. My big bag was half his weight.

He said he can bring beer right to my room, if I want. I think we'll become fast friends.

Sammy said I can get a guide and a car for eight hours for 150 pounds. Perhaps I'll take him up on that for a couple half days. I want to go to the Canadian embassy, and Sammy said it's not a good idea to walk to the pyramids.

"Some young boys might say 'come here, have a drink,'" he said, shrugging his shoulders. The implication was clear. I may be waylaid by some young hoods.

I already miss Linda and the kids, and have tried to call the operator but to no avail. I will go downstairs to the front desk soon, and arrange to make a call.

Stupid me, I forgot to bring a hairbrush, and warm clothes. *Ya big dummy*. I *am* in the desert, and the desert gets cold at night. I'll pick up some clothes tomorrow. Here again, I think Sammy may come in handy.

I plan to start picking trash tomorrow. I hope I find a good place to work.

It is a little unreal, being in Egypt surrounded by Egyptians speaking Arabic, when what seems moments ago I was in Hendersonville, driving Jake to school. Thankfully most people working at the hotel speak some English.

I called the front desk and they said I can use their mobile phone to call home. It'll cost three US dollars per minute. Then the health club called to tell me I could use the gym for 50 pounds an hour, and I could have a massage down there for 200 pounds, or in my room for 300 pounds.

Why is it 100 pounds more in my room? I thought. *Happy ending?* I'll stay away from that.

I went down and picked up my passport from Edward, a comedian with a pony tail and an impressive beer belly working the front desk.

"Is Edward an Egyptian name?" I asked him.

"My parents used English names for all their children," he said, shrugging his shoulders.

Then I met Fatih, who runs the gift shop, and I bought a two-dollar papyrus. He didn't have exact change for my ten dollars, so I'll take one on each of the next four days. It will give me an excuse to converse with him.

In his early sixties, Fatih is probably the equal to at least two Samirs in weight and height. A very affable fellow, he speaks good English.

Appropriately, I met Moxim the bartender at the bar, as well as Figurala, who I think is the number's man, an accountant for the hotel. I also met a woman who has quite the sense of humor herself, Rabbob. She gave me a piece of cake, then disappeared. She was kidding Moxim about wanting to get married again.

"He wants to marry someone from your country," she said, laughing.

Day 1 in the desert
"Police always want money."

I slept fitfully last night, jet-lag. Also, that joy-fear coursing through me. *What the hell am I doing here?*

There's a nightclub on the tenth floor, and it seems the party goes late into the night. That kept me up as well. When I couldn't sleep, I drank a few Stella. I left the TV on all night for company. I was feeling lonely, a stranger in a strange land, on an even stranger mission.

I went down for breakfast and Samir greeted me with a ready smile.

"Have you had breakfast yet?" he asked with concern in his eyes. I guess I was looking a little rough around the edges.

"No, not yet."

"Then go have some," he said, gently touching my arm and turning me in the direction of the restaurant.

The breakfast buffet had croissants, various buns, boiled eggs, tomatoes, cucumbers, an omelet with green and red things in it, what looked like porridge, and jam and honey. A waiter delivered coffee to my table. I ate two eggs and had a croissant with honey.

After breakfast I returned to Samir's station beside the front desk, and he introduced me to Mohamed, my driver for the day. Like Samir, Mohamed was also quick to smile, and I liked him immediately. In his fifties with balding gray hair and a thick gray moustache, his brown eyes seemed to emanate warmth.

We got in his cab and I tried to communicate to him that I wanted to buy a hat and a hairbrush. He didn't get it, despite Samir's earlier assurances to me that he spoke really good English.

He did, however, understand that I wanted to go to the pyramids. I guess that's a universal desire with tourists. He drove through an alley strewn with horses and camels, and riders waiting for tourists. The animals were being fed bright green clover, and I could smell their pungent aroma. The Egyptians were all dressed in traditional garb. With the exception of Mohamed's car and its occupants, the scene could have been played out thousands of years ago.

Mohamed took me to see a very slick salesman who had me on a horse going into the pyramids area within minutes. He was good.

"I like you, you are Canadian, I will give you special deal," and on and on, with constant touching of the shoulder in commiseration and comradery.

After I agreed to do it, (money back guarantee mind you, if I didn't like it) he introduced Nasser, my guide. Nasser and I got on the horses and off we went. It was a good half hour ride to the pyramids. I didn't leave Nasser or my horse Sukkar, for three hours.

I was glad to see there was much litter all around the pyramids and the Sphinx. I have lots of work to do. Months ago someone told me a friend of theirs had been to the pyramids recently and there was no litter at all. Such is not the case.

We walked around the pyramids and I went in a small one, meant for one of Pharaoh Khufu's daughters. Khufu built the largest pyramid, named Khufu's Horizon, and it is the last of the original seven wonders of the world. I have heard it said, "Man fears time, but time fears the pyramids."

I saw lots of garbage walking around the Sphinx as well, mostly plastic bottles and pop cans.

There are three entrances to the Giza plateau for cars and people, and one for horses and camels. Because of where the entrance is situated, we approached the pyramids from the south, coming up to the smallest of the three large pyramids first, Menkaure. This pyramid was named 'Menkaure is Divine.'

It was quite moving, as we traveled across the empty sand-dunes, going down into the trough of a dune, only to rise up over the crest of the . . . wave, if you will . . . and see the mighty pyramids. I'm sure Napoleon's men were completely awed by the sight when they came upon it.

"From atop these pyramids, forty centuries look down upon you," Napoleon Bonaparte said to inspire his soldiers before the Battle of Giza in 1798.

I read a story about Napoleon spending time alone in the king's chamber in the great pyramid, and coming out visibly shaken. Apparently he never told anyone what he saw, but his career went straight downhill. On his deathbed he started to tell a friend what he had seen, and then stopped, saying "what's the use, you'd never believe me."

It is astonishing to think three generations built all the pyramids of Giza and the Sphinx, in the Fourth Dynasty of the Old Kingdom. Khufu built the largest, (the world's tallest building until the 1900's) his son Khafre the middle pyramid, named Khafre is Great, (not as tall as his father's but situated on higher ground so as to appear larger) and the Sphinx, and his grandson Menkaure built the smallest. The three generations of this dynasty ruled Egypt from 2589 BC until 2504 BC, a mere 85 years. Many people know the pyramids by their Greek names, Cheops, Khephren, and Mykerinas respectively. But I will use the Egyptian names in my journal, in deference to the Egyptians.

As for the Sphinx, no one knows what the ancient Egyptians called the magnificent statue. Carved from a single mass of limestone, 66 feet tall and 240 feet long, the Sphinx is named for a human-headed lion in Greek mythology. It was most likely given that name two thousand years after its creators died.

However, ancient hieroglyphic writings of the era of the Sphinx's creation mention 'Roti,' a double lion god that sat at the entrance to the underworld and guarded the horizon where the sun rose and set. Since the Sphinx faces east, it is possible Roti would be an appropriate name, but I will call it the Sphinx.

The Arabic word for Egypt is Misr, but I'll stick with Egypt. Misr sounds too close to misery in English—an unfair association.

When I first realized Khufu's pyramid was built more than 4,500 years ago, the number impressed me. Forty-five centuries seemed an infinity. However, I am fast approaching 50 years of age, half a century. It seems to me to have passed by in moments. I call my time BTE, Bruce's Time on Earth. To go back in time to the age of Khufu—before Columbus, the Dark Ages, Jesus, the Romans, the Greeks, Hannibal, Troy, Moses, the biblical king David—to go through all that, one would only need to travel 90 times my own experience on earth, 90 BTE. I have lived more than one per cent of all the time that has passed since Khufu laid his first stone. It is not so long ago, after all. To meet Jesus in the flesh is only 40 BTE, the prophet Mohamed a scant thirty.

At one point a uniformed official on a camel, with an automatic rifle slung over his shoulder, brow furrowed, got into a bit of a row with Nasser. They barked at one another for a while but Nasser would not back down, and the official finally left.

"What was that all about?" I asked Nasser, as they were speaking Arabic and I didn't understand a word.

"The police always want money," he said, shrugging his shoulders.

Nasser is a short man, with typical Egyptian jet-black hair and dark eyes. He's very dark-skinned. Egyptians would call him a 'black' man, a description with no negative connotations—simply a means of identification. Egyptians come in many shades and there are many Nassers in Egypt.

Nasser was also wearing a heavy jacket, almost a parka, which was mind-boggling to me in the heat of the desert. I wore a T-shirt and was sweating.

He tried getting the horses to gallop, I guess time is money, but after bouncing up and down on what kids these days would call my 'junk,' for five minutes, I asked him to slow down.

It reminded me of a ride I had in New Zealand many years ago. My wife Linda told the guide she was an intermediate rider, which was the truth.

How tough can riding a horse be? I thought. I had the image from an old comic book of Conan the Barbarian pulling back on the reins of his horse, in total command of the steed.

That would be me.

"I'm an intermediate rider as well," I lied.

We were riding English style, with our feet high up on the horse. In retrospect the guide should have clued in that I had lied when my horse wandered over to a patch of grass on a hill and started eating. I didn't know what to do. I was certainly no Conan. But maybe the guide knew what she was doing, teaching me a lesson.

We rode for two hours, jumping over fences and galloping around sharp corners. It was hell. I was screaming all the way. Linda said later she thought I must be having a blast, since I was so loud 'back there.'

The saddle actually wore a hole through the skin on my butt. My inner thighs, stretched to the breaking point trying to keep me on the horse, screamed in pain for weeks with every step I took. This provided much hilarity for Linda, who laughed every time I winced.

On the way back over the sand dunes I pulled back on the reins and amazingly Sukkar stopped. Maybe I will be like Conan someday. Or perhaps the horse is better trained. I dismounted and pulled a garbage bag out of my backpack and started to fill it with old plastic water bottles that littered the sand. Nasser was ahead of me, and when he looked back to make sure I was still with him, he turned around and came to help. In 15 minutes we had five big bags filled. In that short time I found a horseshoe, and took that as a good sign. Perhaps God approves of what I'm doing here.

Several Egyptians passed by on horses and camels and spoke to Nasser, who always responded jovially.

"You are a good man," one camel rider said to me, which made me feel a little less an idiot.

"Where can we leave the bags?" I asked Nasser.

"We must take them with us," he said, "or the foxes will tear them apart."

I thought differently since there was nothing organic in the bags—I don't pick up organic material because it will decompose on its own—but agreed we really should take them out.

We hoisted them up to our saddles and this spooked Sukkar because the bouncing plastic made a loud rustling noise as we rode. Sukkar took off in a panic, bolting downhill, shades of New Zealand. The more we bounced, the more noise the bags made, the faster she went, the more we bounced, the more noise the bags made, the faster she went . . . Uh-oh!

There I was, two big garbage bags in my lap, bouncing on a horse galloping down a sand dune at the pyramids of Giza. Linda would have loved it.

I was terrified I'd fall off the horse and my big trip to Egypt would end with broken bones and a cracked skull on day one. So much for 40 days in the desert! Would I feel like an idiot going home all busted up? Ah-yuh!

Ya big dummy.

Fortunately, in classic hero style, Nasser caught up to me and took hold of the reins of my horse, and though it was difficult for him to keep her from galloping off, he somehow managed it. Clearly a skilled horseman.

The stone fence securing the Giza plateau from heavily populated Cairo, the largest city in Africa with seventeen million people, is about ten feet high, and guarded well. We had trouble leaving because the police did not believe the bags contained plastic. Who would bother picking up plastic bottles and take them away in garbage bags?

"They think we take parts of mummy with us," Nasser said with a chuckle, an aside to me during his deliberations with the guards.

Once outside Nasser gave the bags to an old man.

"He will sell the plastic," said Nasser.

As we made our way down the street, we saw an old woman sifting through garbage piled against the fence. Recycling Egyptian style. Nasser spoke to her in Arabic.

"What did you say to her?" I asked.

"I said you could give her lots of plastic," said Nasser. "She said plastic only buys cheap rice."

At 32, Nasser has been married 10 months. He's happy about it. He said he has been working the pyramids for 20 years, starting as a boy handling the horses for scared tourists. That explains his skill with horses, and scared tourists.

I was hot, and we were both sweating, but Nasser didn't take off his parka, or his baseball cap.

He showed me the pedestrian entrance in front of the Sphinx, called the Sphinx Gate. Tomorrow I will go there by 9:00 a.m. and stay to 4:00 p.m.. The Giza plateau is only open for those hours. That will be the test to see if they will let me do this. I'm debating whether I should ask the head of the police that manage the area for permission, or just go ahead and do it. Forgiveness or permission?

Mohamed took me back to the hotel on another harrowing journey of near-misses on the road. There I had a shower and collected my things. We went to the Canadian Embassy and I was able to procure a bunch of hand sized Canadian flags. I'll use them to mark off the area of sand I'm cleaning. They were quite friendly at the Embassy, mostly Egyptians though I did see the odd Caucasian walk in.

I had yet to get my hairbrush or a hat. I tried to tell Mohamed this, and he took me to a hairdresser thinking I wanted a haircut. Fortunately, next door was a pharmacy and for eight pounds I bought a hairbrush.

I still need a good hat, but Nasser gave me one of those tacky tourist 'Egyptian' hats—a white cloth folded and draped over the head, with a colorful tassel tied around. It makes you look like an

Arabian Sheik, simple but effective. I can use that for tomorrow. However, it might draw attention to me. None of the Egyptians wear hats like that. Perhaps it's just a way to identify tourists— marks, if you will. I'm not sure I want to stick out.

On the way back to Siag we got stuck in traffic, and I found myself beside a transit microbus, really a van, with a beautiful woman sitting by the window just next to me. She was wearing the headdress of the Muslim faith, the hijab, but her face was clearly visible. I smiled at her, and she smiled at me. Moments later, traffic as it was, we were again next to each other. We smiled at each other again, somewhat warmer, but still simply friendly.

A few minutes later it happened once more, and we smiled at each other with both humor and warmth. Then what I assumed was her husband, or a male relative sitting on the far side of her, leaned forward into view and gave me a stern gaze. He made some 'what the hell is your problem?' gesture, shrugging his shoulders, and lifting up his hands, palms up, glaring menacingly. She turned to see what I was looking at, then turned back to me. She brushed her hand over her brow in a 'screw him, he's an idiot' motion.

It made me think of some of the tragedies I have read about, where a Muslim man's machismo just goes way out of control. I was worried she might pay for smiling at me, and I was also worried he might jump out of the van and come at me. I made sure my door was unlocked so I could get out quickly if I had to defend myself. I didn't want to be a sitting duck in Mohamed's car. But nothing came of it.

We tried to get a 'sim' card, a card that enables my cell phone from Canada to work in Egypt. Mohamed took me to three different street vendors selling sim cards and the outcome was unanimous. My phone could not take a sim card.

I was looking through the instruction manual.

"There's nothing in here about a sim card," I told Mohamed.

"Can I see?" he asked, holding out his hand.

"It's all in English," I said, handing it to him. "You won't understand it."

He took it anyway, and from the picture on the cover quickly deduced that I was looking at the instruction manual for my camera, not my phone.

"Why you do that?" he asked, handing it back to me.

Ya big dummy.

Day 2 in the desert-acceptance?
"What are you doing?"

I called Linda, and she explained that our phone company, Media-com, restricted international calls, except for Canada. She said they will lift the restriction in a few days. Apparently the furnace broke down, but her sister's husband Joop turned on the gas fireplace, and in fact, the bastard was sitting in my kitchen drinking my beer as we were speaking. She seemed all stressed out, and I've only been gone four days. This could be a problem.

I'm looking forward to talking to the kids soon.

Samir came to my room for a few beers last night.

"This hotel, it used to be five-star," he said.

It sure looks like a hotel that *used to be* five-star. All the accouterments are here, it's just they haven't been maintained.

I just went downstairs to the lobby looking for a quiet place to write in my journal, and some men are still treating the marble floor with some liquid and a very loud floor polisher. It has to be more than 80 decibels.

Searching for some semblance of silence, I went out the back door, down the steps to the pool. There were many chairs and tables set up around the pool, with a round bar off to the side. It looked and felt as if the revelers, sitting in chairs or at the round bar, or swimming in the pool, had just vanished in an instant. It reminded me of the Overlook Hotel in the movie The Shining.

The place looked dirty so I checked the table with my finger, and it had a quarter inch of sand and dust on it, understandable when you consider the Sahara desert is a few blocks away. What did I expect in a country that is 95 per cent desert?

I went to the bar which looked just as abandoned but not quite as dusty, and set up my computer. But in ten minutes the smell from the cars on the other side of the wall was too much, so I've retreated back to my room.

Samir said the hotel was owned by three brothers, one of whom is dead, another lives elsewhere, and the third, the playboy, is on the bad side of Egyptian president Hosni Mubarek, and is not allowed in Egypt. Apparently the playboy is responsible for the decline.

"He used to like bitch women," said Samir.

"What?" I asked.

"You know, bitch women, who love the cock, and him acting like a big shot because he owns the hotel."

Samir has been working in hotels for more than 20 years. He's one and a half years younger than I.

My time at the pyramids today was fantastic. I was going to walk there, but the directions from Magdy the morning bellhop differed from Fatih's, whose description differed from Samir's, so after about five minutes walking somewhat aimlessly, I turned around and got Mohamed to give me a ride for twenty pounds.

Pedestrians enter the Giza plateau through a small building about 500 yards in front of the Sphinx. On the left side of the building is a small window where tickets are sold, and then visitors enter through two doors in the middle of the building. Once through a metal detector, bags are searched.

I paid 60 pounds ($12) for my ticket, and then I noticed three people getting ready to sit down and eat falafels just inside the ticket window.

"My goodness, that looks really good," I casually commented.

"You like?" one of the men asked, holding a falafel out to me.

He insisted I take one. It tasted great, but I saved most of it for lunch. Such generosity.

Once inside I stood looking at the Sphinx for a long time, wondering where to start. I thought about how I came to be there.

The thought to spend 40 days in the desert picking up garbage came to me a few years ago. I do not know where it came from, but it was an evolution. It began when I was here two years ago with my son Jake. We were near the step pyramids of Sakkara, built by Imhotep for Pharaoh Djoser, and our guide was using a stick to draw an example of a step pyramid in the sand. We were in an area off the beaten path, yet as she pulled the stick through the sand, cigarette butts bobbed to the surface.

What? I thought. *Is all of Egypt an ashtray?*

After months of picking garbage in Hendersonville, I have come to despise cigarette butts, they are simply *everywhere*.

It's ironic that the idea to come here evolved from the sands at Sakkara, as the pyramids of Giza evolved from the step pyramids of Sakkara.

I had planned to be here last year but Linda gave me so much grief that I postponed it until now. She even threatened to go to the courts and say I abandoned my children. But I could not leave it undone any longer. She knows I would have divorced her if she said I couldn't go. Like she told Ally, it's something I feel I must do. To what end, I don't know.

We moved to Hendersonville to escape the cold prairie winters, and be near Linda's sister Marianne. It was Linda's idea, but I readily agreed to it. I was sick of the long cold winters as much as she was, and having visited Hendersonville many times to see Marianne and her family, I liked the town.

More than 15 years of back-breaking work, we have built up our fishing operation to such a degree that we can afford to fish 45 days in the spring and again in the fall. We don't work in the summer or winter. I am not skipping out of work to go to Egypt.

Venturing into real estate, taking huge risks most people wouldn't even consider, we created three residential subdivisions for a total of 56 lots, and sold them all.

While initially a nail-biter, commercial real estate eventually proved even more profitable. Though always juggling cash flow because of our fishing schedule, we are sound financially. The cost of going to Egypt is not prohibitive.

Every spring and every fall I leave the family to go fishing, so my absence is nothing new.

"It's a lot of work," said Linda, "being a single parent while you go off to pick up *garbage*."

"Hire somebody to help you with the kids, or to clean the house," I answered. "Better yet, hire two people."

Linda almost convinced me not to do it.

I asked my kids what they thought about their Dad picking up garbage.

"I think it's cool," said Ti.

"Yeah," said Jake.

Ally didn't really answer.

Why Linda was so against Egypt baffles me, but she did eventually come around. For Christmas she bought me a hand-held translator and a book on Arabic.

Still gazing at the Sphinx, I thought about the embrace. It was an epiphany, really. It came to me when I was returning from Canada after receiving an award from the Government of Canada for volunteer work I have done for the past 11 years.

When I was told I was getting an award, it made me wonder— why do I do all this work for free? In my life, most of what I do, I do not get paid for. I do it because I feel it is the right thing to do.

I thought back to a private boys' school I attended as a young man, St. John's Cathedral Boys' School. There we did physically challenging things most people never do. Snowshoeing 50 miles in a day, paddling canoes for 900 miles, very difficult things meant to be challenges to overcome. A 'mock battleground' the headmaster, Frank Wiens, called it. The school was often referred to as 'the toughest boys' school in North America.'

In order for the students to do these difficult things, the staff had to do them as well. They were paid one dollar per day, so it was really volunteer work. I believe it was watching the staff that I almost recognized a force I now call 'the embrace.' For the staff at that school, their lives were all about volunteer work, self-sacrifice for others. It was there at the school I first sensed the embrace, but it would be more than thirty years before I recognized it for what it is, in its utter simplicity. Thinking back further, I saw it in my parents, but somehow expected it to be there. I'm sure most children have seen the embrace in their parents, but take it for granted. I know I did. It was there for me to see, but I was blind to it for so long.

I remembered drinking with Frank Wiens, co-founder and headmaster of the school, and some fellow St. John's alumni some ten years after I graduated.

"I feel like there's something I just about understand," I told Frank. "As if some veil is about to be lifted, and I'll somehow 'get it', but I'm not quite there yet."

I felt like I do when I can't remember a name, or a word. Understanding was 'on the tip of my tongue.' I was frustrated, and excited at the same time.

Whatever it is, I can't wait to see it, I thought. *It's gonna be good.*

Frank laughed, we drank, and the concept of the embrace, small and weak as it was in my frail mind, retreated.

The veil was lifted on that flight back to Canada, and I came to believe there is a force for good out there, much like 'the force' in George Lucas's Star Wars movies. To me the analogy is clear. In Star Wars, Yoda, a seemingly weak and helpless creature is instead very powerful, as he is strong in 'the force.' In our world, Mother Theresa comes to mind, as someone who appeared to be small and weak, but was instead, and I'm sure none would argue, very powerful. She was strong in 'the embrace.' Her life was all about that force, the embrace.

The embrace needs to be shown. You can talk about it all you want, but it must be shown in order to be strong. The staff at the boys' school did not tell me what they were doing. They just did it. Likewise Mother Theresa just did what she did, no great hullaballoo. The answer to the question of why I volunteer is that I saw it as a boy, and was in fact the recipient of the embrace. So now I in my turn contribute to that force.

The religions of the world know this, none more than Islam, arguably the youngest of the world's great religions. It's very early in the Quran that it talks about prayer. It asks the question 'can't I just study?' and the answer is no, you must *go to the mosque* and pray.

What an impact it must have on the young in such a culture, when five times a day the adults, who themselves appear godlike to children, are seen to prostrate themselves to an unseen, all-knowing, and all-powerful entity. I believe this hard-wires Islam into the brains of the children.

It's the same in nature. Not having verbal abilities, a mother wolf can only teach by doing. This might relate back to our own evolutionary ancestors, and a deep part of our brain, back when we, too, could only learn by seeing and teach by example, far back in our evolutionary path before we had the capacity for speech—a state we held for millions of years.

The embrace must be shown in order to be strong, as Mother Theresa did, and millions of people the world over are doing right now. And every kind act contributes to the embrace.

How different would the world be, if countries, instead of believing in a pre-emptive strike, believed in a pre-emptive embrace? If rich countries reached out to poorer ones and embraced them, helped them understand the embrace by demonstrating it to them, because that is the only way to teach the embrace, asking for and wanting nothing in return, no oil or natural resources, simply enhancing that force.

All the religions in the world, in their truest form, uncorrupted, teach the embrace. It is the one commonality upon which all can agree, and because of that I believe the embrace is the answer to so many of the world's problems today. Religious conflict makes no sense if all involved practice the embrace. We don't.

But we must. We must, as a people, as a civilization, we must make this force stronger, and have it shine into the dark corners of this world. Light up the darkness, as Bob Marley said.

I have had a recurring dream since I was a child. In the dream I'm in a large house with several other people my age, all boys when I was a child, all men as I became an adult. There is no embrace in the house. The house is dark, pitch black. We are on the main floor near the exit. My little brother is on the second floor. There is evil in the house, deadly evil. There are four of us, standing huddled together. One of the other people with me is decapitated with a flash of light, I can see his head slowing falling off his neck before darkness is again complete. Another companion is whisked away, as if a giant hook from some twisted talent show had reached around his waist and pulled him away. Whoosh, is what I hear. I see nothing. Then I can hear him screaming until he is, presumably, dead. Another just dissolves in front of me for no apparent reason. I am utterly terrified.

The door to leave is to my right, and not far away. To stay in this house any longer would be suicide, but I have to get my little brother. To do that, I'll need to use the tiny flashlight in my hand. But if I use the flashlight I will draw attention to myself.

The chances of success in finding my little brother on the second floor, and then coming back down and out the door are almost zero. But it *is* my little brother up there. I hesitate, unsure of what to do, so very afraid. Then I wake up.

I always wake up before I have decided what to do.

I do have a little brother, but I think the little brother in the dream represents future generations. They need to be taken from this dark place. We need to shine our tiny little flashlights, light up the darkness, draw attention to ourselves, against all the evil of the world, and lead them out of the house, and into the light. The chances of success are slim, death probable, and yet we must do it. Will we?

Watching television months back all I heard from the US government and George Bush was where to invade next. They, the government not the people, have no concept of the embrace, because they think the embrace does nothing for the national interest. And there's the irony, because the embrace is the *only* thing that can truly protect the national interest of any country. If the US and so many other countries had not meddled around in the Middle East as they have done for so many years, but instead had been there helping, demonstrating the embrace to the people, they would not be so hated.

It's for lack of the embrace that terrorism thrives. And when terrorists strike, governments pull further away from the embrace, increasing oppression and leading to more terrorist acts. Then governments pull even further away, retaliating yet again and reaping more terrorism for their efforts, and the snowball rolls down to hell. There is only the embrace to save us. Just like Sukkar and the rustling garbage bags, with Nasser to pull on the horse's reins, whoa, there is nothing to fear if we just stop.

The Holy Quran:
"But if the enemy inclines towards peace, you (also) incline towards peace, and trust in Allah, for He is One who knows and hears (all things)."

I came to Egypt to embrace Egypt and the Egyptian people, and by extension the Muslim people of the world, and by further extension, Egypt being the cradle of human civilization, all the peoples of the world.

Deep thinking is all well and good, Benson, I thought to myself, *but you've got a job to do.*

Ya big dummy.

With not a little trepidation, I started picking garbage just to the left of the Sphinx, as you face it directly. A clean-shaven, husky Egyptian was leaning against the Valley Temple of Khafre, just south of the Temple of the Sphinx. He was wearing a white calabaya, the one-piece gown Egyptian men wear.

"Is it okay if I pick some stuff up?" I asked him.

"No problem," said Saman, with a thick Egyptian accent.

He was obviously curious about me. I wasn't Egyptian, and yet I didn't act like any of the other tourists.

Who is this big dummy?

Plastic water bottles, empty food containers, disposable cups, spoons, newspapers, pop cans—there was lots of garbage. Behind and under boulders and granite blocks that might have fallen from the Temple hundreds or thousands of years ago, was a shocking array of debris that clearly had been there for a long time.

I tried to stay under the radar, just some guy picking stuff up, don't mind me.

I'm just a soul whose intentions are good, oh Lord please don't let me be misunderstood.

I kept my head down.

I wasn't sure I would be allowed to pick garbage. Would I be chased off? Arrested? What would I do with the bags of garbage I filled up? I had no idea. It would be very difficult to drag them all the way out of the fenced-in area. And then what would I do with them? Again, I had no idea.

I felt so uncertain about what I was doing, that I was tempted to just go home and tell Linda she was right, it was a stupid thing to do, and walk around with my tail between my legs for a few weeks.

"They're just going to laugh at you," she said often. "'Look at the stupid Canadian picking up our garbage!'"

But I pushed those bad thoughts deep into my brain, back into that bad part that always thought the worst, and just kept working. I imagined if I was in a movie, there would be a song playing. Perhaps Eye of the Tiger from Rocky fame to inspire me. Or maybe something from The Three Stooges. Something to let me know what genre I'm playing in, drama or farce. But alas, in real life there is no soundtrack to go by, only our hearts and minds, the warring reason and passion.

Lebanese poet Kahlil Gibran wrote of reason and passion in his famous book The Prophet:

"Your soul is oftentimes a battlefield, upon which your reason and your judgement wage war against your passion and your appetite."

". . . reason, ruling alone, is a force confining; and passion, unattended, is a flame that burns to its own destruction. Therefore let your soul exalt your reason to the height of passion, that it may sing; And let it direct your passion with reason, that your passion may live through its own daily resurrection . . ."

I read that portion of The Prophet this morning, looking for some assurance. My passion demands I be here. My reason is skeptical.

As I was picking, a few Egyptian men on camels and horses, and some just walking around, would say something kind, like 'you a good man, where you from?'

"Canada."

I felt encouraged, but then this short person in overalls approached me. Walid. He spoke no English at all, but by flashing an official-looking badge, and his hand gestures, I soon deduced that he is responsible for cleaning this area of the Sphinx site. I think he's in charge of one-third of the site.

I tried playing dumb, but it wasn't working. Was he going to toss me out? Thankfully Saman came to my rescue.

"What did he say to you?" he asked me.

"I have no idea."

He spoke to Walid and then turned to me.

"Continue what you were doing."

I asked him to say that I love Egypt and being at the pyramids, and this is my way to say thanks. He spoke Arabic again, and I think he conveyed the message as I got the thumbs up from Walid.

I have met three guys who clean up, Walid, Ramadan and Hassanan. We evolved a working relationship, communicating without the benefit of language, like our common ancestors. I filled a few bags, and then they came and took them, explaining what they were doing with hand gestures. Sometimes they would come and ask for a 'sack' and I would give them one of my bags. I'm glad I brought 90 bags with me.

At one point Walid and Hassanan led me to an underground area, through a small trench dug out of the rock thousands of years ago, and showed me a huge pile of garbage. This was an ancient tomb for nobles, an area out of bounds for tourists. The garbage and debris were several feet thick, possibly 50 years of accumulation. Who knows, maybe a hundred? A thousand? I tried to get to the bottom of it, but didn't reach it. The dust dispersed into the air by moving the debris was choking me. We will need masks. I put my hand to my face to indicate a mask, and they both nodded.

I'm going to try to find some masks this afternoon. I conveyed to the guys that we could do a little of the big pile each day, but with masks.

All in all, a wonderful day. As I left, I was surprised to see some cans and bottles in the area I had already cleaned, but that represented half a day. I think what we need (how presumptuous, 'we') are garbage barrels that can be emptied every day, and signs all over the place asking people not to litter. I think after ten days or so, I might mention it, maybe ask the Canadian Embassy to foot the bill. If not, I probably could. But it would be better coming from Canada.

The highlight of my day came when a young Egyptian woman named Myhrna approached me.

"What are you doing?" she asked me. Apparently she and her two friends had been watching me for several minutes.

"Just cleaning up," I told her.

"Why?"

"I love Egypt, and this area in particular. This is my way of saying thank-you to the Egyptian people for allowing me to be here."

She shrank back as if struck, and put her hand to her mouth. Then she moved toward me and grasped my right forearm with both her hands.

"Thank-you, thank-you so much, for what you are doing," she said, almost crying.

I was so moved, that I had to hold back tears myself. She was clearly touched and a little shocked by my picking up a little garbage. For that, it was all worth it. This whole trip! It was a defining moment, and I will never forget it. To get such a response for just picking up garbage . . . what an embrace!

Later, a group of young men came by, and the scene was repeated. The pre-emptive embrace is a concept I know will work. I have seen it today.

A young boy, maybe eight years old, helped me for about half an hour. I told him I would see him tomorrow, and I wonder if I will.

A sudden burning of my forearms had me worried. I was wearing a short-sleeved shirt. *Ya big dummy.*

I lathered on some sun-screen, but my arms still hurt. I had sun-screened my face in the morning, but not my arms. So, discretion being the better part of valor, I left. In the past I have burned my arms so badly I couldn't go outside for days, even with a long-sleeved shirt. I can't afford that now.

As I was leaving, I was accosted by only one persistent postcard hawker, but was able to convince him that I had no money. That's my story and I'm sticking to it.

Just as I exited the area, a taxi driver asked if I wanted a ride.

"Twenty pounds to Siag," he said, and I took him up on it. That was what I had paid Mohamed in the morning. I will try to walk again tomorrow, perhaps get better directions, maybe leave a little earlier.

Now it's near four o'clock, and I'm going to try to find a pharmacy. I need those masks, and some athlete foot powder or ointment. The hat I have works well enough. I would like to get an Egyptian robe, but not just yet. I don't want to appear to be a 'poser.'

The first time I ran for Member of Parliament in Canada, one of my advisors wanted me to wear a cowboy hat in a parade in Teulon, a cattle town. I refused, on the grounds I'm a fisherman, not a cowboy, so I won't pretend to be one. I probably shouldn't pretend to be an Egyptian, either.

I went out to find a pharmacy and as often happens here, I met another Mohamed. He works in a tourist shop selling statues of Egyptian artifacts. He offered me tea.

"Tourist is dead," he said, meaning tourism is way down, not threatening to kill me. He has traveled to England and America.

"In Egypt, all they want is to eat and have sex," he said, pouring tea. "In the West they just want to smoke and drink."

We touched on the subject of religion, gingerly. Neither of us wanted to jeopardize our thoroughly enjoyable exchange. I mentioned the embrace, the commonality of all religions, and he leaned back in his chair and looked at the ceiling, puffing on his cigarette.

Day 3 in the desert-where do I begin?

"I help you. I help you."

When I woke up, I was feeling a little rough, once again doubting my purpose here, wondering if it was worthless, if I was being an idiot. Should I just go home?

I was feeling a cold coming on, so I took one of the vitamin C pouches meant for travelers, and felt better. Off I went, and returned moments later to put on a long-sleeved shirt. I didn't think my forearms needed it, but once I was out in the sun they started stinging, despite the SPF 30 I had put on.

I walked to the Sphinx without getting lost, though I had to ask directions from an Egyptian fellow. After I left him I promptly turned the wrong way, but he was watching and whistled at me. I turned around and he pointed to the correct path. I think I'll be okay tomorrow.

I stopped on the way and bought a bottle of water for 1.25 pounds, 25 cents, from a street vendor. They could have ripped me off, but didn't. In fact, the vendor and his friend at first said one and a half pounds. I gave them that, and then they told me 1.25 and gave me change.

Once again I bought my ticket, and said to the guys eating in the back, "boy, that looks really good."

A fellow inside gestured me in to eat with them.

"No thanks, I've already eaten," I said, not wanting to take advantage of his hospitality.

Inside I went, back to where I began the day before. It took mere minutes to clean up the areas I had done before, as there was not the years of accumulation of garbage.

Unfortunately this Egyptian guy was following me around, trying to be my guide, and he stuck with me for 20 minutes. Then he asked for money for being my 'guide.' He was very persistent and I finally gave him some money to make him go away. After that, I vowed never to take money with me again. I should've stuck to my story.

With the bothersome dude gone, I went to work on a new area, along the outside of the fence on the south side of the Sphinx.

There is a causeway that leads some 600 meters from the Mortuary temple in front of Khafre, the middle pyramid, downhill to the Valley Temple, next to the Temple of the Sphinx. This causeway is fenced for about 100 meters, to allow tourists to marvel at the Sphinx unmolested by vendors hawking their wares.

As I was working on the outside of the fence, a portly gentleman on the inside of the Sphinx area called to me. With a big camera around his neck and a bright Hawaiian shirt he looked every bit the tourist, and I was wondering where he was from.

"I want to thank you from the bottom of my heart for what you are doing," he said, touching the left side of his chest with the palm of his hand.

"I don't know what to say," he added, shaking his head. "It is not the tourist, it is us Egyptians who do this."

He helped me for about twenty minutes, passing trash from the inside of the fence outside to me.

"I should be doing this with you," he said."Can I take your picture?"

Heartily emboldened, I went on about my business. Many of the camel drivers passing by would say 'good man' or give me the thumbs up.

At one point this little girl and boy came up to me, children of men and women who work the site selling souvenirs. They wanted to help. The older boy picked up a few things and put them in my bag and soon lost interest, but the little girl was quite the worker. She came back again and again asking for bags, and she filled them. Quite the trooper for an eight or nine-year-old.

"I help you, I help you," she kept saying. She was so enthusiastic about filling the bags, that she led me to a tomb that was just loaded with garbage. I had seen it before but I wanted to get a mask first.

"Only pick outside," I told her. "Don't go inside."

She understood and went to work. Just then, a group of seven or eight teenage Egyptian schoolboys saw what I was doing and some of them wanted to help. I invited them down into the ravine outside the tomb, and some of them filled bags. They were kids having fun, very respectful. Several of them had their picture taken with me. One of them wanted a pair of gloves to use, but I only had one pair.

The teenagers were playing music and asked me to dance with them, but I bowed out claiming I couldn't dance. In retrospect I should have.

How does the song go?

If you get the chance to sit it out or dance, I hope you dance.

Unfortunately, the little girl cut her finger on a piece of glass. It was just two small punctures, but I felt horrible. She was unfazed.

"No more today, okay?" I told the darling little girl.

"Okay." She seemed to speak and understand English quite well. I offered her 50 piastres, but she refused it. I have decided to name her 'little tiger.'

During the morning, as several kids would pick up the odd piece for me, this one boy, maybe ten or eleven, kept coming by and speaking Arabic. I thought he was telling me to go away, but I just smiled at him. Well, damned if the kid didn't finally come by with some garbage, put it in my bag, and give me 50 piastres. I was flabbergasted! I tried to give it back to him but he refused.

I know this, whatever money I gave the bothersome dude earlier, my 'guide,' was worth nothing to the 50 piastres, half an Egyptian pound, a mere ten cents, this little boy gave me. It really touched my heart. He isn't a tourist, his parents work the site. He has no money to spare. That's why I wanted to give the note to the girl, to pass it on. Yet she refused! I will treasure that 50-piastre note.

Shortly after twelve, these two Egyptian men stopped and asked me what I was doing. I told them.

"You mean, you clean, and no get paid?" asked Rabihr Noss.

He asked me to sit and talk with him.

"Just two minutes," he said.

"Sure."

Rabihr and his friend Hassan and I sat down on a rocky ledge. After a few minutes he invited me to eat supper with him.

"I will not eat until you come to my home," Rabihr said, putting on the pressure.

"Neither will I," added Hassan.

Rabihr gave me his cell number.

"Call me when you are outside the gate, and Hassan will come for you."

Just as I was finishing up, an old vendor sitting outside the Sphinx fence called me over to him. He was dressed in traditional Egyptian clothing.

"Here, here," he said, sweeping his arm in a circle, indicating garbage around him that he wanted me to pick up.

It was what I had intended in the first place, but I was worried about offending. I had seen him often, hands reaching inside the gate pleading with some tourist to buy his wares, and sometimes playing a flute to attract a customer.

Next to him was a man named Nasser, dressed in today's attire.

"If the young people were taught about the importance of the pyramids," said Nasser, "they would not make such a mess."

"I don't know, Nasser," I said. "Many young people have helped me. They really seem to want to help, but there is no place to put trash."

He agreed that was the problem, and we commiserated on where to put trash barrels 'one here, there, there,' etc.

As I left, I saw some garbage in areas where I had cleaned earlier, work I would have tomorrow. But, they didn't ask me to come here and do this. Who am I to judge? That must be rule number one of being a Trashman, don't judge. You are just there to clean up.

Cleaning along a road in Hendersonville, day one or two, I noticed a big white plastic bag blowing around in the ditch in front of me.

How can people walk by and not pick it up? I thought, in judgement. When I grabbed it, I realized it was one of my bags that had blown out of my own pocket.

Ya big dummy!

I went out the gates and looked for a phone. I was accosted in the typical way, 'taxi, car, you come to my shop, special deal for you.' One character, another Walid, spoke to me for a while. I said I wanted to use a phone. He tried his cell but it didn't work, so his buddy led me down the street to a phone shop. I had learned from Rabihr they charge 50 piastres per minute. I didn't use the money the little boy gave me. I will save that.

I called Rabihr and he said he would send Hassan to get me immediately.

I returned to the area by the gate, and the landmark Pizza Hut/ Kentucky Fried Chicken incongruously meters from the entrance to, and in eyesight of, the pyramids and Sphinx. Walid offered me tea, and when he went to get it, the owner of the local souvenir shop told me to only pay ten pounds for a taxi to Siag.

"If they ask for more, walk away," he advised.

I had paid twenty, so that's some useful intelligence.

The tea was great, company as well. I did give Walid's buddy one pound baksheesh, or tip, for showing me where the phone was.

Hassan's cell ran out of juice and Rabihr couldn't contact him, so he came to get me himself on his friend's motorcycle. I hopped on behind him and went for one hell of a ride—a very dangerous ride. We were weaving in and out of traffic at breakneck speeds, barely missing people and cars, trucks, horses, carts, donkeys and camels. I was terrified. What would happen if I broke an arm? Or busted my head? Where would I go? I shudder to think. But Rabihr got me there uninjured. Damn they live dangerously.

He did a lot of yelling at others on the road. "You have to be loud, or they won't listen," he shouted over his shoulder to me.

His friend's father, who runs a tire repair shop/bicycle shop, met me with a huge smile and a handshake, and offered me tea. A very stocky, bearded fellow wearing dirty overalls, he spoke no English. I never did get his name. The whole family seemed to be hanging out at the shop, including two very little girls. One of them, perhaps four or five years old, had a remarkable face, a very light complexion with flashing blue-green eyes. One could tell, even at this young age, that she would be a striking woman. She reminded me of Cleopatra, or Nefertiti, the bloodline of the Egyptians.

The tire shop was small, maybe ten feet by ten feet, crammed with all sorts of tires, bicycle parts, and whatever tools of the trade the man needed. Very typical. Egypt, at least this part of it, hasn't gone for the big box concept yet. You can still find a tailor, baker, pottery maker, and bicycle repair shop all on one side of the street. Each has a small store, and each manages to feed his family. I prefer that to going to a giant Wal-mart. It also makes for a better sense of community.

I was the center of attention, and felt like an honored guest. After tea at the shop, we went through a maze of narrow alleyways to Rabihr's house. Apparently the family has just bought it. His room is in the front, with a bed sitting on bricks and a wardrobe as the only furnishings. We sat on the floor on cushions. I met his father, but was not introduced to anyone else, though there were several women milling about in the next room. When Hassan arrived Rabihr gave him 50 pounds and off he went to get some food.

In typical Egyptian generosity, Rabihr gave me a T-shirt and a baseball hat. He showed me pictures of his friends and family while we waited for Hassan to return with dinner. The food was fantastic. We had chicken and some other type of meat called Kafta, with pita bread and sauce. The three of us ate sitting on the floor, and after we had finished Rabihr took the remaining food to the rest of the family in the other room.

After dinner Rabihr's brother came by, and he and Rabihr and Hassan smoked some hashish. He had a small cube of it that he softened up with a lighter and mixed with tobacco. He got three joints out of it, and they smoked them all. I asked Rabihr if I could take his picture.

"Why? So you could show government?" he asked jokingly, exhaling hashish smoke. But he made sure no hash was to be seen when I took his photo.

Rabihr showed me upstairs about three flights where he will live in two to three months after he gets married.

"What is the name of the woman you will marry?" I asked him.

"I won't tell you," he said, smiling. "It is secret."

I had absolutely no intention of getting back on a motorcycle with a *now-stoned* Rabihr to get back to Siag, but needn't have worried. After they toked up, we left and got a ride on one of the trikes, called a tok-tok. It took us part way, and from there I took a van for 50 piastres that dropped me a few blocks from Siag. I walked the rest of the way.

It was an incredibly eventful day. It gave me great insights into the Egyptian people. Rabihr told me that he works the pyramids because his father did, and his father before him. He also told me he would be in trouble if his father caught him smoking hash. That's why he was careful to blow the smoke out the window.

So, well fed, I returned to Siag. I wrote here a little, had a nap, woke up and had a shower, then napped again. Then I went downstairs to use the internet. I now have an e-mail address— *bensonegypt@hotmail.com*

I sent the family a message. I tried calling, but just got the machine, so I called Marianne and left a message, telling them about the e-mail address.

Each morning I feel I have a cold coming on, but once I get to the Sphinx I feel great, somehow re-energized. But now I am tired. It is close to midnight, and I will go to sleep.

I was reading the Egyptian Gazette that I picked up at a news stand in the morning, and it had a story about how the government wants to restrict Fatwas, or religious decrees, to those religious leaders who have graduated from a religious university. Apparently there have been frivolous Fatwas.

I quote, "One preacher issued a Fatwa two years ago, giving licence to females to breast-feed their male colleagues in work."

We in the West hear of Fatwas as always against us and very dangerous, but this puts them in a different perspective. I imagine many Fatwas that make headlines in the Western media only produce chuckles and derision here.

The Fatwa allowing women to breast-feed their colleagues was merely an attempt to get around religious laws about men and women working together. There was never the intent to actually have any breast-feeding take place.

I hope nothing goes awry in Hendersonville, as I do not want to return . . . yet.

Day 4 in the desert—another great day

"You come have dinner with me."

I found my way to the site no problem, and even found it back.

It took me about an hour to redo all the area I had done in the past two days. The police at the locked gate to the Sphinx at the back of the Valley Temple of Khafre offered me some food. I just took a piece of falafel. Damn that's good. Then off I went to

continue around the Sphinx. My goal was to make it to the end of
the fence.

Walid, the shorter garbage collector, came by, and with Saman
to interpret said the government is okay with me working there.
Nice to know. I have to admit it's a little presumptuous to just
show up one day and start picking up garbage.

Hassanan, the tall collector I often see with Walid, found me
working behind the Valley Temple and motioned that he wanted
me to go back to the front of the Sphinx with him, but I gestured
I wanted to continue where I was. He seemed okay with that. I
helped him move the bags I filled yesterday to a small pit outside
the stone fence that separates the tourists from the horses and
camels and their riders. From there someone else will take it away.
I think. I hope.

The kids came around me a lot today, to talk, or to help. Little
Tiger came by. Her name is Omniah, that's how I spell it. She
wrote her name in Arabic in my notebook. She is ten years old.
I'm not exactly sure what she does at the pyramids. I've never seen
her trying to sell anything. I think she, like many other children,
just hang out all day with their parents, who sell souvenirs.

Many of the children want to help, such must be the nature
of children, and many did today. Young girls and older women
would call me over, and hand me some trash they had collected.
Another group of teen boys came by to shake my hand. They were
inside the fence of the Sphinx, and then came out to meet me.
Egyptian tourists.

Around noon, Nasser, the older guy who was selling figurines—
he must stay outside the fence but is able to place his wares
through the bars and inside the fence—took me for tea over near
the entrance to the Sphinx Temple, where I first began picking
trash day one. I call him Nasser the Old so as not to confuse him
with Nasser the Horseman. He offered to buy me food as well,
but the man was out of food. This is food sold to the Egyptian
vendors, not the tourists—authentic Egyptian food.

Saman came by as we were enjoying our tea.

"You come have dinner with me, tomorrow, at my house," he
said.

I went back to work, and soon saw a man with a donkey in tow,
selling food to the Egyptians. Some kids bought me two bottles
of Pepsi and one Egyptian sandwich—a pita, with egg, cheese,
tomato, some sort of sauce and some plant.

The man with the donkey, Maharab, magically pulled the drinks and the ingredients for the sandwich out of hidden pockets in a sack draped across the donkey's back. I wondered if the beast could trace its ancestry back five thousand years when the species was first tamed in the Nile valley.

As I was getting my free lunch, a little girl threw her juice bag on the ground. Without thinking, I grunted.

She quickly picked it up and put it in my bag. "Sorry."

These kids want to please, and want to do what's right, but there is no place to put the garbage, in the whole damn city, almost.

Little Tiger got into a fight with another girl, a little bigger than her. They really went at it. Some of the boys tried to break it up. I was unsure what to do. A guy on a camel thought it was amusing. Then a woman came by, hollered something in Arabic and it stopped. Moments later the two had completely forgotten it, and were giggling together about something.

I spent a little time on the one underground area, picked three bags worth, but I need to wear something over my mouth. This is a place where people have been going to the bathroom for years. It is interesting that there is not one garbage can, or washroom in the entire site. Of course it's a mess! I have spoken to many of the people who work the site, and they say the same. There is no place to put garbage.

I left around 1:30 and had tea with the owner of the souvenir shop beside the Pizza Hut, the guy who said to only pay ten pounds to the Siag. I met a few other men, including one who seems very fluent in English and drinks beer every day. A man after my own heart.

I walked home and didn't get lost. I checked my e-mails, had one from Linda and Ally. Ally signed off love Ally, Linda just Linda. Nothing from Jake or Ti. I hope their swim meet went well. When we moved to Hendersonville the boys couldn't swim beyond the dog paddle, Gimli doesn't have a pool. After two courses at the YMCA in Hendersonville they fly though the water. Hendersonville definitely provides more opportunities for our children at this age. Which is not to say Gimli is a bad place.

Jake was born in Berkeley, California. A few weeks after he was born, I was in San Francisco filming a movie called *Zoli's Brain*. I had a bit part, albeit a speaking role. Filming went longer than expected, so I called Linda from the subway station to say I would be late.

"Man, you wouldn't believe what's been going on here!"

"What, what is it?" I asked, with new-father nervousness. "Is Jake okay?"

"Yeah, he's fine."

"Well, what happened?"

"I'll tell you when you get here," she said. "It's a long story, but everybody's okay."

Jake was sleeping when I got home.

"I came home from the store, and Jake was crying," explained Linda. "He was really loud. Eric was in the parking lot holding his briefcase. He pulled out two hand guns, and started yelling something about 'kill the fucking baby, kill the fucking baby.'"

Eric was a neighbor who lived across the parking lot from us. A doctoral student in astronomy, we knew he was a little crazy. We were living in Berkeley, after all. Just about everybody is a little crazy in Berkeley.

Both Linda and I worked as street vendors selling colorful tie-dyed T-shirts and other clothing on busy Telegraph Avenue, along with hundreds of other vendors hawking a vast array of wares. I was what they called a 'frost-back.' Like the wet-backs, illegal Mexicans still wet from crossing the Rio Grande, it's said Canadians still have the frost on their back when they come down to work illegally. I went by the name Larry, the name my brother-in-law went by until he married a Dutch girl and changed it to the more formal Laurence. He thought Larry was too lowbrow for his Dutch in-laws.

"I'll call you Laurence if you call me Sir Bruce," I told him. I used his social security number, memorized it, but never got used to the name.

I still remember this one vendor calling my name as I went into a store.

"Larry . . . Larry . . . " no response. Louder then "Larry . . . Larry . . . " I still did not turn around. But she had heard some people call me Bruce.

"Bruce!"

I turned around immediately.

"Which name do you go by anyway?"

"Well, actually both, you see I . . . " I babbled, trying to explain why I didn't answer to my own name. I was sure she wouldn't rat me out, but someone listening might.

"Forget it," she said, waving her hand. "Just grab me a Pepsi, will you?"

"Sure."

We saw crazy people every day. The panhandlers, homeless vets a little touched in the head, naked people walking in groups of five to 25, all strolled by our vendor stands. I wasn't in Kansas anymore, and it was fascinating. We took it all in stride.

Eric had been in our house drinking wine in the past. Other than a penchant for drifting off in the middle of a conversation to talk to an imaginary person, we thought him harmless.

"What did you do?" I asked Linda.

"I ran into our apartment, and locked the door. Then I went into our bedroom in the back and called the landlord."

The landlord couldn't do much, but one of our neighbors saw Eric waving the guns around and called the cops.

"It took only a few minutes for the SWAT team to arrive. I could see them walking along the fence beside the parking lot, guns drawn," said Linda, calmly. "They took him down fast. They said his bag was full of ammunition."

I was lucky I didn't come home to a 'Police Line-Do Not Cross.'

I went to court when Eric's charges came up. I explained to the Judge my concerns about Eric, and they remanded him in custody. His father was there, a retired UC Berkeley professor.

"My son needs help," he said. "He's been in institutions before."

It turned out Eric had the legal right to carry guns because he was never institutionalized *in the state of California*, and he collected and transported rare coins.

About a month before the Eric incident, I woke up to a bloodcurdling scream, a woman's voice. I quickly put my pants on and ran out the door. Across the back lane a woman was standing beside her car, keys in hand, weeping.

"What happened?" I asked her.

"I'm going on a trip, and some homeless guy grabbed my purse," she moaned. "It had everything in it; my ticket, my money, my passport."

"Which way did he go?"

"That way," she pointed.

"What did he look like?"

"A black guy," is all she said.

I took off looking for the purse snatcher in the direction she pointed, looking in places I normally never would—under low-hanging branches, behind fences, empty lots, anyplace a person might hide. To my surprise, within a one block radius of our apartment I found dozens of sleeping homeless people.

"You see a black guy run by here?" I asked a few.

"No, sorry," was the universal reply.

To have that many homeless people staying so close to our apartment was unsettling, considering the purse snatching that morning. Nonetheless, I shrugged it off.

But after the incident with Eric, I said to Linda, "Screw it. Let's move to Gimli. I know it's safe to raise kids there, and I know I can make money fishing."

Gimli is a great place to raise small kids, and we did catch a lot of fish. But the kids are older now, and their needs are different. So are mine and Linda's.

My mind is in two different worlds.

I wonder how my kids would like to hang out at the pyramids all day, waiting for their lifelong career selling trinkets to tourists, then passing that opportunity onto their own children. I don't think my kids know how lucky they are.

I met an English fellow named Nick in the Dominican Republic when we were escaping the Canadian winter for a few months some 12 years ago. He talked of a friend wanting to win the lottery.

"I told him, 'you silly bastard, you already won the lottery. What are the odds your mother and father would meet, have sex, and that one egg would meet that one sperm? Just by being alive, you've won the bloody lottery!'"

Take it a step further, being born on earth, the odds are a person would be born into poverty in India or China, not in a first world nation. Most likely anyone reading this has won the lottery on several levels. I know I have.

Day 5 in the desert

"Some people are good, some people are bad."

Last night I drank too much, as this couple and their friends, in Cairo from England to go to a wedding today, were pounding back the beers.

As I'm walking to work, this young Egyptian man locked strides with mine. It reminded me of my 'guide' some days ago.

"How are you, my friend?" he asked.

I didn't remember him, and wasn't sure if he was some hustler looking for a few pounds.

"I don't have any money."

"Do you need money?" he asked, and reached into his pocket.

I soon discovered he's one of the horsemen, and was willing to give me money if I didn't have any. We walked together to the site.

"Cigarette?" he asked, holding one out to me.

"No," I said, intentionally coughing. "My lungs."

"Me, my lungs are good, strong," he said, holding his fists out in front of him. "I fuck my wife every night for one, maybe two hours. Then I have a shower and go to sleep."

He was clearly happy about that, and I could see every one of his teeth as he grinned madly. I howled with laughter. To be so young and in lust.

My mood was up and down again today. In the morning I was feeling a little depressed, and then cheered up as I saw Saman at the Sphinx. I started picking trash, quickly combing over the area I had done before. It took me mere minutes today, as there wasn't all that much to pick up.

Many vendors were milling about, as one guy, Hassan, showed up with koshery, 'Egyptian macaroni.' Macaroni noodles, rice and lentil beans, with a pasta sauce on top, koshery is sold in small plastic containers. I recognized the containers, as I have picked up hundreds of them.

"Would you like one?" asked Hassan. It was delicious. It cost two and a half pounds, 50 cents, and you could get a hot or not-so-hot sauce with it. Hassan had two bottles, and he put a little in the plastic bowl. Under instruction, I mixed it thoroughly.

I had one and a half pounds and a five-pound note, so I gave him the fiver, but he didn't have change.

"Give him one and a half, I will pay the rest," said one of the men I had never seen before. The embrace.

I sat there and ate with the vendors, surrounded by friendly Egyptians. They asked a few questions, where I was staying, did I buy a ticket to get in, etc.

"Every day?"

"Yes."

They all agreed I shouldn't have to buy a ticket to get in, and some said Saman would talk to the boss and see what he could do. I was hoping he would, but when I left today, he told me to take my tickets I had purchased for previous days to the ticket counter in the morning.

"You tell them you help the people," he said. "You shouldn't have to pay."

I'm not so sure about that.

"I want to show you something," he said suddenly, motioning with his left hand for me to follow him.

He lead me over to some tombs full of garbage. We crawled into one tomb through a round opening two feet in diameter.

"It's really dark in here," I said to Saman.

"But you have just come inside, in a few minutes your eyes adjust," said Saman, and of course they did and I could see the trash. Across the trench it was a lot worse. There were five distinct areas, five burial chambers.

Then Saman turned serious, perhaps the true purpose of taking me into the tombs.

"Bruce, don't trust anybody," he said, with conviction in his voice. "One man say you must be very rich, because you stay at Siag. But I told him you are a poor man. Don't trust anybody. Some people are good, some people are bad."

I thanked him for the advice and started cleaning while Saman went back to work selling camel rides. Walid and Ramadan found me and indicated for me to follow them. I was reluctant as I knew what *I* wanted to do, and I knew what *they* wanted me to do. It was the cesspool, the worst place I have found yet. Sure enough, they took me there, (these guys speak no English) and one asked for a garbage bag. I gave it to him, and he picked up a few things and then they started walking away.

"No, no, no, you stay here," I said, and with hand signals told him to stay and help me. They both started giving me directions about what to pick up. Walid picked up a rock, and said "no" and then tossed it back on the ground. Then he picked up a piece of plastic, and put it in the garbage bag.

I got mad and angrily waved them off. They tried to appease me with words I didn't understand, but I waved them off again, and they left. I filled one bag, then went back to the tombs Saman had asked me to clean. I started at the worst end of it, and after about half an hour bent over, I decided to piece it out over a few days, five to be precise. The ceiling of the tomb is only about four feet high, so I'm bent over all the time. Since I've had two back operations, I'm cautious about injuring my back. I did one-fifth, and will space it out over four more days. The darker side I completed in no time.

As I was in there, Hassanan and Ramadan came in and were trying to communicate, I'm still not sure what they were on about. Several young Egyptians that spoke English came by and I asked them to interpret. Even from that, all I could gather was that they were worried about me for some reason. I still have no idea why.

I started to pick up the bags I had filled when Ramadan and Hassanan signaled they would take them, so I went and started working behind the Sphinx. Half an hour later, Nasser the Old approached me.

"I need to go pray to my God," he said. "Can you watch . . . ?" he pointed to the figurines he had lined up neatly on a blanket inside the Sphinx fence.

"You want me to watch your stuff?" I asked.

"Yes," he answered, nodding.

I asked him the prices of his wares, and I think he told me the high end, because I have heard him haggle in the past and the prices were much lower.

I only had one serious inquiry in my short career as an Egyptian souvenir salesman at the Sphinx. A German couple asked my price. I think they thought I said the price in euros, as the man snorted and they left. I think the vendors have to put up with a lot of that.

Then up comes donkey man, Maharab, with food and drink. I still wasn't hungry but I bought a drink.

"How much?" I asked.

"Not worry, you give me five, ten, no worry," he said, shrugging his shoulders.

"Egyptian price," I said, smiling.

He shrugged his shoulders again.

"Five pounds is not Egyptian price," I said, still smiling.

"Give me four," he said, smiling back.

"Two. I give you two."

"I give it to you for three," he said, rolling his eyes.

I gave him the three, and later found out Egyptian price for drink or falafel is two pounds, 40 cents.

At the end of my day, I gathered up the filled bags and took them outside the stone fence behind the horses. I saw Saman again.

"I will work those tombs you showed me a little more," I told him. "Then I will go home."

He said he was hoping he would see the engineer. Apparently the engineer can get me in for free. But we never saw him.

"Meet me at five at Pizza Hut," said Saman. "Then we go to my home to eat."

I went to clean up Saman's tombs and saw that Ramadan and Hassanan had not moved the garbage bags that they said they would. Instead they just rolled them down into another tomb. I took them away.

I went to have tea outside the gate, and the store-owner took me to see Walid a few blocks away where I had an enjoyable tea on the street with his friends. It was at the stable area, on Pyramid Road, very pleasant. When I saw Walid, he shook my hand, and then did the cheek to cheek thing the French do, without the kissing. I guess that's how they do things around here.

I walked home. Mohamed the taxi driver honked his horn and waved at me as he drove by in the opposite direction, and Samir and Magdy were here to greet me as I got back to the hotel. This made me feel at home, like I belonged, at least a little.

Once again today I was amazed at how my feelings can be affected by a negative comment or a positive one.

"So you're just picking up stuff?" said an English woman.

"Yeah."

"Do you belong to a group?"

"No, just me."

"Well, good on ya."

But the lazy boys who just shoved the full bags back into another tomb bummed me out.

Saman and I ate off a round serving tray on the carpet on the floor. I just caught glimpses of his wife. She wears the hijab, but not the veil, the niqaab. He has three daughters, 10 months, two years, and six years—little darlings that he very obviously adores. I was a hit with the kids and soon they were joined by cousins and seven kids were hanging around me, watching Tom and Gerry on the TV. They were all looking at me and smiling shyly.

Saman lives within a block of the Sphinx, in a square four-story cement house he shares with his parents and three brothers and their families.

Other than the television, I saw no furniture, though I was only in the living room. We ate almost immediately after we got to his home.

"Egyptian food, that OK?" asked Saman as the food arrived.

We had canned tuna, pita bread, beans, tomatoes and homemade french fries.

"You like?"

"Yes."

"Really?"

Later we had some type of pea that you bite open and then squeeze out, casting away the thin transparent casing. I think it must be a treat because the kids scarfed it big time after Saman and I finished eating.

As in Rabihr's house, the leftovers were taken out of the room as soon as we finished.

Saman fell asleep a few times watching television after we had eaten.

After a Pepsi and then some tea, I excused myself. It was close to seven, and he had prayers at seven. Plus, I knew he was tired. He's a hardworking man. He told me he gets up at five to get the camels ready, feed them, clean them, etc. Then he's at the Sphinx by eight.

It was news to me that it opens at eight! I will try to be there by eight tomorrow, take some materials to begin learning Arabic in earnest. Now is the perfect time.

I took a cab home. I was tired. I e-mailed Linda and the kids. I had e-mails from the kids, but none from my wife.

I had my heart touched again by an Egyptian. I started loading up my backpack for tomorrow, and realized that I only had two bags left. Panic city!

I went downstairs and talked to the two guys behind the desk, Edward the comedian and another guy. I explained the problem. The bellhop Bono came over, and the three discussed what to do, in Arabic. Finally, it was determined that Bono would go get some bags. They are sold by the kilogram.

"Can I go with you?" I asked Bono, as I wanted to make sure I got what I wanted.

It was a long walk through the streets of Giza. The first store didn't have what we wanted. The second store had two types of bags that would do. I bought two kilos of the thicker ones for 19 pounds, then took one of the thinner bags just to check it out. If the thinner ones are strong enough, I'll get more bags per kilogram.

Once we got back, Edward asked Bono something in Arabic, then Bono reached into his pocket, pulled out 20 pounds and handed it to me.

I didn't understand, and looked at Bono quizzically.

"Edward wants to pay for the bags," said Bono.

I was stepping into the elevator by then, and turned around to look at the comedian, and held my chest where my heart is.

"What? You are doing something for my country . . ." I heard as the elevator doors closed. Once again, the embrace. Twenty pounds is less than four dollars, not much to me, but lots to Edward.

Day 6 in the desert—hot today

"Some people ask why you do this. They think you have some reason, not what you say."

My first day to start at eight a.m., and I was nearly on time. I followed Saman's advice, but could only find three ticket stubs.

"From yesterday," was all the ticket-taker said when I showed him my old tickets.

Some new-age older European woman, in love with Leonard Cohen, saw me and started asking questions.

"Who are you? What are you doing here? Why?"

A Canadian. Picking up garbage. To help.

"Can I help you?" She sure talked a lot.

Apparently she gave up all her worldly wealth some time ago and moved to Egypt. She lives down the street from the Sphinx Gate. She's from Sweden, a writer, a poet, etc. She was interesting, and I'll look her up some day, but I wanted to get in to go to work, so I just paid and went in. I told the Swedish woman I'd be to the left of the Sphinx.

She was waiting for some Egyptian friend who worked there and could get her in for free. I guess when you give up all your worldly goods, you need friends like that.

Typical day, I started to the left of the Sphinx, then worked toward Khafre along the stone fence where the vendors sit. They always leave a mess, so I went at it. Later Ramadan and Walid showed up. That Ramadan sure is a lazy guy. One thing that strikes me is that these guys don't have any garbage bags to put the garbage in. They're always getting them from me. Talk about a flaw in the system!

Saman showed up and told me to go work in the tombs he showed me because I was just doing Ramadan's work for him.

"Look at him," he said pointing to Ramadan sitting on his ass. "He wants get paid, but not want to work."

I met a couple guys from Seattle early in the morning. They wanted sunset and sunrise shots of the pyramids. Since I was picking up trash, they must have assumed I was Egyptian.

"Good morning," I said, and freaked them out.

"Whoa, I didn't expect to hear that accent," said the taller of the two.

"No, eh," I said.

"Canadian?" he guessed accurately. That 'eh' is so universally Canadian.

"Did you pay today?" Saman asked me.

"Yes."

"Maybe I will talk to them," he said, pointing to a tourist office, the entrance to which I had just cleaned, "if he shows up." I have never seen anyone in that tourist office.

Later, Saman called me over. He had a change of plan.

"You must talk to the big boss, Kamal Wahid, General Director of Giza Pyramids, on the other side of Khufu, the big pyramid."

Saman went over the name several times with me so I would remember.

I worked my way to the back, or west side of the big pyramid, picking garbage as I went. I filled one bag, then went straight to the office. I had to ask a few police, but they all knew Kamal Wahid.

There were many entrances to the unassuming one-story building tucked away up a hill a few hundred yards from Khufu. I went in the first entrance, looked in the first door I found, and saw a stately-looking man, maybe mid fifties, sitting at a huge desk. There were many other men in the room.

To be honest, I was worried about seeing this guy because he could say "who the hell do you think you are?" I was strongly tempted to bail, just go back to paying the 60 Egyptian, and not draw attention to myself. This guy might kick me out.

"Are you Kamal Wahid?" I asked, carefully repeating the name Saman had taught me.

"Yes," he said.

"Can I come in?"

"Yes."

"*Arabic shwya, shwya,*" I said. Arabic little, little.

"In English," he said.

I explained what I have been doing, and showed him the tickets.

"Some of the guys said maybe I could talk to you and I wouldn't have to buy a ticket every day."

"I'll take care of it," he said immediately, and picked up his cell phone.

Then one of the many men in the room, Ahmed, a civil engineer, rose and came forward and shook my hand.

"I want to thank you for all of Egypt for what you are doing," he said. "I wish I could help you."

After Mr. Wahid finished his calls, he directed me to go with one of the men in the office to the Sphinx Gate. Ahmed came with us, which was good as Ahmed is fluent in English, and the other guy speaks not a word.

Ahmed wants to be an archeological engineer, takes four more semesters, two years, as he is an engineer already. He's 23, unmarried, perhaps he'll marry in five years. This was his first day on the job.

"The government wants to improve this area greatly," he said, waving his arm over the Giza Plateau.

"According to Mr. Kamal Wahid," said Ahmed, "you are the first person to come to Egypt to do this, ever, from all the world."

I know this isn't exactly true as I saw some Oriental people one day with surgical gloves, masks and tweezers picking up garbage in an area I had already covered. Though I had gone over the area once already, they still filled some six or seven black bags. I think they might have done a little inside the fence by the Sphinx as well. That got me thinking, rule number two of being a Trashman should be "You'll never get it all."

Back in Hendersonville, I wouldn't bother picking up cigarette butts, they were so plentiful. I wonder what chemicals a cigarette filter breaks down into as it decomposes. Is it harmful to human health? I'm willing to bet it is. Worldwide, billions of pounds of cigarette butts become litter each year. Studies have shown when cigarette butts eventually make it to water, they kill microorganisms essential to all life on earth, and take up to 15 years to fully decompose. I think a class-action suit against tobacco companies is in order. They should make the filters from a safe and fast-decomposing material so the streets aren't littered with them. But more importantly, smokers need to be educated as to how to dispose of the filters properly.

My friend James is a smoker. He used to work for me in the fishing industry years ago. I remember one summer day he came by to talk about something, I can't remember what. We were standing in my driveway, and as he was leaving he threw his cigarette butt down on the ground, stepped on it, and with a smile and a wave, he drove off. Now there is no way on earth James would intentionally litter my yard like that. To James, cigarette butts are not litter.

I also spent many hours picking up the Styrofoam packing 'peanuts' used to protect items during shipping. I know there's an organic substitute. The Styrofoam peanuts should be outlawed. One bag of peanuts can litter a football field, and last damn near forever. They take *two hundred years* to decompose.

One pet peeve of mine with garbage on the ground is bright colors, particularly bright blue, as it does not appear often in nature. Even a tiny piece of bright blue plastic can ruin a landscape, as I discovered in northern Canada.

I was working as the editor of the Opasquia Times in The Pas, Manitoba, a twice weekly newspaper of 40-60 pages, when a local photographer walked into my office.

"I'm taking the train up to Churchill," she said. "Would you be willing to buy some pictures of polar bears in the wild?"

On the shore of Hudson's Bay, Churchill is renowned as the polar bear capital of the world, and a Mecca for polar bear watching. Frontiers North Adventures custom builds Tundra Buggies, trucks with tires more than five feet tall and three feet across designed to keep photographers and gawkers up out of harms way, as they drive out onto the ice and into the polar bear's territory. I heard a story once, whether truth or urban myth I don't know, about a tourist reaching his hand out the window wanting to pet a cute polar bear. The polar bear tore his arm off with a swipe of his paw.

"Maybe I'd buy one," I said to her. I can't remember her name, but I do remember she was very good-looking. I was a lot more interested in a date than a picture of a polar bear.

"What would it cost me?" I asked, lacking the courage to ask for what I really wanted.

"One hundred dollars."

She came back a week later with a great shot of a polar bear in its natural habitat. We ran it on the front page, and I gave a color copy to my older brother for Christmas. When he opened it,

I noticed a small speck of blue in front of the bear's face. I didn't notice it in the black and white newspaper, but here it was plain to see. I looked closer, and sure enough, a small piece of bright blue plastic surveyor's tape completely spoiled the all-white landscape.

Ahmed and the other guy introduced me to several people inside the gate on the left side of the Sphinx.

"They say if you bring a copy of your passport for them you won't need to buy a ticket," said Ahmed.

I walked with Ahmed along the sand to show him where I wanted to pick up garbage inside the fence, beside and behind the Sphinx, an area completely off limits to tourists.

"Do you think I could put out some baskets for people to put trash in?" I asked Ahmed. "Here, alongside the Sphinx?"

"I will check with Mr. Kamal Wahid."

I went back to work in the tombs beside the Mortuary Temple of Khafre, and Hassanan called out to me. He showed me a myriad of small tombs and passageways filled with debris. I started to pick up some of the garbage, with Hassanan following me around and watching me, and helping me the odd time. He would tie up a garbage bag, or move it out of the way. I thought he was supposed to be picking up garbage and was being lazy, and with my little Arabic and mimicry, I was giving him a hard time about it.

"Hassanan work," I said. I even had him pick up some garbage while I held the bag.

Well, my bad. Rabihr comes by riding a camel. He translates, and it turns out Hassanan's job is not picking up garbage, it's keeping people out of the areas where they are not to go because there may be antiquities there. These are the same places Hassanan just finished showing me and asking me to clean. I felt terrible, but Hassanan was patient with me. I shouldn't make assumptions. Another rule for a Trashman?

It was after one, and five hours of working hard was wearing on me, so I decided to go home. Rabihr and I hopped on his camel and off we went. It's always a thrill when the camel stands up. He raises his hind legs first, pitching his passengers roughly forward so they must hang on or go flying over the camel's head, and then raising his forelegs, rises to a surprising height. I wouldn't want to fall from such an elevation.

Rabihr wanted me to go to his place, but I wanted to go home for a shower. It gets quite dusty in the tombs, and I was quite rank.

"Why you not bring clean clothes to go home?" Rabihr asked.

I tried to explain that I am dirty, and if I change into clean clothes, those clothes will become dirty. But he is into being clean, as are most Egyptians, it seems. He doesn't go into the dirty tombs either, or sweat as he fills bag after bag in the hot sun.

He dropped me off just outside the site and I walked home. I went downstairs to get my beer, and a copy of my passport to give the people at the Sphinx.

"You should be on TV, a hero to the Egyptian people," said Edward the comedian. "I will call someone to do that tomorrow."

Whoa! This is scaring me now.

The bags work well, so I ordered five more kilograms. Bono (real name Mohamed) will get them today or tomorrow. I have enough for a few days.

No e-mails from home, but I sent one, asking for e-mails. I do miss home.

I bought five more papyruses from Fatih, just taking one. Then I got him to order some Egyptian food, half a chicken, with bread, pickled carrots and peppers, and salad, only 20 pounds.

Rabihr came over and we drank a few beers. He brought a friend, Hamdy, who had a smoke on my balcony and then left. Rabihr stayed for a few hours.

"The police will not be good to me," he said, when I invited him over.

"I will tell hotel security you are coming," I said. "It will be all right."

Sure enough, I got a phone call from the front desk.

"Did you invite Rabihr Noss?"

"Yes, send him up."

Unfortunately Rabihr had forgotten the number to my room, so he came up to the sixth floor, stood around for a while, and then went back into the lobby. He was nervous as a cat. Before its great decline, the hotel was off limits to Egyptians. I couldn't understand what was taking him so long, so I went down to the lobby and caught him before he left.

"Some people ask why you do this," Rabihr told me. "They think you have some reason, not what you say."

Day 7 in the desert—What a day!
Good and bad, up and down, ending on a hopeful note.

"This is the way to do it, soft."

I was there by eight. I'm glad I went to bed at ten the night before. I was allowed through without paying after dropping Mr. Kamal's name. I think the Mr. is used on the first name here. Once through, the fellow who had said simply "from yesterday" when I showed him the tickets I had previously paid for, approached me.

"You no buy ticket, today, tomorrow and after that," he said.

I started in front of the Sphinx Gate today, a little change as good as a rest. I worked there for only half an hour, maybe 45 minutes. As I was working a short woman, with sunglasses and a wide-brimmed hat, called out to me. I had seen her before, and suspect she does not like me. I think she is in charge of the cleaners who rarely clean, and so I am a threat to her.

"*Sba al Hair*," I said as nicely as possible. Good morning.

"Why you do this?" she asked tersely, but with a smile.

"My way to say thanks to the Egyptian people for letting me be here. To embrace them, and all the people of the world."

She smiled, and I went back to work.

I was in the tombs Saman had shown me, when Walid and Ramadan showed up. They told me again with words I did not understand and gestures I could sometimes make out, first, not to put glass in the bags because glass would cut the bags. Okay, I got that. Second, there is a lot of dust down here. I know that. Third, you have to watch out for snakes.

Snakes?

At that point I decided to take a break from the tomb, and I went over to the other bad spot, just to the right of Saman's tombs, where

Little Tiger cut herself. At least that area has seven foot ceilings and easy exits should a snake rear its ugly head. Unfortunately the area has been used as a bathroom for possibly generations, so it was a tradeoff.

The lady that doesn't like me reappeared, this time with a tall lanky man named Mohamed. (There are so many Mohameds.)

"Why you here?" she asked once again. "Egypt is big place, why you not go to Alexandria, or Aswan, or Luxor?"

It became clear that she wanted to get rid of me. I pretended I did not know that, and instead told her we needed a rake to make it easier to clean that area.

"Can I see pictures on your camera?" she asked, completely changing the topic of conversation.

How did she know I had a camera? Then it dawned on me. I had asked Hassanan to take my picture when I was in Saman's tombs. He must have told this woman.

I took out my digital camera and showed her the pictures I had taken. She asked me to delete the ones that showed garbage on the ground.

"It is dangerous for me," she said.

The writing on the wall was as clear as it ever could be. She was covering her butt. But I deleted the offending photos, there were only four that seemed to worry her. While I was doing this, she was looking over my shoulder. It's a new camera, and I have never read the instruction manual, (except when Mohamed the cab driver was helping me find a sim card for my phone) so it took me a while to figure out how to do it. This made her even more suspicious. I guess Rabihr was right. No, I don't guess, I *know* Rabihr was right.

Some people ask why you do this. They think you have some reason, not what you say.

Hassanan brought a rake, and the four of us, Hassanan, Ramadan, Walid and I worked on the bad area. I should call it bad area A as it was the first really bad spot I saw at the pyramids. As we were working, Walid suddenly jumped back. An animated conversation ensued between Walid and Hassanan. From what I could gather Walid was worried the stone slab roof would come crashing down and kill us, but Hassanan struck a pose of a bodybuilder flexing his arms, and said it was strong, no need to worry. Prophetic words.

We continued working, but it always meant one of them raking, me picking up the putrid garbage, and two of them standing around. Periodically I would leave the enclosed area, waiting for the dust to settle.

While waiting, Ramadan asked for some bags and I gave them to him. Then he nudged me on the shoulder to go back in and pick up garbage. I indicated for him to do so. He nudged me again, which angered me. I raised my voice, grabbed the bags from him, all but one, and left. I went about ten yards and then turned around and pulled out my translator Linda had given me for Christmas. I quickly searched the word 'work'.

"*Ramadan hai amal, Ramadan la hai amal, Ramadan hai amal.*" Ramadan work, Ramadan no work, Ramadan work.

Nasser the Old, whose stall I watched while he went to pray, elevating him to Nasser the Devout, came over and asked what was the matter.

Hassanan and Ramadan were following me and I think apologizing.

"He's only a boy, not big," said Nasser. "He doesn't know."

"Tell Ramadan that he has to work," I said to Nasser, pointing to Ramadan the Lazy. "He can't just stand around."

"He is not my boss," I added. "He does not tell me what to do."

I made sure I was loud enough. Rabihr's lesson.

"He's sorry, he's sorry," said Nasser, and Ramadan did seem contrite.

"OKAY?" I said loudly to Ramadan, and he nodded his head.

I had been thinking for some time about how the embrace is not weak, and that guys like Ramadan might mistake kindness for weakness. We shook hands and Hassanan, Ramadan and I went back to help Walid, who was still raking down in bad area A.

Just as we got back into the small tomb Walid came bursting out of the enclosed area, dust chasing after him. About five big stones had fallen from the pillar that holds up the roof of the cavern, but the roof hadn't caved in. Walid had quite the expression on his face, comical really. He had no intentions of going back in there, and it was agreed by all four of us that we had worked in that area enough for one day. We were all laughing the nervous, 'that could have been bad' laugh people sometimes have when escaping injury. To be crushed to death in a five thousand-year-old tomb in Egypt is not how I want to go.

And then I fell into a real pit.

Mahmoud, a fellow I had met with the Lady in the Hat, as I will forever refer to her, called me over. He was with the tall and lanky Mohamed. Mahmoud was dressed in a suit.

"It is great that you have done what you have done," he said, "But you cannot do it any more."

Wham! What the . . . ?

He led me over to the chairs where people sit and watch the light show at night, and we talked. I did not want to stop now. I planned on another 33 days. I can't remember exactly what was said, but I tried explaining that I was just trying to help. He said he loved it that I was doing this and . . . and then he let it out.

"You have to do things in order."

Ah-ha, bureaucracy.

"Then let's do things in order," I said.

Off we went. We hitched a ride up the hill to the administration buildings in a gravel truck and went to see the powers that be.

"Zahi Hawass is in charge of all this," Mahmoud said, waving his arm to indicate everything in sight, "but he is not here now. You will have to see someone else."

I asked to see Mr. Kamal Wahid, but was taken to a different office, to the Chief of Operations, Mohamed Cheoh. We shook hands. He was a short man, with short grey hair and relaxed, kind eyes.

"Can I get you anything?" he asked graciously.

"No, thank-you," I said nervously.

"I'm having tea, will you?"

I had some Egyptian tea as he read some papers on his desk. Then Mr. Kamal Wahid came in, talking on his cell phone. He shook my hand, finished his call, argued with another man, a subordinate I'm sure, then left. Damn, I wish I understood Arabic.

A man came in with a one-foot thick stack of papers for the Chief to sign, and when he finished signing them, he turned his attention to me.

"So tell me, what are you doing in Egypt?" he asked softly.

I told him I had been in Egypt two years before with my son, and loved it. I decided then I wanted to come back and do this, pick up garbage, to say thank-you to Egypt, and to the Egyptian people. I wanted to show my respect for Egypt and the Egyptian people.

"I am not a rich man, I have no money to give," I said. "I am not a powerful man, I can't change things that way, but I can do this. I can pick up garbage. I could say all sorts of nice things about Egypt and the Egyptians . . . "

"Anybody can," he interrupted.

"... but I wanted to demonstrate it. Every time I bend over and pick up a piece of garbage, I have to bend over and pick up that piece of garbage. It's more than words."

He seemed to get it, and said he appreciated what I was doing, thought it was great, but . . . oh-oh here it comes . . .

"You have to get permission from Dr. Zahi Hawass."

Not impossible, I thought. *But Mahmoud said Dr. Zahi was out of town.*

"Is he around?" I asked.

"Yes, he is at the office in Cairo."

The Chief gave me the address in Arabic and English, and said he didn't think there would be any problem.

"This is the way to do it," he said, "soft."

Jubilant once more, I thanked everyone and went out the door to get a cab. The Chief said to pay no more than 20 pounds for a taxi to Dr. Zahi Hawass's office. The first cab driver I saw said 60, the second said 30, so I took it.

An interesting driver. He lives in a town 60 kilometers away, and four months ago married his second wife. He has two now. Egyptians are allowed up to four wives. He works one month in Cairo, then spends one week with the first wife and five kids.

"It's good, it's very good," he said grinning, and I thought about the young man and his lungs. We both laughed. Egyptians love to laugh.

Dr. Zahi Hawass's office is at The Center for Antiquities in downtown Cairo. He is the Secretary-General of The Supreme Council of Antiquities. I found my way to his office, and met his assistant Wafaa, a beautiful young woman wearing a shawl. I told her what I was doing and she thanked me. They all do that. Then I explained what I needed.

"It will not be a problem," said Wafaa, "but Dr. Zahi is not in."

She gave me her phone number to use if I needed anything.

"I will call you after I have spoken to him," she assured me.

It was another negotiation back to Siag, the price of my skin color. The taxi driver first agreed to 40, then on destination asked for 50. I was in an amiable mood, and we settled on 45.

"Good for you and good for me," I said.

I had a shower and ate the last of my chicken from the night before. Then I went down and called Wafaa, gave her the number to Siag, and used the internet, e-mailed home, and to Ahmed, then had a nap. At 4:30 I called Wafaa.

"Have you spoken to Dr. Zahi Hawass?" I asked her.

"I am sorry, he is not here," she said.

"When do you expect him back?"

"Maybe two days."

No!

Then I had a brainwave, and I phoned Ahmed.

"I will call Mr. Kamal Wahid now, and call you back," said Ahmed.

In five minutes he called back.

"You can meet Mr. Kamal tomorrow and he will sort everything out."

Great.

So now I really don't know what will happen to me tomorrow, but apparently Mr. Kamal gets in around ten, so I'll get there by nine, or nine-thirty.

Samir will come over for beer in about an hour and a half, and I'm going to get Fatih to order me some more chicken, or maybe a kebab.

Day 8 in the desert—spent in the office of the Chief of Operations

"One guy came here and said he was Jesus."

I went to the Sphinx around eight, and the guy who told me the day before that I no longer have to pay, was there to tell me he couldn't let me in *at all* until I saw Dr. Z.

I said I would go to Mr. Kamal Wahid's office, and he ordered a subordinate to take me. But instead of taking me to Mr. Kamal Wahid's office, he wanted to take me to the Lady in the Hat. Once I saw where we were heading, I turned around and walked back out. This one cab driver, (at least I think he's a cab driver, he's there every day) asked me what was wrong. I told him. Then several guys had a conversation about me. The taxi driver introduced himself as Ali, and told me to go back in.

"She will not help me," I said to Ali.

"We want to help you, because you clean up the shit," he said. "They take the money but do nothing. It's fucking bullshit!"

Against my better judgement, I let the guy take me in to see the Lady in the Hat.

"I am going to see Mr. Kamal Wahid," I told her.

"He does not come here until ten o'clock," she said.

"I know, I am going to talk to a friend while I wait for him."

"And who is this friend of yours?" she asked, with a threatening smile.

I became worried she might make things bad for Rabihr, so I shut up.

"You stay with me until Mr. Wahid come, you understand?" she said.

"I think we understand each other perfectly well," I replied, smiling back at her. Then I turned and left the site again.

"The Lady in the Hat is no help to me," I told Ali when I was out. "She will not let me go to Mr. Kamal Wahid's office."

"Take a taxi to the other entrance," he told me, "The Mena House gate." He waved a cab over, and opened the door for me. "Pay only ten pounds."

At the Mena House gate, about a half mile north, I had to explain who I wanted to see. They all know Mr. Kamal Wahid, but I was not escorted to his office. I was moved from office to office a few times, and each time they asked me questions, very informally. They were all very friendly, and one guy looked at the pictures on my camera.

They explained that nobody had ever done anything like I was doing.

"I am in shock, and don't know what to say," said one woman.

I spent most of the day in the Chief's office, Mohamed Cheoh, the nice guy with the kind eyes and good English.

The Chief ordered me tea, and shared his food with me. He had probably a hundred people come into his office during the day. For almost every person he pressed a button and the sound of a bird chirping sounded outside, summoning a young man. The Chief would say something to him, and the young man would disappear, then reappear with tea and other drinks. The kid was fast.

Laughter all day, wished I knew what the hell they were talking about. They sure were having fun. Lo and behold in comes an American woman, Sandra, about my age. She's working on her dissertation about false doors. These doors were believed to be a threshold between the living and the dead, through which the dearly departed and the Gods could interact. They were usually the focus of a tomb's offering chapel, and were placed on the west side of a tomb, because the 'land of the dead' was to the west.

Sandra and I had a good conversation in English, a lovely woman.

"What are *you* doing here?" she asked, after explaining false doors to me.

"I doubt you're going to believe me," I said, chuckling, "The Egyptians certainly don't."

At four o'clock Mr. Kamal Wahid came back out of the many meetings he had all day, and argued with the Chief and a third man (whom I call the Third Man) for twenty minutes outside the office. Then the Chief yelled back at me, standing in the doorstep, "You can go, Bruce."

I had been pacing the floor in front of Sandra wondering what my fate would be, talking to her but my mind was wandering. I went over to see the three of them.

"Come back tomorrow and ask for Mahmoud El Al," said Mr. Kamal Wahid.

"No camera," he warned.

I was thrilled. I hope this is the end of that, and I can just go about my business. Sandra, who has been here seven times, said she was amazed I got away with it as long as I did. I admit it was hugely arrogant to just come here and start picking up debris at this sacred site. But I'm okay now.

I learned something of the culture of Egypt today. I was sitting with my right ankle over my left knee, exposing the bottom of my foot to the room.

"In our country it is an insult to sit like that," the Third Man said to me, pointing at the sole of my shoe. "To show the bottom of your foot to someone is very bad, but I know you do not know that, so I am not angry."

"I know it now," I said, putting my foot back on the ground.

My watch died on me, water resistant my ass. I need more bags, and to do some laundry. I think I'll just wash some socks in the sink. They should be dry by tomorrow afternoon.

I have to mention something surprising. The Chief told Sandra and myself a joke.

"This Australian comes to America, and crosses the street without looking. He's almost hit by a car. The driver of the car rolls down his window and yells out, 'What? Did you come here to die?'

'No,' yells the Aussie, 'I came here yesterdie.'"

An Egyptian joke. Quite clever to make a joke based on dialect differences in another language.

I think they kept me there all day to determine if I was a good guy or not, sane or insane. The Chief told me they have had a lot of different people come to the site.

"One guy came here and said he was Jesus."

I just came back from getting some more bags and a watch with Bono. The watch cost 3.5 pounds, about 70 cents. Made in China, of course. As we were setting it in the store, the lights went out. The merchant coolly lit a candle, and things continued. Minutes later the lights came back on, and we finished the deal and left. Business as usual in this chaotic place.

Bono hailed one of the tok-toks and he took us for bags. Lights were still out there. A kid was running the store using his cell phone. We couldn't find what we wanted, both his and Bono's phones kicked out. But a minute later the owner showed up on a motorcycle, and we had two kilos of bags—one of the tough bags, and one of the weaker ones. That's the last of the tougher, but he'll have some more in two days. I told him I may need fifty kilos. It would cost a hundred dollars but would last until I go home.

Day 9 in the desert—great to be back

"She think you take Sphinx back to Canada."

Whoa, the power just died. A good thing this computer has a surge protector because I usually leave it plugged in all day. I'm sure the power goes off and on several times a day.

I had an early start, and was there by eight. They let me in when I asked for Mahmoud El Al, but then they saw the Lady in the Hat coming. Her name I discovered is Madame Boudry. The guards made me wait for her.

She was a little weird but okay today. Nasser the Devout explained to me that she just does not believe someone would do this for free. She did say to me that I should take the next two days off, as it is the weekend.

"Ramadan and Walid will not be here, and you are just like them," she said.

"I am here for forty days, and if I take days off I will never leave," I said, smiling. It had the desired effect. She wants me gone as soon as possible.

I started work in front of the Sphinx. There was one area I'm sure nobody has touched for a long time. It was the inside of a curved wall, only sand there, and no reason for a tourist, or anybody else for that matter, to walk there. However the wind often blows in that direction, filling the area with debris.

Ahmed the engineer came by, and I talked with him for a while. I invited him to Canada for fishing. I will have to ask if he gets seasick. He certainly seems a good guy. I told him about the Lady in the Hat.

"I will ask if you can work tomorrow and the day after," said Ahmed.

"I worked those days last week," I said.

"Well then, if you worked those days last week, it should not be a problem," he said, shaking his head vigorously. "Do not worry."

I promised Ahmed a copy of Skufty, and I have just put it in my bag.

I finished more than half of the curved wall by ten thirty, then went to the Sphinx.

"Where have you been for two days?" asked Saman.

"The day before yesterday security took me to see Mohamed Cheoh, the Chief of Operations, and he sent me to see Dr. Zahi Hawass," I explained. "But the Doctor was not in. Yesterday I was in the Chief's office."

"Why you in the Chief's office?"

"I don't know," I said, shrugging."To see if I am a terrorist?"

There were two Egyptian women sitting on the stone fence next to the exit from the Valley Temple of Khafre, one with the niqaab, the other with just the hijab. The one with the niqaab called me over as soon as she saw me, ripped off a small piece of the sandwich she was preparing to eat, and then gave me the lion's share. I sat and ate with them, and they laughed and laughed.

The woman with the hijab sat beside me and handed me potatoes and pickled vegetables. She spoke English quite well.

"What is your religggg . . . religiii . . . religion?" She asked, struggling over the word. That was a tough one. I didn't quite know what to say.

"I believe in all the religions," I eventually said. (Though I don't identify myself as a Christian, because of my experience at St. John's many of the people I admire in this world are Christians.)

At that she and Saman said something to each other, (I will have to ask Saman what it was) and they agreed, nodding their heads. What they agreed on I have no idea. I may have been interpreted as an atheist, which is far from the truth. Or maybe an idiot, not quite so far from the truth. *Ya big dummy.*

"My religion is Islam," she said, leaning toward me, and then back again, smiling proudly.

They came by bus from a town 200 kilometers away, and would return that day. I wished I was allowed to take pictures.

These ladies were a blast, laughing all the time. Their kids gathered around and took my picture with their cell phones. I didn't think to ask them to e-mail the pictures to me. One of the girls gave me a pineapple drink, and I shared my water with the veiled woman. She would remove her niqaab from time to time, and I got a clear look at her face. She was always smiling that 'whole-face' smile, unlike the Lady in the Hat. She'll have crows feet galore when she's older and she'll laugh about that too, I'm sure.

"You will have to take an Egyptian wife the next time you come," joked Saman.

"Will you marry me?" asked the woman with the hijab, laughing.

I didn't want to say goodby.

The ladies offered me tea.

"You have two minutes to drink it," said Saman, playing the taskmaster, "and then get back to work."

I'm sure I will never meet them again, but I hope I never forget them. They gave me a free lunch, a pile of laughs, and a warm feeling toward Egyptians and Muslims. Wonderful people. Here I am, Heinlein's proverbial stranger in a strange land, and they embraced me.

It's interesting to note that we in the West are often told the veil and headdress subjugates women, and yet these women seemed as liberated and free to express themselves as anyone I have ever met. There is a view that the wearing of the hijab and the veil is to show honor to an object, or a place. Certainly all the depictions of Jesus's mother Mary have her head covered.

When I was picking up trash along Highway 64 that runs through Hendersonville, I found a concrete statue of Mother Mary, 18 inches tall. It was broken in two, but I took it home and my kids and I glued her back together. We scraped the old paint off and repainted her bright white. She glistens in the sun in our back yard now, watching over my family while I'm in Egypt. Lady Madonna, my children at her feet. She has a hijab. Is she Muslim?

I worked my way around to Nasser the Devout's spot, and spoke with him briefly.

"I don't think the Lady in the Hat likes me," I said to him.

"No, this is good," he replied, looking over my shoulder.

I turned to see what he was looking at, and sure enough, she was right behind me, with Hassanan in tow. I'm sure she heard me. Ha-ha on me.

Nasser spoke with her briefly, and later explained her suspicions.

"She think you take Sphinx back to Canada," he said, smiling.

The Lady in the Hat and Hassanan showed me a tomb just behind Nasser that needed a lot of work, and I put my back into it. It took six bags to clean up. I took the bags to the drop off point, in a little pit in the horse and camel area far outside the tourist area. The Lady in the Hat reappeared with her tall and lanky companion, and followed me. They watched as I returned to the back of the Sphinx and worked my way along to the pyramids. I do not understand why they follow me. It must be because she is so suspicious of my motives.

After working my way up the walkway to Khufu, I went in to see the Chief, Mohamed Cheoh. He was sitting there with the Third Man, saying goodby to Sandra, the American woman.

"I'm just checking in," I said to the Chief.

"But you have skipped a few bosses," he said, smiling widely. "You should see Madame Boudry first, not come straight to the big boss."

So I have to submit to her authority. That's fine. As much as it pains me, I will do it. Maybe that is the lesson here for me. One of them, anyway.

Mohamed had offered me tea, but I declined, wanting a cold beer. It may have been a mistake, as the Lady in the Hat showed up as I was leaving. Who knows what she will tell the Chief.

I saw Mr. Kamal Wahid on my way out and gave him the copy of Skufty as a gift. I'll pack another one to give to Ahmed tomorrow.

On my way down to the Sphinx and home, I picked up the three bags I had filled on the way to see the Chief, and dragged them down. When I got close to the wall that separates the horse and camel people from the tourists, Little Tiger came alongside.

"Give me," she said, grabbing one bag.

"It is too heavy," I said.

"No problem," she said. She dragged it along the ground with great effort.

Then two other kids came along and took a bag each. Empty-handed, I stopped walking and watched them carry and drag the bags across the sand to the drop-off spot. It was a beautiful sight.

"Would you like some tea?" a stranger yelled out as I was walking to Siag.

"Yes, I love Egyptian tea."

He was a cab driver having tea with a friend. Random act of kindness.

The maintenance boys are here to check on my refrigerator. Of everything in this room, bed, blankets, shower, toilet, power source, lights, and even television, my refrigerator is the most important. *Cold beer.*

Day 10 in the desert—a great day, no Lady in the Hat

"It's commendable, but at the end of the day, after you leave, it'll all be the same."

The Lady in the Hat was not in as today and tomorrow are holidays. Yahoo!

I was met at the Sphinx Gate by Ali, who greeted me warmly with "this is your place" and led me inside. That felt good. I was worried again that I may not get in. I count my blessings every day I get past security.

I was feeling a little rough this morning. Last night Fatih bought me dinner, and I ate and fell asleep until 11:30. Then I went down and drank with the English people.

Archie and George had me laughing until 3:00 a.m.. Good old Andy Capp that George, and his wife Flo was there too, and she does look a bit like Flo. Archie's wife was not impressed by the comparison.

"That's hawdly flattering," she said, looking every bit the prim and proper Englishwomen with her hands on her lap, looking down her nose at me.

I met a fellow named Mohawk at security. He was sweeping the floor. A big beefy guy with an honest face and a friendly smile, he's been working here for years.

I started where I had left off in the semicircle, but after about an hour the tall lanky Mohamed that pals around with 'the hatted one,' came by and from his gesticulations I determined the good Dr. Zahi Hawass was here, and he didn't want the Doc to see me.

Fine by me. I worked in Saman's tombs, and then took ten bags out of the out-house, (bad area A) so named because it's clear that's where people have been going to the bathroom.

Wanting a change, I worked my way to the middle pyramid that still has some limestone casing stones near the top, Khafre. The casing stones are fitted together so expertly that a knife blade cannot fit between them.

Egyptologist Sir Flinders Petrie wrote in 1880 that the precision of the casing stones was "equal to opticians' work of the present day, but on a scale of acres."

In ancient Egyptian times the pyramids appeared as shimmering white mountains. Mind-blowing to anyone who saw them, I'm sure.

A massive earthquake in 1300 AD, or less than 15 BTE ago, loosened the casing stones from the pyramids, and they were carted away to be used to build mosques and fortresses in Cairo.

There is plenty of garbage around Khafre. I could easily spend a day there.

Halfway up to Khafre, a vendor, Hya-hya, selling water and such, called to me. He had stashed a pile of garbage behind a rock, and he took my bag and filled it. He wanted to keep the area clean, but hadn't the technology, if you will. I left him with a bag for later.

"*Shokrun*," he said. Thank-you.

Continuing uphill to Khafre, an Egyptian tourist tapped me on the shoulder, and I turned around.

"What are you doing?"

"I love Egypt," I said, simply.

"Egypt love you."

A minute later he brought me a sandwich, and had his wife take a photo of the two of us.

I went to see Rabihr, who said he was working at the entrance to the modern building that houses Khufu's ship.

Khufu's ship was discovered in 1954. The sailboat, 143 feet long and 19.5 feet wide, was disassembled and laid out in a logical manner in 1,224 pieces, and buried in a pit beside Khufu's pyramid. Nobody knows the history or function of the ship, but there is speculation it is a 'solar barge' a ritual vessel to carry the resurrected king with the sun god Ra across the heavens. It might have been a funerary barge, carrying the kings embalmed body from Memphis to Giza. Maybe Khufu used it to visit holy sites, and it was buried for his use in the afterlife.

It was painstakingly reassembled over several years, and has been on display since 1982. It has been described as a masterpiece of woodcraft that could sail today if put in water.

Thousands of tourists visit the ship each day, so it's a good spot for Rabihr to sell his wares, but again he wasn't there.

"Do you know where he lives?" asked one of the vendors.

I thought of that motorcycle ride. Like I was paying attention to where I was going? My God, I was trying to stay alive!

I ended the day taking four bags to the outside pit. I was tempted to do a bit more at the semicircle, but I was feeling dead tired, so I went home.

I was thinking about my daily expenditures, and beer is definitely the highest. For instance, yesterday I bought no food. I had no breakfast, though it's provided here at Siag. The Islam ladies bought me lunch, and Fatih bought me supper. However, I spent at least 20 bucks on beer. Today I had the sandwich the fellow gave me, and will eat the remainder of Fatih's gift for supper. But I've already spent eight dollars on beer. I will have to make a graph of my daily expenses. (Appendix D)

It's unfortunate I don't have a camera at work. In about ten days I'll ask again if I can have it. I have always felt that I wouldn't get any real respect until after 20 days. Like snowshoeing.

I ran in two federal elections in Canada for the ruling Liberal party. The first time there was no incumbent and I thought I had a chance. A five-way race, I lost with less than 25 per cent of the vote. The second time, the party approached me and asked me to run.

"I'll run if I can do it my way," I said, knowing I had no chance of winning.

They were cool with that, and so it being a winter election, (one reason for being cool) I snowshoed some 300 miles around the riding.

Paul Martin, Canada's Prime Minister and the leader of my party, actually said "Let's strap on our snowshoes and get to work," on national television to inspire the troops the day the election was called. I was the only candidate to take his words literally.

I thought I had to do 100 miles before anybody would notice. Sure enough, the media showed up the day I passed the 100-mile mark.

I snowshoed a circular route, ending back in Gimli on election day. I spoke to my kids as I was taking off my snowshoes to go into the school gymnasium to vote.

"I want you guys to tell your children that *their* grandfather once snowshoed three hundred miles to cast his vote. That's how important it was to him."

It was worth the pain of the 300 miles just to be able to say that. I try to take every opportunity to teach my children. And to assure them that I love them.

"I'm glad you're my son, son," I've often said to each of the boys, words I have yet to hear from my own father.

"I'm glad you're my daughter," to Ally.

I get paid back in spades.

"I'm glad you're my Dad, Dad."

"We sure got lucky, didn't we? I could've ended up with some other kids, but I didn't. I got you guys."

"Yeah, we sure got lucky."

Another thought I had yesterday was that radical Islam is not Islam at all, and needs to be denounced by Muslim clerics. I saw a Muslim woman on TV, crying out how she was ashamed of Muslims who beheaded a Polish engineer. But she needn't be. That is not Islam at all. What shall we call them? Islamic Defilers? Demons?

UN Secretary General Koffi Annan hit the nail on the head at the Global Ethic Lecture in Tubingen in 2003, when he said "No religion or ethical system should ever be condemned because of the moral lapses of some of its adherents. If I, as a Christian, for instance, do not wish my faith to be judged by the actions of the Crusaders or the Inquisition, I should be very careful not to judge anyone else's faith by the actions that a few terrorists may commit in its name."

I was talking with Archie last night, about my time picking up garbage, my forty days in the desert.

"It's commendable, but really, at the end of the day, after you leave, it'll all be the same," he said.

That may be true, but maybe that's the purpose. Really, why get out of bed? You're just going to return to it in the evening. I don't know.

When I was ten years old, I had a small tin box hidden in the closet underneath the stairs. This box held all my little treasures that I wanted to keep forever. Then my grandfather died, and I realized my own mortality. I, too, would die, and these treasures would be meaningless. Only I cherished them. I remember walking to the garbage cans out by the back lane and throwing the box away. If I could not keep them for eternity, what was the point? Why waste energy on them?

Linda might call tonight, but I have no interest in talking to her. I appreciate that she's looking after things back home, but she's mad that I'm here, and just bums me out when we talk. I do want to talk to my children.

Today as I was struggling to carry four bags a kid on a horse asked to take one, and I gave him one. Then a man did as well, lightening my load.

Day 11 in the desert—I met Hya-hya again

"They say they are poor, but they are not poor."

Where to start? I went to the ACE club last night, the expatriate club I found on the internet. I needed some time in a pub!

I flagged down a cab outside the hotel. The driver was a really happy guy, just grinning away, his face lit right up. He didn't speak much English, but he quoted me 30 pounds, read the address I had written in English, and off we went. When he wasn't grinning he was singing to the music on the radio, really blissing out. All the cabs seem to play the same music.

I'm suffering from music deprivation, I need to hear some classic rock or folk music, "the kinda music just soothes the soul."

When Jake was almost two years' old, and Ti was on the way, we wanted to buy a house in Gimli. We searched for months, but couldn't find anything suitable.

I was a member of the Kinsmen of Gimli, a service club, and at our annual meeting Linda was lamenting the lack of housing choices in Gimli to the mayor's wife, Jocelyn.

"Why don't you see if you can buy the old Tergesen house across the street from us?" asked Jocelyn. "It's been empty for two years."

We called the owners and agreed to agree on a fair price, keeping realtors out of the transaction. Possession was to be June 1st.

But we didn't have any money.

I went looking for fishing jobs in British Columbia, hoping to make enough for a down-payment. Before I left, I spent months in the gym getting into shape. I wanted to bounce as I walked the docks looking for work. There were lots of guy pounding the docks for a job, but I knew *I* would hire me in a heartbeat, and wanted the fishermen in BC to feel the same way. I cut my hair to look as clean-cut as possible, and quit smoking.

I landed two jobs, a month on a freezer prawn boat that ended just before my spring season on Lake Winnipeg began, and a season on a salmon gill-netter that started when my spring season ended, and was over a few days before my fall season began in Gimli. I was able to fish seven months consecutively, and we got the house.

Buying groceries for the salmon boat in Prince Rupert, just south of Alaska, I was startled to hear music playing from the store's speakers. It was marvelous! It seemed to fill me up, and I was dancing in the aisles.

I needed that music. I didn't mind my skipper, Greg Bolderson, but he didn't like me, and there were just the two of us on the boat. In all my commercial fishing experience, in three different countries and six or seven different fisheries, Bolderson was the only skipper that took a dislike to me.

Most of his deck-hands in the past were in their late teens or early 20's, while I was 33.

"I want someone a little older," he said when he hired me. "I'm sick of hearing how fast their truck can go, or how drunk they get. I need some mature conversation."

Be careful of what you ask for, or you just might get it.

The problem with mature conversation is someone can disagree with you, and have the facts to back it up. In the past Bolderson could rattle off any amount of inanities to his young crewmen, and never be challenged. To my detriment, I had my own thoughts on most matters, and would politely share them.

Bolderson didn't share many of my beliefs, but we were already into the season, and he'd have trouble finding a new man. Besides, I was polite, and worked like a bastard. Since he had recently changed from a lifetime of trolling—catching fish with hooks—to gill-netting, I knew gill-nets much better than he did.

I didn't share many of Bolderson's beliefs, but we were already into the season, and I'd have trouble finding a new job. Everybody had their crews and I needed the money to buy the house. Besides, he was polite, and appreciated my hard work. He also had a nose for the fish, and since I was on commission, I could do worse than working on his boat.

Certain incidents exacerbated the situation.

We were allowed one net, 200 fathoms, or 1200 feet long. One end was attached to the boat, but the other had to be free-flowing. Unlike Lake Winnipeg, fishermen were not allowed to anchor the net. Fish openings were 24, 36, or 48 hours long, and many fishermen would fish through the opening without sleep. To his credit, Bolderson was a practical man, and since the daytime produced a fraction of the fish caught at sundown and sunup, he insisted we rest during the day, to be sharp when fishing was the heaviest.

"I'm going down for a nap," he said one day.

I looked at him questioningly. We had the net floating off the back.

"Don't worry," he said, reading my look, "the net will be fine. But wake me up if we start moving toward those rocks. It's probably not a problem, just watch the tide."

"You sure?" I asked, looking at the rocky island he had pointed to. I had never fished here before, and had no idea of the strength of the tides. I didn't even know when it was high or low tide!

"Yeah, it'll be fine."

It was a beautiful day, so I sat on the deck and read a book, glancing at the rocks from time to time.

Judging distance over water can be tricky, but soon I began to think we were moving closer to the rocks. I debated waking up the skipper for some time, unsure of what I was seeing. Finally, I went below deck and shook him awake.

We pulled the net in as quickly as we could, but the tide was faster. We lost the end of the net, causing $1500 damage.

"It's a good thing you woke me up," said Bolderson, "or we would've lost the entire net, not just a portion."

"That won't happen again," I vowed. If I had woken him sooner, we would still have the whole net.

Two weeks later we were at the same spot, in the same conditions.

"Let's both catch some sleep so we're ready for sunset," said Bolderson.

I looked at the rocks where we lost some of our net a fortnight before. Then I looked at him. Was he crazy? Instead of asking him if he was, I shrugged my shoulders.

He's the skipper, I thought. *Perhaps he knows something I don't.*

I lay in my bunk, unable to sleep. I had vowed it wouldn't happen again, and yet here we were, both in our bunks, while we're drifting God only knows where with 1200 feet of net worth $5000 trailing behind us.

I went up to take a leak and quickly came back down to wake the skipper.

"It's happening again. I'm sure of it."

Once again we cranked in the net at full speed, but this time we got it all, just as our boat was 20 feet from shore. If we had stayed below deck for another 20 minutes, the net would be gone and the boat would've been on the rocks.

Normally I picked all the fish out of the net while the skipper drove the boat, and told me what to do. But once in a while he would come out on deck to work the net with me. One time we hit a school of red jellyfish.

Jelly fish tend to come apart easily when handled and are easy to get out of the net. But contact with red jellyfish burns the skin, and can really burn the eyes. Flush with water and it goes away in a few minutes.

The skipper was helping me on deck as the drum pulled in the net, activated by a bar at our feet. Stand on the bar and the hydraulics rotates the drum drawing the net into the boat.

The bar is a safety feature required by law on gill-netters after a fisherman fishing alone was caught up in his net and coiled on the drum along with the net. He was broken in half and buried by his net. With nobody on board to turn it off, the drum kept going around and around. The boat was found out of fuel, the fisherman assumed to have fallen overboard. They towed the boat to harbor. It was weeks later someone walked by the vessel in port and noticed a strange smell coming from the net. Uncoiling the net revealed the unfortunate victim.

The skipper was trying to squeeze a red jellyfish through the mesh of the net. If a jellyfish is tangled in a mass of mesh, or web as we call it, squeezing it through is easier than flipping the mesh back and forth and trying to find it to flip it overboard. But this takes time, and reduces the creature to, well, a mass of jelly looking for some skin to burn.

I could see the creature was merely caught in one flap of mesh, or web, near the cork-line. Flipping the line would release it and send it back into the water. A simple process, but because of our tense relationship, I didn't want to tell Bolderson how to do it. Instead I tried to show him by flipping the line ever so slightly, hoping he would see what needed to be done without me telling him, and we could get moving again. Time is money, and I had a house to buy.

Instead, he lifted the jellyfish into the air still in the net, and slammed it down on the deck, sending red jellyfish pieces flying in all directions, including into both our faces.

"Are you working with me or against me?" he yelled.

My face burning for two reasons, I swore I'd never again try to teach him anything. But that didn't mean *I* couldn't learn from *him*.

Though I knew more about handling gill-nets, he knew infinitely more about his fishing grounds than I did.

One opening we caught a school of a dogfish, a type of shark.

"Watch out," he said, "they can stick you." He pointed out they had small spikes on their body.

Big deal, I thought. *Most of the fish on Lake Winnipeg have those. Fishermen often get a spine or bone in their hands.*

Moments later I had a spine go under my thumbnail. It hurt, but no more than I expected. I kept working.

Twenty minutes later it hurt even more.

"Man, that bone must have broken off under there," I said, examining my thumb. "It hurts way more than it should."

"They're poisonous as well," he said.

If I'd known that I would've been more careful.

The first sea urchin we caught in the net confounded me. All those spikes, I thought it would take forever to get it out, as I gingerly rotated it in my hand, examining it to determine my course of action.

"I'll show you how to deal with these," said Bolderson. He smashed it to bits with a baseball bat, and the pieces fell out of the net and onto the deck like magic. I never would've thought of that.

We evolved a working relationship based on our mutual desire to catch as much fish as possible. We didn't discuss anything of real importance. We stuck to the job at hand, and small talk. We never mentioned the elephant in the galley, and we got along.

The ever-present cloud that hung about the boat, and my head, was depressing, but the music in the grocery store just chased it away. I danced in the aisles as I shopped for grub for the boat, blissing out like the cab driver yesterday.

Once we got close to the ACE club my cabbie had to ask directions a few times. I didn't mind. I was in no hurry. Once there I gave him 40 pounds, ten pounds more than we had agreed on, glad to have his upbeat company.

The club was entertaining. Everyone who works there is black, which I commented on as I sat at the bar.

"What, a white guy's not good enough to work here?" I said. "You have to be black? That's racism."

"Uhh . . . It's a Sudanese club, buddy."

You must hold a foreign passport to enter. The first visit is free, after that it's 20 pounds, and after three more visits you have to join or not come back. This was my free visit.

The first guy I met was Tony, a short Englishman, 62 years old, and a dead-ringer for the actor Bob Hoskins. In a few minutes he explained that when his wife died at 55, he came to Egypt.

"I felt like I had two pricks, I screwed everything," he said, adding that he never cheated on his wife in England. He has a new wife, a much younger black woman about a foot taller than him. They've been together for many years.

"I'll get you some clean women, don't you worry," he said to me, unsolicited. "I won't get you any dirty women, nobody needs that." So I guess that's taken care of.

Tony wandered off and I met a German couple, Michael and Katja. At least I think they were a couple. Very informative. He's been here off and on for 22 years, her only two and a half. Engaging conversation. She has very little respect for the intellect of Egyptians.

"They all have only one brain cell, and most of them have lost it," she said with a thick German accent. And yet she was in a relationship with an Egyptian once. She also said that many European women in their fifties and sixties come to Egypt to have sex with men in their twenties.

The beer was cheap, only 12 pounds. They have a card system where you buy a card worth 100 pounds. It has a bunch of numbers on it that add up to 100. When you buy a beer they scribble over 12 pounds worth.

I had about six beers and then left. I was tired, and it was quite smoky in there. The Germans chain-smoked all night. It looked interesting, lots of people from all over the world. Next to me was what I think was a drunk German, groping a black woman with so much rouge on her cheeks she looked cartoonish. I imagined she was from some poor African country, and that since she had a foreign passport she could enter the Ace club to try and improve her lot in life.

"He is grabbing me," she complained to Michael, squirming out of the German's grip.

"Where is your husband?" he said, and for some reason that shut her up.

When I left, Michael was wandering around, and Katja was trying to talk me into staying.

"I have to work at eight in the morning," I said.

"You can't be late?"

The cab ride back was uneventful, and Hassan the Egypt-Israeli war veteran bellhop came up to my room with my laundry.

"You are like me when I was in the army," he said, hunching his shoulders and flexing his arms. "Strong."

I went straight to sleep, and was I ever tired in the morning.

Ali met me again after I went through security.

"No camera?"asked security.

"No camera."

I went to work at the semicircle, and finished my work along the wall. I worked the sand in front of the Sphinx for a while, keeping a good eye on my backpack. I would hate to see it disappear. I also have to keep it fairly close because if I wander too far from it security suspects there's a bomb inside.

Bombs are a real concern here. In fact, yesterday I had left some bags against the vendor's wall, and today Walid came up to me, and with his charade skills let me know I couldn't leave the full garbage bags where they were because security was concerned about an explosion.

"Boom," said Walid, putting his hands together as if holding a basketball, then moving them apart.

So I moved the bags. He didn't offer to help. Here I am judging again. Walid didn't ask me to come here. Rule number one, Benson.

Ramadan, Hassanan, and Mohawk appeared. Mohawk did some interpreting, and he told me that Ramadan and Walid were "bad people."

"They say they are poor, but they are not poor," he said. "They have a cow, chickens, sheep."

I continued talking to Mohawk as Ramadan and Walid walked over to the Sphinx. Mohawk looked up, then nodded his head in their direction.

"Look at them, they are fighting," he said. Sure enough, there were Ramadan and Walid, slapping each other in front of the entrance to the Sphinx Temple like Curly and Moe from the Three Stooges. It was hilarious. I laughed, but Mohawk just shook his head with obvious disgust. Then he asked for my mobile number, and was incredulous when I said I didn't have one.

"I will see you tomorrow," I said. "*Bokra, Enshallah.*" Tomorrow, God willing.

I was hung-over. I counted the beers I had last night. It wasn't that many, maybe eight, but I guess it was the night before with the Englishmen that was getting me.

Near the end of the day I met Hya-hya and I gave him a garbage bag. He sells water and soda out of a two-gallon metal pail. He led me over to a pile of trash in the remnants of a tomb. It was an area only about eight feet by twenty, but we filled at least twelve bags. He helped me until the job was done, the first time that has happened. He has some other areas to do tomorrow, and I'll meet him at ten. It was great to run into him because I was tired, really beat, and wondering what the hell I was doing. I was really doubting myself. I don't show it to anybody, but I battle with reason every day. Am I being an idiot, wasting time and money in Egypt, when I should be with my wife and kids?

As we were walking, a very old man wearing a grey calibaya quite similar to Hya-hya's came over and shook my hand.

"*Ana Bruce*," I said.

"*Ana Rabihr*," he answered.

I think he's a caretaker of a guardhouse to the south of the causeway to Khafre, two thirds of the distance from the Sphinx to the pyramid. I call him Rabihr the Elder.

I called home today and all is well. Linda got the flowers and chocolate I ordered on-line for Valentine's Day, and was in a good mood.

I walked home and drank a few beers before I had a shower. Damn good, that beer.

Rabihr came up to me on a horse just as I was finishing today. He wants me to go by his place tonight, but I'm too tired. I still have writing to do, and I have to go get more bags. The thin ones just aren't tough enough, and they rip so easily. I will have lunch with Rabihr tomorrow, at Khufu, the big pyramid.

I went with Samir to get bags, it was a different place with white bags instead of black, but they seem strong. I'm sure they'll do.

"How many bags you use in one day?" Edward the comedian asked when we returned.

"About one and a half kilos."

"How many more days you go to pyramids?"

"Twenty-nine."

"Why don't you just get 45 kilos of what you want, and keep them in your room?" he asked. "Whatever is left, leave it for the hotel." *Ya big dummy.*

I speak with Fatih nearly every night. Tonight he told me that ten years ago he had a small problem with his heart.

"I had to quit smoking cigarettes, and hashish," he said, "and beer, whiskey and women."

"Outside of my marriage, that is," he added, grinning.

Yesterday he told me he met a woman from Turkey, 51 years old. I saw her at his shop a few days ago. She looked older than that. Fatih said he was thinking of marrying her, a second wife. I guess he's not *too* concerned about his heart.

"Are you really getting married?" I asked him last night.

"She wants me to send her money to come to Egypt," he said, "but I want her to come to Egypt first, then I will give her the money."

"I'm not stupid," he added, tapping his head and smiling.

Day 12 in the desert—feeling good

"Bruce!"

I went to bed last night at eight o'clock, and I felt great today. Too many late nights, I guess, and it is hard work, givin'er all day. I actually went down for breakfast for the first time in many days. There's not much there I like, but apparently you can order an omelet or boiled eggs, so I might try that tomorrow. A Spanish omelet would be good.

A watershed moment—today was the first day security did not open my backpack. They just handed it back to me with a smile and some words in Arabic.

I went to work right away, cleaning up an overflowing garbage container first, (in all the site, there are only three small trash containers at the Sphinx Gate) then working on the large area in front of the Sphinx, a way to keep away from the Lady in the Hat, though she did wander around for a while and just lingered nearby.

Hassanan came up and hugged me and said something, I think, about Doc Zahi. Maybe the Doc gave me approval. I'll have to check downstairs at the front desk of Siag for a message from Wafaa.

I had lunch from the donkey man, Maharab. Such a wicked sandwich, I could eat one every day. It costs four pounds but I gave him five, almost a whole dollar in total for a sandwich and a seven-up. But he still must make a profit.

Maharab is very enterprising, and a fine example of minimal packaging. He reuses everything he can, and always takes the bottles back to recycle because he gets a deposit back on them. The only waste he leaves behind is biodegradable eggshells, and the odd pile of manure his donkey produces. He doesn't drive a car to work, he walks leading his donkey that doesn't use gasoline, but runs on fresh, green clover. I'm sure 50 to 100 people are fed by this man each day, and zero non-biodegradable waste is produced from it.

Compare that to 100 people going to McDonalds. First, most people drive to McDonalds burning non-renewable fuels. These fuels were pumped out of the bowels of the earth and refined from crude oil using energy and polluting hundreds of gallons of water in the process, then polluting the air as they are burned.

And the packaging! Energy was used to produce every bit of packaging, and everything is packaged. *Everything!*

Maharab should be looked at as an example of how we can greatly reduce our dependance on energy, consumption of natural resources, and packaging waste that clogs our landfills taking decades to decompose. And what does he do it with? A freakin' donkey!

Rabihr showed up on a camel again after lunch. He found me near the Mortuary Temple of Khafre. I am now going to a party tonight behind Rabihr's house.

I was taking three bags down to the pit as I was leaving and a young girl about 13 or 14 helped me by grabbing two of the bags. I was happy when she didn't ask for any money in return. You never know. I hope it has become understood that I have no money to pay for help.

Walking down the street on my way home I was assailed with the usual countless—"Taxi? Hello, where you going? You need something?" And little children following me, trying to sell me something, when one kid yells out "Bruce!"

I stopped and we shook hands, he was beaming. I didn't recognize him, but I must know him from inside the site. I must make a better effort to remember names and faces.

I went to the embassy again, got a few flags, apparently that's all they have. No more flags or any other paraphernalia.

"It's cheaper to go to a dollar store," said Christian, my contact at the embassy.

"Where is there a dollar store in Egypt?" I asked.

"Not in Egypt, in Canada."

He gave me everything he had, some flags, balloons and pins. The trip took one and a half hours, through congested, exhaust-filled streets. Tough on the lungs. Tough on vehicles too, there's hardly a car or truck on the street that hasn't a dent or scrape on it and side-view mirrors have a short life-span.

Bono went to get the bags and order another 35 kilos. That should last me until I go home.

Fatih exchanged some money for me, and let me use his phone. I picked up a papyrus. He owes me four now. Apparently the woman from Turkey is planning on coming within two weeks.

"She wants to meet my family and see my house," said Fatih.

After the party . . .

Rabihr showed up early, and we went to his buddy's place to wait for the party to begin. They were really into their appearance. Young Ali was worried his jeans were too long, Rabihr thought his jacket was dirty, and their other buddy Bolla polished his shoes so bright you could shave by them.

The back streets are really interesting. I can imagine that in most instances, each neighbor knows what the other is up to. It was really neat to see that they have goats on the third floor roof. They try to utilize every bit of space they can. I guess they must, with so many people, and so little room.

I got back from the party at eleven or so. It was like a wedding social in Canada, except the only woman was a fat-bottomed girl who wore a large sequin-blue bra and shorts, and boogied up on the stage. No great dancer, but she could shake her boobs a little. She really didn't seem to interest very many of the guys.

At our table the boys smoked hashish steady all night. In fact, it was part of the accouterments. There was fruit, and bread, and hashish. I saw someone go from table to table tossing little pieces of aluminum foil on each table.

"What is that?" I asked Rabihr.

"Hashish," said Rabihr. "Go ahead, open it."

It looked like Egyptian blond hash. I had seen it before when a friend's brother-in-law, in the Canadian military and stationed in Egypt, smuggled some to Canada in a camera he sent by mail. That was more than half a BTE ago.

We were in a tent, with maybe fifty tables inside. White lights were strung in a semicircular pattern throughout. The sound system was tinny, and there was a band of maybe 11 or 12 playing Egyptian music. The smoke was amazing, if they weren't smoking hashish, it was cigarettes or sheesha—tobacco smoked with a water-pipe. But everyone got along. They were hugging each other and shaking hands and often kissing each other on the cheek. These people get along with each other, and they did everything they could to make me feel welcome. I couldn't help but compare it to social events back home where so often people start fighting. But then, back home they're drinking alcohol, not smoking hashish. Could that be the difference?

Eventually I was feeling stoned myself from all the smoke in the air, my first ever contact high. I took a tok-tok home—five pounds, one dollar, and another wild ride.

Day 13 in the desert—another day at the office

"My name is Ozymandias, king of kings:
Look on my works, ye Mighty, and despair!"

With trepidation I put the 'clean my room' sign on my door this morning. I was worried the maid may throw away some important stuff, as I have my writing and reading materials all over the place in here. I needn't have worried. It was fine when I got home.

I went in and worked the area in front of the Sphinx. It seems so much cleaner now that I've gone over it a few times, and it goes quicker every day. I saw Meek, whom I call Mr. Meek. I'm sure I'm spelling his name wrong. He's a cleaner at the Sphinx Gate area.

As I was working in front of the Sphinx, Entrance Ali called out to me.

"Come here Bruce, I need you." Alexander Graham Bell's famous words.

The Swedish lady I had met before wanted to see me. She was outside the site. I guess Ali is her friend that can sometimes get her in for free.

I went to talk to her, a little peeved that my work was interrupted. But my mind was open.

"You have received a letter," she said to me through the bars of the exit gate.

"No," I replied somewhat warily, wondering what she was up to. "I didn't."

"We have a mutual friend," she said. She does not speak directly for some reason.

"Who?"

"Walid."

It was the young Walid I met outside the Sphinx, not the lazy trash picker inside. She had given Walid a letter to give to me, as Mr. Sayed, Walid's boss, had mentioned my name to her. I haven't seen Walid for a while, so I have not received the letter.

She had mentioned when I first met her that she wanted to come pick trash with me. Since I feel I am on probation, I was afraid she might somehow mess things up for me.

"I want to know what you are doing, and why," she said. "From your own mouth."

"Well," I said, looking at my watch, "I'll be out of here at exactly two o'clock. I could meet you then."

"I will see you here at two, then."

I walked back in and saw Saman, and had koshery for breakfast with some of the vendors. They were very protective of me, and made sure I got seven and a half pounds back from a tenner.

I started back uphill and Mohamed, the lanky deputy of the Lady in the Hat, met me and invited me for tea in the antiquities office. There were two women inside, one who speaks good English.

"Hello Bruce," she said off the hop. She had heard of me. I had tea after introductions. I felt the tall lanky fellow was hurt because I asked his name. Mohamed. Hurt because I didn't remember it. But I have met so many Mohameds. However, he did say "You are my friend," with a big grin, and the grin was genuine. I must learn more Arabic, like "Mohamed, you are my friend."

I worked until ten on the outside of the wall that separates the tourists from the horses. It wasn't as bad as I had first thought. I made some real progress. Then over to the new bad spot, on the left of the path to Khafre.

Walid came up and asked for a bag, and I gave him one. Then he asked for one for Ramadan, but Ramadan the Lazy didn't want it. One would be enough for the both of them all day.

I saw Hya-hya on my way, and he and Rabihr the Elder met me at one of the sites I picked yesterday. They moved the bags to what is becoming our bag storage area. I don't know what will become of them.

I went down to the Sphinx for lunch from Maharab, who was in the process of feeding about five people. He is a popular man at the Giza plateau.

"If Maharab die, nobody eat at the pyramids," one young man said to me. Then he kissed Maharab on the cheek, laughing.

I worked a little more outside the wall, and a young man came and helped. The two of us really did a lot, the kid was game to go. I was worried he would want money, but after 20 minutes he said he had to go, waved and left. Beautiful.

I still had time to kill before two so I went inside the Sphinx for the first time since I have been here. There was a cleaner standing against the wall, and I waved to him. He waved back. I could see he had been doing a good job. The only part that really needed it was the thin area between the bars of the fence and the stone. I did about half before I had to go meet Karen, the Swedish woman. One bag was only half full, so I left it between the bars and stone to use tomorrow when I'll finish up.

Karen was there waiting for me at exactly two. I showed her on my watch.

"You are on German time," she said. "I am on Swedish time, and have been here for 15 minutes."

"Where shall we go for tea?"

"You decide, a café or my place. My place is very close."

We decided on her place, and she led me into a neat little courtyard just off the main drag, then down a few alleys and finally to the house she is renting for two thousand Egyptian pounds a month.

It was Spartan, basically four rooms of equal size, with hardly any furniture.

"Do you want to sit, or lay down?" she asked me.

We sat at the one table in one room, until she said she wanted to sit on the floor. She laid out a blanket and we sat and had tea. She gave me a tour of the place and told me of her desire to turn it into a guesthouse.

"I wouldn't charge money, I'd just want gifts in exchange."

Very funky-dunky this lady. She's 57, gets some pension from Sweden, has a sister that is somehow into economics, and apparently has a system for redistribution of the wealth of the world. Apparently people are trying to stop her, or help her. I'm not sure as Karen is somewhat cryptic. She has a son and I think she wants me to hire him to go fishing.

"Everybody loves him," she said.

She has been writing copiously, good stuff she says. She had paints and a half-finished painting on the table. She said she is very allergic to chemicals, but she smokes. She rented out her place to a film crew, and that explained the grass I saw in the front yard, the only grass I have seen in Giza. The "pig Egyptian men" crapped all over her bathtub, apparently.

"I couldn't even go in to brush my teeth." Somehow she cleaned it up.

We had a good conversation, and she was particularly interested in the Center for Civilization.

My wife and kids and I were living in Paris when I wrote a Universal Declaration of Human Duties and Responsibilities that I'd like the United Nations to adopt. I was studying the UN, reading it's charter and whatever information I could get at the American Library in Paris, when I was shocked to discover there was no such declaration. I had assumed, since there was a Universal Declaration of Human Rights, there would be one for responsibilities, as rights and responsibilities go hand in hand.

I decided to write such a declaration, and over the course of several months, and many, many drafts, I completed it. (Appendix A)

The flat we rented in Paris in the 11th Arrondissement was huge, about 2,000 square feet. With Linda and me and the three kids, and our friend Irena from Australia, who came to help us with the children, we needed the room. Linda was studying cuisine at Le Cordon Bleu, and I had to make frequent trips back to Canada.

(It cost a small fortune and entailed a lot of work to move the entire family to Paris so she could study cuisine. But it was her dream, so I did what I could to help her realize it, the whole family did. After that, how could she be so against me wandering off by myself to Egypt for a month and a half? It was, and remains, inexplicable to me.)

Above the kitchen in our Paris flat was a loft, where I did my work. The floor was covered in various versions of the Declaration, as I struggled with it. Papers were strewn all over. My kids used the back of discarded pages to draw pictures, and made hundreds of paper airplanes, which they flew all over the apartment.

The Universal Declaration of Human Duties and Responsibilities is based on four principles, what I call The Four Principles of Humanity.

> Firstly, human beings are responsible for the Earth, for without the Earth they cannot bear any other burden, or responsibility. *Human beings are responsible for the earth.*

> Secondly, each person is responsible for their fellows, that is each and all members of the human race, for if their fellows are unable to tend to the Earth, they will not be able to be responsible to the Earth, thus if human beings ignore the plight of their fellows, they are not being responsible to the Earth. *Human beings are responsible for their fellows.*

> Thirdly, human beings are responsible for their offspring for if their offspring are not taught of their own responsibility to the earth and their fellows, they are not being responsible to the Earth or their fellows. *Human beings are responsible for their offspring.*

> Fourthly, human beings are responsible for their own actions. *Human beings are responsible for themselves.*

After completing the Declaration, I went looking for some organization to take it forward to the United Nations. I again assumed (I know, making an ass of 'u', and 'me') there must be some Center for Civilization.

We know that every civilization humans have ever created, has collapsed. What would make ours any different? Surely someone, or some organization, must be 'minding the store' so to speak. What would be the cost of the collapse of our civilization? Is it billions? Trillions? No, it is more. It is *everything*. In my humble opinion, if our civilization collapses, man will most likely not rise again. We have used up all the readily available oil and minerals that enabled us to get to where we are now. For instance, a more primitive people would be unable to drill five miles beneath the floor of the ocean to access oil and natural gas.

I searched and searched and could find no such entity, so I decided to create one. I and two of my fellows incorporated The Center for Civilization (CFC), dedicated to the continuation of human civilization on Earth, in the spring of 2007.

Presently the focus of the CFC is to get the United Nations to adopt the Universal Declaration of Human Duties and Responsibilities. What would our world be like three generations from now if the children of all nations were taught, not only of their rights, but also their responsibilities to the earth, their fellows, their children, and for themselves? Would the Doomsday Clock, now set at six minutes to midnight, turn backwards a little?

The CFC also seeks to establish a human flag—a flag that can be flown in every country of the world to celebrate membership in the human race. To embrace one another. And perhaps more importantly, for our children to see a banner of kinship amongst all peoples. Again, who knows what the impact would be on our world three generations from now?

I drew a template for such a flag while hiking through the Appalachian Mountains last summer with my son Ti. (Appendix B) The design for the flag is a simple bald figure of an adult human handing the world to an identical smaller version, a child. The child has a hopeful smile, the adult a serious one. Both figures have many layers from black to white. The adult's color increases in darkness from head to toe, the child the opposite.

I thought each country could turn the globe to place themselves in the middle, making each flag unique to each country.

Lofty goals for a simple fisherman from Gimli, and I often feel like I'm banging my head against a wall, or tilting at windmills Don Quixote style—but I draw some inspiration from what may seem an unlikely source. A man named Gord Gowie.

An ex-military man and former prison guard, Gord ended up on the Recreation Authority in Gimli. The Rec Authority was charged with overseeing the Rec Center, really just a skating rink and a curling rink. Ever a proponent of physical fitness, he suggested putting a fitness center in some unused space in the basement of the Rec Center.

"Gord can be a little long-winded," said my wife, a citizen representative on the Rec Authority at the time, "and some of the others would just roll their eyes or yawn, whenever he began to speak. He couldn't have missed it, but he just didn't let it bother him."

The local distillery, Diageo, formerly Seagrams, (Gimli is the only place on earth where Crown Royal whiskey is made, the bootlegging Bronfman's chose the site for the quality of the artesian well water) was throwing out some workout equipment, and Gord could get it for free.

"It was a close vote, but we got it," said Linda.

Gord's work was done.

The workout equipment was pathetic, antiquated stuff that belonged in a museum, and some cheap machines in need of repair. Garbage, really.

But it was something.

Slowly people began coming in to work out. A few donated some quality machines, some barbells and dumbells. A volunteer fitness center board was put in place, and they approached various service groups for funding. One by one every piece Gord brought in was replaced. In a few years, thanks to the work of dozens of people, it was a topnotch fitness center.

Not very many people know Gord's role in the evolution of the fitness center. He doesn't get much credit for what he did, nor does he care for acknowledgment. But the truth is, if Gord hadn't brought the crap in and called it a fitness center in the first place, it might still be empty space.

The Center for Civilization is not much now, but there is, on this planet, a Center for Civilization, dedicated to the continuation of human civilization on earth. *It is something.*

Karen reminded me once again of her distant relative Dag Hammarskjold, the first Secretary General of the United Nations. Then I left. I had been with her a little over an hour. I think she may be going a little batty with no television or radio, no Arabic, (she said she refuses to learn Arabic) and such an empty house. Alone too much. The only furniture was the one desk and two chairs, with one mattress in each of two rooms.

She is right that there is much she could do with the place. The roof has a great view of the pyramids. It would be a great place to party. A little music, BBQ, sleeping bag . . . perfect.

Back home Edward the comedian behind the desk said he was doing a good job for me, talking to television people.

"Everyone I talk to asks 'why, why would he do this?' It's like you said, there is only one pyramids in the world, one of the seven wonders of the world."

In fact, of the original seven wonders of the world, only the pyramids of Giza remain. The disappearance of the other six 'wonders' reminds me of Percy Shelley's poem, Ozymandias, about Rameses the Great, who ruled Egypt from 1279 to 1213 BC, a thousand years, or 20 BTE, after the pyramids of Giza were built. Ozymandias was another name for Rameses the Great.

I met a traveler from an antique land
Who said: Two vast and trunkless legs of stone
Stand in the desert. Near them, on the sand,
Half sunk, a shattered visage lies, whose frown
And wrinkled lip, and sneer of cold command
Tell that its sculptor well those passions read
Which yet survive, stamped on these lifeless things,
The hand that mocked them and the heart that fed.
And on the pedestal these words appear:
"My name is Ozymandias, king of kings:
Look on my works, ye Mighty, and despair!"
Nothing beside remains. Round the decay
Of that colossal wreck, boundless and bare
The lone and level sands stretch far away

The central theme of Ozymandias is the inevitable collapse of any empire, or civilization, and ancient Egypt is arguably the greatest example of that. Look west from the Giza Plateau, and 'the lone and level sands stretch far away.' I see it every day. I guess nobody was minding the store.

An interesting thing happened today. I lost one AA battery to the remote for my TV yesterday. It must be in this room somewhere, but I can't find it. Sure enough I found a battery in the sand today. It was a little rusty, but I brought it back, put it in the remote, and it worked! The sands of the Sahara provided. I have a remote for what my father calls 'the idiot box.'

I also found some Austrian shillings today. Find a shilling, pick it up, and all the day you'll have good luck.

I just helped Fatih write a letter to his potential new wife. He dictated to me as I used the hotel's computer. She wants to come with a relative to meet his family. She speaks German and he doesn't. I used the internet to translate from English into German, so there's less chance of a mistake. He finished his letter bellowing to me "I love you too much!"

So now it looks like she'll pay for the flight, and he will look after her and her relative once they get here. I hope his heart can take it.

Fatih ordered me some food, and has promised to teach me Arabic tomorrow. He's here every night, a resource I would be nuts not to utilize.

Rabbob let me use the computer again for free. She is such a dear. She also gave me a bunch of food, so I'm sitting here with my food from Fatih, and I'm not hungry.

Edward the comedian told a funny story about a gay man, but I just caught a bit of it. "He's a man, but not a man," he said, then he made his wrists go limp. "He fell into Lake Nasser and crocodiles were coming toward him. 'Ooh, I'm in the water, baby, mama help me.'"

I have never spent so long in a hotel before, and I'm realizing the complexity of the relationships in this hotel. It should be interesting for the next four weeks.

Rabbob said an Egyptian television crew might show up tomorrow. I hope not.

Day 14 in the desert—many horseshoes today-enshallah? (God willing)

"Does he want me to bring him a boat, too?"

I saw Walid and Ramadan this morning, sitting and talking, and I called Walid over and offered him a garbage bag. He took it, making motions to his ear, and the crossing of the arms to indicate something was over, or finished. In my paronoia I thought someone had called and said to get rid of the Canadian. But the Lady in the Hat came by and explained that Walid has hearing problems. I remembered seeing his hearing aids. I guess they're on the fritz.

I smooth-talked the Lady in the Hat for a while, and then went to work. I picked my way to the Sphinx but the guard would not let me in.

"Hassanan cleans inside," he said. Bummer.

I guess Hassanan, a different Hassanan from the guy I know, doesn't want me in there.

Yesterday I noticed the area inside the Sphinx was very clean. It's just that Hassanan seems to leave the area between the bars and the stone alone. I did notice that the bag I left in there yesterday was gone.

I worked the area of the horses and camels and then waded into the pit. It's where we put our garbage bags once they're full. When I first saw this area, I thought it would take forever to clean, but I am a little more confident now that I have done so much picking. I went to work. Doing a little each day, I think I could finish it in less than a week.

At ten I went to the tomb Hya-hya had shown me the day before. At first sight it looked like a ten-bag job, maybe an hour's work. But after two hours and 22 bags I was not done yet.

I walked up to the big pyramid and took a quick look for Rabihr but couldn't find him. He's somewhat of an elusive character.

Maharab was near the Sphinx and I had a great lunch. I swear his sandwiches get better every day.

I bought Saman a drink. His friend was there, an avid fisherman, according to Saman.

"Can you bring me some fish to cook when you come back to Egypt?" Saman asked me.

"Sure."

He spoke in Arabic to his friend the fisherman, then turned to me.

"My friend would like some fishing line. Can you bring some?"

"Sure."

"And he needs the machine."

"The reel?" I asked, pretending to reel in a fish.

"Yes, and a stick," he said, and made the motions of pulling on a fishing rod.

"A fishing rod?" I asked.

"Yes."

"Does he want me to bring him a boat, too?" I asked.

Saman's eyes went wide.

"No, no," he said, waving his hands back and forth.

He looked at me and saw my smile and we both laughed. He interpreted for his friend and we all had a good chuckle.

I worked my way toward Khufu after lunch, expecting to make it to the pyramid, but the wind had blown in a lot of garbage, so it took me a while. For the first time in many days an antiquities officer on a camel asked me what I was doing. They can be a little intimidating at first, sitting way up on a camel with an automatic rifle.

"What is that?" he demanded to know, pointing to my garbage bag.

"I am picking up garbage, rubbish," I said.

He couldn't understand so he asked a young Egyptian standing nearby. I could see him explaining it, complete with hand gestures of picking something off the ground and placing it in a bag.

"Okay," said the officer, and wandered away.

Once I had two bags filled, I took them to the pit. I can't leave them laying around or security will freak.

On my way to the pit with the last two bags I was approached by a young man on a camel.

"My friend, my friend," he yelled to me, but I didn't recognize him.

"Big party in three days," he said as he got closer.

That struck a chord with me. I looked again and I saw it was Rabihr's friend Ali, who was partying with us the other day, smoking hash like a trooper.

He offered to carry a bag, then to help me in the pit. Great kid, probably twenty or so. Off he went on his camel, with two friends on another, waving goodby.

"Party in three days," he yelled back at me.

I bought three water bottles on the way home. I could fit only two in the backpack, but for three pounds each, it's a deal. They cost ten pounds at the Siag. The backpack hurt my back, as it sat funny, and when I started getting shooting pains in my legs and back, I jumped in a tok-tok.

Both my back surgeries were preceded by weeks in the fetal position in excruciating pain, unable to move or defecate, dropping all the painkillers I could get my hands on. The pain was intense, such as I have never felt before or since.

At the first operation, the surgeon removed three pieces of my lowest disc, L-5 S-1, that were broken off and touching my spinal chord. Four months later I was jogging, and two months after that I was back in the hospital. *Ya big dummy!*

The rest of my disc had come shooting out. I think of it like standing on a bar of soap. Now misshapen, it was just a matter of time before the disc would move from the pressure put upon it.

I was scheduled to have my second surgery on a Friday, a day surgery. I'd be home by nightfall. From past experience, I knew the pain would be gone immediately following the operation. But things ran late that day, and I was told I'd have to wait until Monday for the operation. They found me a bed on the cardiac ward.

"You'll give me some painkillers, though. Won't you?"

"Oh yes. Don't worry. We have some Tylenol 3's for you."

"What?" I said, horrified. "That's not good enough! I need a morphine drip!"

"Sorry, all you get is T-3's."

"You can't do that! The pain is just too much! Tylenol does nothing!"

"Sorry," was all the nurse said.

(I related this conversation to my psychiatrist cousin Wray months later. "Some nurses believe the road to heaven is paved with pain medication *they did not give*," is all he said.)

I was terrified. A weekend in unbearable pain, unnecessary pain. I had to get through to this nurse. I had to let them know I needed to have a morphine drip, or regular shots of something exponentially stronger than T-3's. But I couldn't sit upright, let alone get out of bed and find the nurse's superior.

Attached to the bed was a metal arm with the remote control for a television. I started punching it.

"I need a morphine drip," I yelled, punching away.

"Stop that, you'll hurt yourself."

After three punches blood started to fly. I picked up the pace.

"I need a morphine drip," I yelled again. Pieces of flesh were hanging loosely from my battered hand, blood arcing in a semicircle up to ten feet away. All my medication had worn off, and I felt nothing in my hand. My back was in such pain that I cannot imagine torture being worse.

I prayed that punching my fist to smithereens would get me the Holy Grail, a morphine drip. I'm sure anyone who has experienced torture would gladly do the same to escape a weekend in hell.

"Remember Bruce," said my uncle Tom when I first hurt my back. "You get as much from our health care system as you demand. Did you hear me Bruce? As you *demand*."

A retired neurosurgeon, uncle Tom knew the Canadian health care system intimately.

"I *demand* a morphine drip," I shouted, still pumping my fist.

The nurse came to my bed with two other people. I don't know if she called them over, or if they saw me and thought I had gone insane. They made motions to restrain me, so I relaxed, and lay back in the bed.

"Okay, okay. We'll get you one," said someone.

A morphine drip allows the patient to self-administer for pain. An IV needle goes in the arm, and to get a shot, the patient presses a button. A safety feature ensures the button only works once every five minutes. In ten minutes, with three shots of morphine, I was out of pain. I fell asleep while the nurse was bandaging my hand.

On Monday morning I went into surgery. When I woke up, the surgeon was standing over me.

"How did it go?" I asked weakly.

"Well, we had some problems."

"What do you mean?"

"We accidentally cut your spinal sac and all your spinal fluid drained out," he said.

"What does that mean?" I asked, afraid of the answer.

"Oh, don't worry," he said quickly, no doubt noticing the concern in my face. "We patched it."

"Will I be able to walk?"

"Sure. It just means that you can't sit up for 48 hours while your body replenishes the spinal fluid."

"So I have to stay laying down for two days?"

"Yes. You should be fine in two days. If you get up after 48 hours and get an incredible headache, worse than you have ever had in your life, that means there's no spinal fluid in your brain and our patch didn't work. If that happens lay down immediately, and we'll have to figure out what to do."

So I lay in that bed worrying for exactly 48 hours. When I sat up, I felt a little dizzy, but at least I didn't have a headache. I got out of bed and walked woozily down the hall, struggling to keep my balance.

"No headache, no headache," I said to myself, willing it so.

I hadn't used my legs for weeks, but getting up and active immediately after surgery is very important for recovery. I had lost two days, so I stumbled up and down that hospital hallway dozens of times, grateful to be on my feet, and out of pain.

If my back went here in Egypt, I'd be in deep trouble. Not to mention my mission would end.

I should buy thirty bottles one day and take a tok-tok. I'd save a fortune, and I'd always have water. *Ya big dummy.*

I had some thoughts today. Many people have said "It's too bad that when you leave it will go right back to the way it was."

But perhaps that's reason enough. Every day I am here, I know it's a little better. Every day I work on it, it improves, if only just a little. That may be a lesson for us all. Every day we work on making this world a better place, it improves, if only a little. And each day we do not, it gets worse, if only just a little. There is no Utopian society. The work will never end. We can work our entire lives, and never get there. But to not work is unconscionable, because it will get worse. So yes, I return some days to see more garbage where I had cleaned the day before. But it's always less than it was when I first cleaned. Every day I work, it gets better.

Edward mentioned the television crew again yesterday, and so did Rabbob. I hope not to see them for at least a week or two. It could put the mission in jeopardy. Also, I need to get my words straight, get ready for the questions. *Mon dieu*, I have difficulty articulating what I'm doing to myself.

I found four horseshoes today, I now have eight for the 14 days I've been here. *Enshallah?*

I just spoke with Fatih. He's having second thoughts about the Turkish woman.

"She wants to come here for four weeks, but after that she could say she does not want to marry me," he said, "and I'll be out many thousands of pounds. I think I'll say I'll pay for one week or two."

He's still thinking about it. He only knew her for the one week she stayed in the hotel.

I picked up 15 kilos of bags today, and in a few days will get another 15. I took the guy's card so I can go there myself in a tok-tok next time. Bono came with me today, and I gave him ten pounds. I think I have been negligent in the baksheesh department. I'll talk to Samir about it.

Day 15 in the desert—what a day

"And there's my pay."

Ali was at the Sphinx gate, and hustled me through quickly. As I walked in I could hear this chubby blond woman talking beside me. She was dressed all in black, including delicate black gloves. She looked over at me.

"Where are you from?" she asked, with what I thought was an Italian accent.

She kept talking to me, but I saw Mr. Meek and went over to shake his hand. He seemed a little preoccupied. Normally we shake hands vigorously, and he speaks to me in Arabic with a wide grin, and then goes on his way.

"They don't speak English," the woman said to me.

I continued walking and she continued talking. She has a friend in Ottawa, the home of Canada's government.

I stopped walking to start work, stooping to pick up some plastic koshery containers and empty drink cans.

"What are you doing?" she asked.

"I pick up the garbage," I said. "Just helping out."

"Can I help too?" she asked.

"You're not really dressed for it."

She had been up all night partying and wanted to party tonight with me. She was with three guys she identified as her driver, interpreter and guide. They looked Egyptian to me. They all watched me as she kept talking about partying. One of them groaned and another rolled his eyes. I guess this is her constant modus operandi.

"You don't mind partying with black people, girls I mean?" she asked.

It seemed a strange thing to ask since she was as white as milk, with blond hair, a product of an Italian father and American mother.

She wanted to give me her phone number but her guys didn't have a pen or paper, so she ripped out the identifying sticker from her phone and gave it to me. Her guys wanted to have their picture taken with me, so I obliged.

"I will never forget you," said one.

It was great to hear as I was a little despondent when I woke up, questioning what I was doing. I guess my digestive problems last night and this morning didn't help. The last thing I wanted was to have the trots and be at the pyramids all day without a bathroom.

"Are you going to party with me?" she kept asking.

"I don't know," I said, "I have to be at work at eight in the morning."

"You can't be late?"

"No," I said.

When she left to go for a horse ride, she turned and gave me the most lascivious look of lust I have ever seen *in my life*. She wanted me. Boy, was I glad to see her go.

Four Egyptian men had watched the whole thing, and after she was gone, they walked over to me. We yucked it up a bit.

"The men with that woman were not Egyptian, but Arabian," said one of the guys. An important distinction, it seems.

"So, did she like your work, or your face?" he asked me, laughing.

As I picked my way across the front of the Sphinx, I could see Ramadan the Lazy doing his best to stay hidden from sight. I filled a bag on my way around to where the wall drops down and the horses and camels poke their heads over, and jumped the wall and worked the other side.

An Egyptian dressed in a grey calibaya and a white turban came up to me, and speaking no English, indicated for me to follow him. I did, wondering what he was up to. He took me to an area that had a single strand of barbed-wire strung around it about 18 inches high. We easily hopped over, and into an excavation site that seemed abandoned. I certainly haven't seen anyone digging there in the two weeks I've been here.

We went down a gradual slope for about sixty feet, then made a right turn and went down another sixty feet. My guide then jumped some four feet down to the next level. I followed suit. There at the foot of the four-foot 'step' was much debris that had blown in over the course of time. Going further down into the excavation site the path again made a right angle turn, and a four-foot high column of rock blocked the way. There was garbage on both sides of this column. We worked both places and filled ten bags.

"*Ana Bruce*," I said, introducing myself.

"*Ana Sadek*."

Ten minutes into the work I noticed something that looked like a skull under a rock. I pulled it out and looked at it. It was indeed a human skull! There was a hole in the back of it, which I assumed was the cause of death—presumably a blunt instrument.

Here I was in Egypt, in a pit between the Sphinx and the mighty Pyramids of Giza, more than forty centuries gazing down upon me, and I had unearthed a human skull? That's the stuff of dreams!

However my guide, Mr. Sadek, was not so impressed. When I showed it to him, he gently took it from my hands, *and put it right back where I found it.*

It was still early in the day when we were done, and I was already quite dusty. It gets so dusty that my wrists and face, the only exposed parts of my upper body, become covered in a grime of sweat and sand and dust that's tough to get off because it's wet and sticks to my skin.

I went into the pit for a while, where I met Mohamed, the tall lanky sidekick of the Lady in the Hat. (I had seen her earlier, but only briefly, a few words.)

"*Mohamed Ana Sadek*," I said, (Mohamed I friends, the best I could do) and he smiled.

I explained how I was doing one piece of the pit per day, and he seemed to get it. I gave him one of the Canada pins, pinned it on his shirt. He was smiling widely again. I think I am forgiven for forgetting his name.

I left the pit with Mohamed and showed him the nine foot by six foot tomb that produced 22 bags and was still not clean. I worked there for some time, took another six bags out, but I really need a rake.

I was on my way to see Maharab for lunch, but Rabihr the Elder stopped me and showed me another spot that needed some work. It looked like some stairs going down into a tomb, but it may be a false door. The stairwell was filled up to the top with garbage, for all I know six to eight feet deep. But I figured I'm here to serve, so I started. Another fellow was there, named—what are the odds—Mohamed. He spoke a little English, and he translated that Rabihr was asking if I wanted tea. Absolutely.

Off Rabihr went to make tea, and Ahmed appeared.

I hadn't seen Ahmed for a few days. I gave him his copy of *A Season for Skufty*. We talked about the Center for Civilization, and the Universal Declaration of Human Duties and Responsibilities. He said he will translate it into Arabic. We will meet tomorrow at ten for tea.

Ahmed works at the middle pyramid where they are building a wooden platform for tourists to walk on.

"It's a bad plan," he said, shaking his head. "The road is a bad plan too, but . . ." he shrugged his shoulders.

Rabihr came with the tea. It was *mumtooz*, excellent.

When I finished, and stood to go find Maharab for lunch, Rabihr the Elder stepped in front of me and pointed to his eyes, and then to me. He said something in Arabic.

"He looks at you with his eyes," interpreted Ahmed. "He says you can look through his eyes. You are a special person."

"And there's my pay," I said softly, turning to Ahmed.

Maharab was not there! I was despondent. I headed back up toward Khufu where I wanted to work, and lo and behold came across a young man in the same business as Maharab, except with a cardboard box and a bucket. *He* was the donkey. He made me a sandwich and did not charge me. I had the money in my outstretched hand, but he refused it. Ah, to feel the embrace.

I worked toward the parking lot where I knew Rabihr the Younger often worked, and met many Egyptians, young and old, selling various trinkets and Egyptian memorabilia. One young man said he would meet me at 12:30 at Khufu tomorrow, and bring me an Arabic-English dictionary. So now I have tea at ten with Rabihr the Old and Ahmed, and 12:30 with the dictionary man at Khufu, a busy day tomorrow. I need to work the pit as well, and a round of Khufu. Lots to do.

Rabihr wanted me to come to his house, but I wanted to go back to my hotel, so he's coming here between seven and eight. He had a car take him out of the site, and picked me up with my two bags of garbage. We put the bags on the roof rack, and then had to quickly jump out and take them to the garbage area behind the guard shed, as we were holding up traffic. Once out the Sphinx gate, we all left the car and walked our separate ways home.

Rabihr and the big guy, Samba. They spend their whole day trying to sell trinkets to tourists, and I guess camel rides as well. I'm sure they have deals with each other all the time. I've seen them swapping money. There's a science to it, or a flow. It's something to watch, like the traffic on the streets—an art form in itself. It looks like chaos, but it works. It reminds me fishing.

When setting a gang of nets on Lake Winnipeg, we tie all the anchors, nets and buoys together before we begin. This can get complicated when setting a big gang with lots of nets and anchors. If you make a mistake you can have a real mess on your hands, and in rough waters, it can be dangerous.

Many years ago I was setting nets with my hired man, Black Joe, so named because he sank my truck in the harbor the first week he worked for me.

"Park the truck over there," I said to Joe, at the Winnipeg Beach harbor some nine miles south of Gimli.

Joe parked the truck, and we loaded up our boats with empty tubs for the fish, and ice to keep it cool. Just as we were pulling out of the harbor, I heard a "SPLASH" behind me. I turned around, and there was my truck, bobbing along in the harbor, and sinking fast.

"What the hell?" I didn't believe my eyes at first. I've heard that expression before, but never fully understood it until then.

I spun my boat around and ran it ashore. My older brother's truck was parked next to where mine used to be, and I jumped in the back to see if I could find a rope. What good that would have done me, I cannot fathom. But I wanted a rope. By the time I realized I was not going to find one, the truck was gone.

"It's right there," said my brother-in-law Ryan, (I taught two of Linda's brothers to fish, Ryan came from California, Laurence from Holland after a divorce) "You can just see the antennae."

Sure enough, looking closely, the top four inches or so of the radio antennae was sticking out of the water, a thin stiletto offered up by the Lady in the Lake.

That was my spare truck. I had blown the engine in my newer truck days before. Now I had no truck. I was feeling under a lot of strain, as I turned and looked at Joe.

"Joooooooeee!" I snarled, clenching my fists, "don't do it again!"

I laughed. It was that, or cry.

I sent my crew out in one boat to start lifting nets and I called a tow truck. I couldn't leave the truck in the harbor because other fishermen would smash their props on the submerged vehicle. Nobody would be looking for a sliver of metal indicating a half-ton truck just beneath the surface. I didn't have to wait long for the tow-truck.

"Where's the vehicle you need towed?" asked Dennis Firman, the tow-truck driver.

"There," I said, pointing, "you can just make out the antennae."

"You gotta be kidding me."

"No, right there. Can you see it?"

"I'm not going in there," he said, emphatically.

"How do we get it out of there, then?"

"*You* go in there and attach this to your trailer hitch," he said, handing me the towing cable.

Later, Black Joe said he was going to quit that day.

"But I felt so guilty when I sank your truck, and you didn't freak on me, I had to stay the season."

We determined that Joe had put the truck in reverse, and then turned off the engine. Once the transmission fluid drained out of the transmission, the truck was essentially in neutral. There being a gentle slope toward the water, the truck slowly rolled downhill, and fell over the bank and three feet down into the water. The gear indicator was broken, so it wasn't really Joe's fault. I was glad I hadn't yelled at him.

Black Joe fished with me for many, many seasons, and we became good friends.

One day we were setting a big gang of nets.

"That looks like chaos!" exclaimed Black Joe, pointing to the myriad lines running to and fro in the front of the boat.

I turned to look where he was pointing.

"That's art to me," I said, and it did look beautiful. It represented the potential to catch fish, and feed my family. Function as art.

As I left Rabihr, three children came up to me, the oldest probably four, grabbing my hand and pleading "one euro please, one euro."

One boy, no more than three, stuck his hand in mine, and the emotional impact was intense. I don't think there's a parent in the world that wouldn't have been affected by it.

"Help me," I called out to Rabihr, who was still in earshot. He just turned around, saw me helpless in the grip of the three-year-old, and laughed.

I bought five waters and took a tok-tok home. The driver held out for seven pounds. He wanted ten, but the price is five. Finally he settled for seven pounds, a whole forty cents more than five. But the price is *supposed* to be five. It is underpriced, at less than one dollar, so rationalizing a slight increase is easy. Still, I didn't like being hosed for two pounds. The driver knew I was pissed, but the kid sitting beside him, probably his younger brother, as he was obviously completely enamored of him and seeking his approval with everything he said (all in Arabic but very obvious) was still as cheerful as ever when I left.

"By-by" he said with a big grin.

Back at the hotel I asked Samir to get me more beer, and went up to drink what beer I had left and write this. Shortly after I closed the door there was a knock. Some gay guy asked about housekeeping. I said tomorrow, then gathered my towels and garbage and took it out to the housekeepers.

I met a young man with housekeeping named Mustafa, who speaks French quite well. We've been communicating that way. He came in while I was writing this journal and cleaned a lot, chatting all the while. He seems a good kid. He said he opened the door this morning, went "*Mon Dieu,*" and left. I guess they were curious as I have only had housekeeping in here twice in 16 days, and it shows. He said he will finish cleaning tomorrow, as he was pulled away because he spent too much time in my room.

Day 16 in the desert—the sand was angry that day my friend

"God put the idea in your head, to do this."

The comedian Edward is no longer with us, along with most of the front desk staff. Fatih told me they embezzled some 1.5 million pounds, about $300,000. I'm not sure I believe that, but the staff has all changed. I'll ask Samir about it. I will miss them, particularly the comedian.

The wind blew all day, the great Sahara desert sandblasting everyone and everything. This is the time of Meshir, I was told, when it will be windy for ten days, cold for ten days, and rain for ten days. (I may have misunderstood the rain part, as it has yet to rain)

Meshir is the sixth month of the Coptic calendar, and is named for Mechir, the Ancient Egyptian God of Wind. It lies between February 8 and March 9. It is also the second month of Proyet, the season of growth and emergence in ancient Egypt, when the flood-waters of the Nile recede, and crops begin to grow throughout the land of Egypt.

The Islamic calendar consists of 12 months, each beginning when the first crescent of a new moon is sighted. The lunar calendar is 11 or 12 days shorter than the solar calendar and since no adjustments are made for the discrepancy, the months migrate through the seasons. Not a big deal, except for Ramadan, the holiest month for Muslims.

"This is a hard time for me," Saman once told me. "Especially in the summer."

Muslims are prohibited from sexual intercourse, eating food and drinking fluids during daylight hours for the entire month of Ramadan. I can imagine Saman and the other Egyptians who work the Giza Plateau getting incredibly thirsty all day in a hot summer sun, with eighteen hours of daylight.

"How do you do it?" I asked Saman, impressed by such devotion.

"It's not easy," he said, smiling.

Fasting during Ramadan, called Sawm, is one of the Five Pillars of Islam. The others are; Shahadah, the profession of faith; Salah, meaning prayers; Zakat, the giving of alms; and Hajj, the well-known once in a lifetime pilgrimage to Mecca. These are not bad things.

"I'm late," I said to Ali at the gate.

"Take your time, this is your home," he said. "The Sphinx is lucky to have you."

I worked around the front, met Mr. Meek who gave me his customary handshake and grin, spoke in Arabic—*how ya doin', ya big dummy*—and left.

I spotted Mohawk walking toward me.

"I look for you last two days but did not see you," he said.

"I was here, over by Khafre," I said, pointing to the middle pyramid. When I think of the thousands of people here every day, it's amazing Mohawk and I see each other as often as we do.

"My grandmother wants to make presents for your children from Egypt," he said. "Symbolic gifts." I have found Egyptians to be extraordinarily friendly to me.

He warned me again about bad people.

"Some people are not good. They are bad people. You must be careful."

"There is a new discovery," he said, suddenly changing the topic. "They found a mummy and some statues behind Menkaure but took no pictures. It is secret."

I made my way to the pit, and up came Ramadan and Walid, with Hassanan cracking the whip. Walid was rattling off Arabic so quick I had no idea what he was saying, but I figured it out by his gestures.

The bags are too heavy.

To show him they weren't I grabbed one and threw it in the air with one hand, then caught it again. He said yes, but you are strong, or lift weights, or are big man, or something like that. He was flexing his muscles and pointing at me.

I guess that's why he twice told me not to put rocks in the bags. He's never felt a bag so stuffed with garbage, so he assumed I was putting rocks in them. Hassanan started yelling at him, and he carried the bag away.

I went up to work on the spot with Rabihr the Elder, and his buddy Mohamed gave me some tea, and helped me with the alphabet and numbers. It took me to near noon to finish the stairs that led to a false door, then off to Khafre, the middle pyramid.

I went down to the Sphinx for some lunch but Maharab was nowhere, and Hassan with the koshery was not in sight, so I mooched a tea from the antiquities office. The woman I call Big Black-eyes as I don't know her real name, taught me to spell Bruce in Arabic. They were very friendly, including the Lady in the Hat. But sitting beside her was the man I have seen with Mr. Kamal Wahid and Mohamed Cheoh. He was in on the conversation outside the office what seems so long ago, as I walked the floor in the office of the Chief Inspector, wondering what my future would hold. The Third Man. I think he's her boss.

I was on my way to Khufu, but saw a kid I knew just as Hassan the koshery guy came by, so I sat and ate. The kid, who called out 'Bruce' on the street so many days ago, spoke to a man sitting beside him, who then turned to me.

"He said you fat when you first got here, but now not so fat," he said.

I burst out laughing.

The kid spoke to the man again, who again translated.

"He's worried you will get angry."

"No, no," I said, looking at the kid and still laughing. "Good joke on me."

I *was* fat when I arrived, and still am, but won't be when I leave.

"You are in a small, special group of people," said the man, "that does what God asks."

"Maybe," I said doubtfully.

"God put the idea in your head," he added, touching my temple, "to do this."

I started toward Khufu, but by the time I filled a bag it was two o'clock. I picked up three bags I had carelessly left at the skull area, and took them to the pit. That leaves two bags still there, I'll get them tomorrow. Strangely, security doesn't seem worried about those bags.

On my way out a kid stepped in front of me, stopping me, and gave me a headdress.

"I have no money," I said.

"Gift," he said, so I accepted. In return I gave him some balloons, and then all the kids around me wanted one, and some adults wanted them for their kids. I gave away everything I had.

Day 17 in the desert—a day of secrets, hope and despair

"Tourist trust tourist."

As I was working in front of the Sphinx, I saw the Italian lady had come back. Fear coursed through my veins like I'd been tasered. She was walking toward the horses, so I dallied a little on the opposite side of the Sphinx. By the time I got around to the horses, she was gone. Three of the boys who witnessed her the day before were quick to tell me she came back with different guys.

"She wants you," one of them said, laughing. But that was the last I saw of her.

I was in one of the many temple enclaves in front of the middle pyramid—the Mortuary Temple of Khafre—when an Iraqi man in a suit and tie stopped me.

"What are you doing?"

"Just cleaning up."

"Why?"

"To say thank-you to Egypt and the Egyptians, for letting me be here. This is my way to embrace Egypt, and all the people of the world."

"Thank-you," he said softly, touching his heart.

Some Egyptians with him had me pose with them, one at a time, and were very encouraging. Those who get it, really get it. Those who don't, simply don't.

I ran into one of Rabihr the Younger's buddies, and he told me to come to the party at 8:30. Then some time later Rabihr showed up.

"Let's have tea," he said, and I followed him to the north side of the Temple. There I noticed a cave under the Temple. Suddenly a man's upper torso appeared out of the cave, holding a tray of plastic cups filled with tea. He seemed to materialize from nowhere. With a small propane stove under the Temple, he sells tea to the Egyptians. I call this teahouse 'the Cave.'

Then Rabihr made the ask.

"I want to talk to you in private," he said. "Follow me."

He led me deep into the Temple of Khafre, away from the people at the Cave.

"Bruce," he said, turning around to face me. "Can you lend me 300 pounds?"

Rabihr the Elder's buddy Mohamed makes 500 pounds a month, so in Egypt 300 pounds is a lot. In fact, Fatih said he would hire his possible Turkish bride-to-be for 300 pounds a month to run his shop. So 300 pounds could be a month's wages.

"I can't ask my friends for money because Egyptian people talk too much," said Rabihr.

He wanted me to promise not to tell anybody.

"It's a secret," he said.

"I'll think about it," I said.

"Come early to the party tonight, six-thirty."

We rejoined his friends, and I quickly left to get back to work. I have decided not to go to his party tonight, as I have no intention of giving him any money. To do so would make me a target again and again. He said he would pay me back in two or three days, but he knows I'm here for a short time, and I will have no recourse if he doesn't pay me back. He also thinks it's not a lot of money for me, and he's right. It's less than US $60, but it's the principle.

Maharab was late today, and I never saw him. Saman said he would come after prayers, devout Muslims pray five times a day, but by then I had started working my way up the left side of the Sphinx toward Khufu.

There were so many people coming down that I debated working up the hill. I thought I'd just walk up and work around the pyramid, but I decided to put my head down and work. As I did so, three young women wearing the hijab stopped me.

"Excuse me, what are you doing?" asked the boldest one, touching my shoulder to get my attention.

"I am just cleaning up. It's my way to say thank-you to Egypt, to embrace the people of Egypt."

"We . . . we want to thank you for this. You make us so very proud."

They were so heartwarming in their gratitude, so sincere. There I was in a dirty shirt, covered in six or seven days grime, and sweat of the same vintage, looking like a bum. I was probably the worst-dressed person on the Giza Plateau, simply picking up garbage, and they were thanking me profusely. People respond to the embrace. They really do. At the end of the day, it's the embrace that reaches, that connects.

"You have made my day, my week, my month," I said. "*Ana Mumtooz.*" I'm perfect. I said it touching my heart to show that I feel perfect, thanks to them. They were beautiful, classy girls, probably in their early 20's. Again, when people get it, they get it. I'm still touched. If these women represent Muslims, I love them. My kingdom for a camera.

Unfortunately, some schmuck whom I didn't recognize but knew me, came up and interrupted us, proffering his hand to me. We ignored him after I first shook his hand. He said something to the girls as they were walking away.

"I told them you like horses and camels," he said.

I'm not sure what he meant by that, but I think the girls thought him an idiot.

I kept working uphill, then reached the end of the knee-high wall, and jumped over and started working back toward the Sphinx. Many women and girls were watching, and they followed me. This was something new. My first stalking.

They were on one side of the wall, me on the other. Finally they called me over. Some of them were working the site selling models of the pyramids and other trinkets. They took a picture of me with my hat off.

One young woman with the veil tousled my hair to make me look better. There were at least eight or ten of them, all excited.

"I go to work now," I finally said.

The girl who tousled my hair held out her hand in front of me. "Money? Money?"

"I have no money, but I have something for you."

I opened my bag and took out the Canadian flag pins. They went wild! They all had their hands out "me, me, me, me." I had the pins in one hand and was pinching them out one at a time. One girl grabbed my elbow and pulled so when the pin dropped, it dropped into her hand. A boy on my left was just as insistent, jerking my arm in the other direction.

"That's it, I have no more," I said, and they cooled down.

"What are they?" someone asked.

"They are pins," I said. I took one from the boy on my left and pinned it on his shirt.

They were still clamoring for more, when I said I had to go. A young man came over to rescue me. He grabbed me by the arm and gently tugged me away.

"They are crazy, those girls," he said.

I kept working until close to two, and was getting ready to take two full bags with me on my way out when a security guy called to me. He introduced himself as Caron, and insisted on looking in the bags. He had obviously not heard of me, as he was confused about what I was doing. I started walking away with the bags, but he stopped me and made a phone call.

All I could make out was "yada, yada, yada, Mister Bruce, yada, yada." Finally he turned and said "it's okay." So now I know I'm good to go. I have it on the highest authority, I hope, that I can work here.

I took the bags and dumped them behind security on the left of the Sphinx, and went around to see if Hassan was at the Sphinx Temple with some koshery, that macaroni concoction I like.

Saman was there and pulled me to the side. Secret number two.

"I need you to help me with my business," he said. "Tourist trust tourist."

At first I thought he wanted me to market for him.

"I can't do that," I told him. "The other camel owners would be angry."

"No, no, no. If you know tourist, you tell them come to me."

"So if I know someone who wants a camel ride," I said, seeking clarification, "I tell them 'come to Sphinx and ask for my friend Saman, and he will treat you right.'"

"Yes, good."

It costs 120 pounds for a one and a half hour camel tour around the pyramid area. About 23 dollars. I wonder what he will charge me for a trip to Sakkara? He has offered to take me there before I go.

Saman made me promise not to tell anybody, just like Rabihr. But Saman's secret is much more digestible.

"Top secret," he said, as I walked away.

Rabihr the Elder's friend Mohamed overheard Saman say "top secret," and just for fun came up and said to me in front of Saman, "We have tea tomorrow, and you tell me."

Little Tiger came up to me with another present, three pyramids and a Sphinx.

"*Shokrun*," I said. Thank-you.

"Your welcome. Please, you give me," she said, curling her fingers into a tunnel and putting it to her lips, making a blowing noise. She wanted a balloon.

"*Waheed*," I said holding up my index finger, and took one out.

"One more," she said, as always.

"Shhh..."

"Okay," she whispered, but sure enough, another kid saw me give her the balloon and ran over. And then there were many. It took a while to extricate myself, but they were happy.

Saman suggested I get koshery outside the pyramid area, as I would get much more for two pounds outside than I get for two and a half inside.

"It's accepted," he said. "Hassan buys koshery for one and a half pound, and sell for two and a half."

So it's acceptable to make a small profit from your fellow Egyptians.

On the way home I found a great little restaurant that the Egyptians use, very busy. But I had no idea what to order, or how. Most of it looked good, though I recognized liver, and knew I didn't want that. I stood there watching for about five minutes when in came the kid who said I was fat when I first arrived. We exchanged greetings, and he helped me order what must be an Egyptian hotdog. I call him Little Buddy.

"You pay one and a half pound," Little Buddy told me and he went his way and I went mine.

I grabbed a tok-tok, because my legs were bothering me. They seem to get worse every day. I'm walking a fine line, between giving away every ounce of energy, and injuring myself.

I e-mailed home to let them know I'm okay. I'll probably call them when I come home from work tomorrow.

Fatih came through with a dozen socks and underwear, tighty-whitey's. Jake and Ti would be proud.

"Nobody wears tighty-whiteys anymore, Dad," they have patiently explained to me.

I also had my shirt and sweats washed. It cost me three dollars, and took only an hour.

Day 18 in the desert—a little hung, makes for a slow day

"This is from my daughters, to encourage you."

I went out last night to the Ace club. I wanted to be somewhere where I knew people weren't after me for my money. Rabihr had really upset me, but I'm over it now. It took forever to get to the Ace because of heavy traffic. For 120 pounds the driver took me there and waited a few hours to take me back.

I had a guy named Vic sign me in. He's a phys-ed teacher at an international school. He loves his smokes and beer. He retired from Windsor, Ontario, and came here on a contract that ends in three months.

Mike from Cyprus joined us after a while. I met him earlier, but his eyes were rubbering round the room presumably looking for sexier table mates than Vic and I. He failed to find such, so returned to us.

I left before I got drunk, and made it back before midnight.

The radio in the cab was playing the same music as the last guy who took me to the Ace club.

"Who sings this?" I asked, pointing at the radio.

"It is Quran."

Turning the radio dial in North Carolina, there is a multitude of Christian stations playing Christian music, and offering various sermons from different preachers. In Egypt, radio stations have someone singing the Quran. These two things are kind of the same. If you can guess which two can go with each other, then it's time to play our game. It's time to play our game.

There was a message for me from Linda at the front desk, and I had to send the bellman Hassan, the Egypt-Israeli war vet, to get a sim card to use on his phone. When I called home Ally answered, and immediately put her four-year-old cousin Melody on the phone. I hung up rather than use the minutes.

I felt a little rough this morning, but I was at work on time. I did the usual work in front of the Sphinx and was up to see Rabihr the Elder's friend Mohamed for tea at ten. He showed me another pile of rubbish, and I worked on it for a while. I might finish it tomorrow. There are so many nooks and crannies, and they're almost all filled with garbage.

I had lunch from a different guy today, who also works out of a box. I had two sandwiches, and a cup of tea. I have been thinking that the sweet tea here may be rotting everybody's teeth, because most people I meet at the site have very rotten teeth, unbelievably so. I have vowed to limit my tea to one a day.

Lunch was great. The Egyptians treat me well. This new sandwich guy didn't even try to rip me off. I gave him a five for two sandwiches and he gave me one pound back without batting an eye.

A couple of young guys sat with me, including Little Buddy. He helped me for a little bit after lunch, then had to run off to work. He was selling postcards and bookmarks.

As I was working my way up to Khufu, Caron, the security guy who stopped me yesterday, stopped me again.

"Mr. Bruce, how are you my friend," he said, shaking my right hand and putting his left hand on my right shoulder.

"Hello Caron," I said. Amazingly, I had remembered his name, which had him smiling broadly as he introduced me to his two friends from Lebanon. *With great power comes great responsibility.*

I continued up, and met another Mohamed, who true to his word, gave me an Arabic-English dictionary. We talked for a while, and looked at the dictionary.

It was close to two when I reached Khufu. I was exhausted, and I guess I looked the part as well. A woman came over to me as I was working along a wall. Pilar Christine Morel Vasquez works for UNESCO.

"Are you working with others from an NGO (non-governmental organization)?" she asked me.

"No, it's just me."

She gave me her card. I looked for one of my Center for Civilization cards in my backpack but I didn't have any. *Ya big dummy.*

"You can just e-mail me," she said, which I will do tonight. Then she gave me a yellow apple.

"This is from my daughters, to encourage you."

Encourage—to give support, confidence, or hope to—that's just what that apple did.

I guess I was looking as tired as I felt. I thanked her, waved a thanks to her daughters standing behind her, and they left.

All day I get Egyptians yelling "hey Canada" and waving at me. One of the regular "hey Canada" boys came over just then, and sat down beside me. I ate the apple while we talked, glad for the company.

I took a tok-tok back to Siag. My legs are getting worse each day, really stiff this morning. My back was bothering me too. I guess 18 days in a row can do that. Another 22 to go.

If my physical downward slide continues, I'm in for a world of hurt.

Day 19 in the desert—injury and inspiration

"Canada, you have tea,"

I talked to Linda and Ally last night, and our friend Lisa as I guess she dropped by the house. Everybody seems to be doing fine, though the boys, or one of them, must be searching porn on the internet. Linda confronted them, and both denied it. She needs to get parental controls on the computer.

I would prefer if she call just once a week, Saturday or Sunday, when I can talk to all the kids too. I like to be able to focus on things here.

"How many more days you come here?" Ali asked me at the entrance this morning.

"Twenty-one."

"That's very good," he said, smiling.

I started working just through security but Ali told me to move further inside as Mr. Meek was coming to clean that area.

Near the Sphinx, Rabihr the Elder's friend Mohamed asked me for a bag, and half-filled it.

"Is that okay?" he asked me.

"Yes." What was I going to say? *No, you bastard, fill it up.*

"Tomorrow I will have three boys to help you," said Mohamed.

"I don't have any money," I said warily.

"I know. This is my city."

So who knows, I may have a small crew tomorrow. If I do, I think we'll start at Khufu, work around it twice. I'll have to make sure I have plenty of bags.

Walid showed up, pointed to his eyes, and said "Ramadan." I showed him where Ramadan was actually cleaning a little, down by the water in the boat pit on the right and in front of the Sphinx. Twenty minutes later Walid asked for two bags. Later I saw the two of them sitting still and resting. I kept looking from time to time for about an hour, and they didn't move. They appeared to be playing 'statue,' a game my father invented for his seven kids to get some peace in the house.

In five years, my parents had five kids, a handful for any couple. Trying to nap on the weekend, my father would invariably find himself with a bunch of kids crawling all over him. We loved playing on his bed as much as we loved him.

"Let's play statue," he would say. "The first one to move or make a sound loses."

The game only ever gave him a short respite, as we all wanted to win, and were carefully watching each other.

"You moved. I saw you."

"No, I didn't."

"Yes you did. He moved Dad!"

"No, I didn't!"

"Okay. Let's start over."

I was working up Khafre's causeway to Rabihr the Elder when two guards asked for bags, and then went about cleaning an area cordoned off with barbed wire. They *want* it clean.

I worked behind the building near Rabihr the Elder, as he made me some tea. As always, Egyptians came by to ask what I was doing, and then gave their approval with a thumbs up, or "you a good man."

Rabihr the Elder helped me a little today. After 45 minutes I said *bokra* (tomorrow) and left.

I worked to the south of Khafre until close to noon, then went around looking for Ahmed, but again he was not there.

I ran into two of Rabihr the Younger's friends.

"You are limping," said Bolla. "I can see you are hurt."

He was right. The tendon on my right foot was giving me grief. It had me seriously worried. I don't want an injury, especially a tendon. But I was able to nurse it for the rest of the day, and it feels good now. I was overcompensating to prevent an injury, so to Bolla it looked worse than it was.

"Four, five days, big party," said the ever-smiling Ali, from atop his camel.

I was back in front of the Sphinx, cleaning an area behind the chain, beside the chairs set up for the nightly light show, when these two little girls came running up to me with garbage in their hands. They helped me almost frantically, each trying to outdo the other. Some guards came over to see what was up.

"How long more you stay here?" asked one.

"Twenty-one days."

"I will miss you."

The reception by the Egyptian people has been incredible.

I gave the girls Canadian flags, three because they have a little sister. I chuckled at that, they all have other siblings, real or imagined, that they need to have 'another one' for.

I went to dump the bag off behind security at the north, and the little girls followed, finding garbage all the way. I was worried they may be wandering too far afield, they were only six or seven years old. But, I guess there is so little crime in Egypt that their parents weren't worried.

As they left, an old man came up to me, classic work

"Rambo," he said. "You are Rambo. What's your name?"

"*Ana Bruce*," I said, shaking his outstretched hand. He held my right hand with his, and with his left he pulled from his pocket two little blue scarabs crudely carved from some soft stone. As he released my hand, he deftly eased the scarabs into my palm, and then closed my hand with both of his.

"For you and your wife," he said. "Gift."

"*Shokrun*," I said, and he released my hand.

"Give me a little money," he pleaded, hands out.

I couldn't give him any money, because if I did word would spread, and every man, woman and child would be looking for money from me, like Rabihr the Younger eventually did. Rabihr's was merely a drawn out approach, but then he was looking for more money.

"No money," I said. I reached for his right hand, opened it up and put the two scarabs in his palm. Then I closed his hand with both of mine.

"*Shokrun*," I said, looking him in the eyes and smiling.

"You smart man," he said with a grin, as he put the scarabs back in his pocket.

I turned to go drop off the bag and who should I see, but the Lady in the Hat. She was close enough that she must have witnessed me with the two girls, and later with the old man.

I wonder if she would resent the rapport I have with people, such as the little girls, and others I talked and laughed with on my way over to where she was sitting.

"I have only 21 days left," I told her.

She is difficult to read, but my guts tell me she is still wondering about my motives. I must be careful at all times, as I'm sure she could purposely misconstrue my actions to others. But it would be difficult for her to make a false accusation stick, as so many people have seen me and talked to me now.

"Canada, you have tea," I heard as I was working behind Khafre. I had tea with three camel men.

"I have seen you many times," said the man who had called out to me. They have their own little set-up on the northwestern side of Khafre—sheesha, a fire for tea, food for camels. It was like their own camp.

"I give you my number," he said, pulling out a business card. "If you know someone wants ride a camel, call me."

I took a tok-tok home because of my sore leg. Tonight I will not walk much at all, give that tendon a rest. If I blow it, what will I do? Go home?

Watching the news, the world looks bleak in so many places.

Day 20 in the desert—halfway there, and halfway home

"The world hates Islam."

I have to mention some things about yesterday. When I met Maharab for lunch, he kissed me on both cheeks, and held his fingers together and pointed to the sky. I had one sandwich and gave him a five.

"Another?" he asked.

"*La, shokrun,*" No, thank-you.

"Water?"

"Yes," I said, as I knew he wanted to keep all of the five.

Mohamed, the assistant manager of the restaurant in Siag, was working the bar last night, and we were talking about religion.

"Why is it, the bible has so many, many versions, but the Quran has only one?" he asked me, narrowing his eyes, and looking at me sideways. "You tell me why."

Of course I couldn't.

"The world hates Islam," he said.

That's a terrible place for us to be, with more than a billion people thinking the other five billion hate them. It is an untenable position, one that needs to be remedied. How did we get to such a state? I believe it's in large part due to the strategy or philosophy of the pre-emptive strike. Certainly the Muslim people I have met are wonderful people.

"Well, *I* love you Mohamed," I said, doing my part to ease global tension.

"I love you too, Bruce," he responded, laughing.

I had a few drinks with a couple from Crete, Rena and Manolis. She's English, he's from Crete.

I discovered 400 pounds missing from my room, taken out of my leather jacket. I mentioned it to Rabbob at the front desk.

"That hasn't happened for a long time," she said.

Fatih lent me 100 pounds, and gave me a tensor bandage, and good thing too. My leg feels much better. Two more days of slow walking and overcompensating and I should be as good as new.

I stretched for a good ten minutes this morning. My back was killing me, and the tendon in my leg was screaming at me. I was feeling like I was wasting my time, like I was stupid to be doing this, a complete moron, but there is no stopping now. I'm halfway there.

Walking to work this morning, I was picked up by a man named Amir in his tok-tok. He works at the pyramids and drives a tok-tok in his spare time.

"I have seen you at the Sphinx," he said. He invited me to supper tonight. A free ride to work, just what I needed, for both my body and spirit.

Mohamed at the Sphinx came through with one kid, named Noor, who, after about 15 minutes, remembered he had a dentist appointment and left. So much for my gang of kids cleaning the Giza plateau.

I worked my way around to the south side of Khafre, and there I met Joel Clark, a Canadian artist specializing in Egyptian art. He introduced me to Nicholas Cashmore, his marketing agent.

Joel has an interesting perspective on ancient Egypt, and I hope to sit down with beers to discuss it. He does not agree with generally accepted theories about the ancient Egyptians, and is convinced they had extraterrestrial help. There are many websites on the internet proclaiming the same theory.

Joel's business card reads:

> *"From the living heart of Eternal Egypt come paintings which unite the past, present and future in visions of cosmic consciousness. For over twenty years Joel Clark has battled the mighty forces of a materialistic world view to manifest the Living Power of Ancient Egypt."*
>
> *"Using traditional methods of ink and tempera with gold leaf on paper, each painting is an act of worship and devotion to the Sacred Wisdom and Higher Awareness so sorely needed at this time by a world gone astray."*

Apparently his works of art take six to 12 months to complete.

Both Joel and Nicholas have great reverence for ancient Egypt and the pyramids, and respect for what I'm doing here.

"The legend," said Nicholas, as he put his arm around my shoulder for Joel to take a picture of us.

They're staying at the Sphinx Tourist Hotel, paying $60 US a night, and it sounds rough. I think I got a good deal at the Siag at $25.

An Egyptian fellow who has been working the pyramids for 30 years started helping me, constantly saying "I'm a good man, I'm a good man." Looking for redemption?

"Want to hear funny story?" he asked me.

"Sure."

"See this statue?" he asked, holding a small figurine of Nefertiti.

"Yeah."

"Engineer, he work over there," he pointed to Menkaure. "He found one of my statues. It was broken, and I threw it away. He found it, and thought it was from ancient times."

How he laughed.

Speaking of engineers, Ahmed and one of his colleagues, Mr. Abd El Fattah appeared just then. They walked with me to drop a bag off in front of Khafre, and then down to the Sphinx where I found Maharab. Ahmed told me to call home because of a bombing one hour away in a café at the El Khalili Bazaar. Apparently terrorists killed a 20-year-old French woman.

"Your family will be worried about you," he said.

They left me there with Maharab, and I had a sandwich and a Fanta.

Some loud kid came by, jabbering away in Arabic to Maharab, who made him a sandwich. He was maybe 14 years old, with a cigarette behind his ear.

"You're too young to smoke," I said.

"No, smoking good," he said. "Smoking hashish better."

Then he pretended to have a hit of some hash. He sucked in some air like pulling on a joint, then coughed a little, as if trying to keep the smoke in, one hand still holding the imaginary joint, the other against his chest. Then a long exhale of satisfaction. Hilarious, his imitation was perfect. I burst out laughing.

Ahmed returned while I was still eating and paid for my lunch— five pounds for the Maharab special. It really should be four, but I always pay five. Through Ahmed, Maharab invited me to his house for supper, and I'll go tomorrow, as I'm at Amir's tonight. After Ahmed left, a policeman came over and spoke to Maharab.

"You no pay, okay?" the policeman said to me with a smile.

"*Shokrun*," I said to him, and looked at Maharab. He was looking down and smiling. Maharab had just been paid twice, once by Ahmed and again by the policeman.

I went up to work with Rabihr the Elder, and the 'boys' called me over to this security shack where five of them were sitting on the floor having tea. As I walked over, I found a horseshoe, I now have 19 for the 20 days I have been here. *Enshallah*. They gave me tea, laughed and laughed, another tea, laughed some more, and tried to get me to imitate words in Arabic. I suspect some of the words made me or others the butt of a joke. But such good nature. They always have a cup of tea for you.

On my way back down to the Sphinx, one of Rabihr the Younger's buddies came by with a friend, each on a camel. I rode with his friend on the back of his camel as close as I could get to the exit. How cool is that?

Walking home I hear this "Bruce!" and it's the Swedish woman sitting at a café, so I joined her for tea. She has such a disjointed way of talking and follows her own unique train of thought that it's difficult to have a conversation. But she's charming and eccentric and it's easy to enjoy her company. I had tried to pop into her place the day before, but got lost in the maze. My leg was hurting, so I bailed and went home. She was told about it. I guess everybody knows what everybody else is doing in such crowded situations.

"Everyone watches everyone else," said Karen.

"I heard about the bombing," she added. "Tourism in Egypt will suffer enormously because of it."

I don't think it'll make the news back home.

I told Karen what the German woman, Katja, had told me about older women coming to Egypt to have sex with young Egyptian men.

"Oh dear God, yes, happens all the time," she said. "They pay for it too. Why, a good-looking young Egyptian man can support his whole family from 'gifts' from older women."

I hugged her when I left.

"They're thinking we're fucking now for sure," she said.

"Was it good for you?" I asked.

Tomorrow after work I will ask to bring a camera. I hope they let me.

Day 21 in the desert—up and down, I get my picture taken by a professional and chicken out about the camera

"I think they say they are rubbish people."

Fatih was bragging last night about how he and his friend would sometimes drink 24 beers between them in a sitting. Clearly he has no idea who he is talking to.

I thanked him for the tensor bandage he gave me yesterday.

"I'm a doctor," he said with a straight face.

"No, I don't think so," I said, and he smiled.

I was e-mailing Linda about our bank account and was late calling Amir to come get me for dinner. I said we could make it another time, but he insisted on coming right over to get me.

At his house he unlocked what must be the greeting room. He introduced me to his kids, but I had no glimpse of his wife. His brother came in, and I recognized him from the Sphinx area. Amir and his brother both work many jobs to make ends meet. His brother said he was tired and went to sleep.

Food came on a big platter.

"Eat," said Amir, and he left the room and closed the door. I waited, expecting him to come back and eat with me. When he finally did, he saw I hadn't touched the food.

"We have already eaten," he told me. "You eat now," and he left again.

I ate, and when finished, I called him and he came and took the tray. Weird, he could've sat there and talked with me while I ate. Strange custom.

I was just interrupted by Mustafa and the head guy for cleaning this floor, asking where the lost money was, when did I see it last, etcetera. I just want to forget about it.

"I was not here that day," said Mustafa.

But he was. I remember he knocked on the door to ask if everything was fine with how he cleaned the room, and I said yes, as I hadn't discovered the money missing yet.

Last night Manolis from Crete said that pyramids don't make a shadow. I found that fascinating. But alas, they do. I was working in the shadow of the middle pyramid today. I guess everything makes a shadow. It is known, though, that at noon at the spring equinox the pyramids cast no shadow. But there is more to the great pyramid of Khufu than that.

Forty years ago Peter Tompkins wrote in his book *Secrets of the Great Pyramid*:

"Recent studies of ancient Egyptian hieroglyphs and the cuneiform mathematical tablets of the Babylonians and Sumerians have established that an advanced science did flourish in the Middle East at least three thousand years before Christ, and that Pythagoras, Eratoshenes, Hipparchus and other Greeks reputed to have originated mathematics on this planet merely picked up fragments of an ancient science evolved by remote and unknown predecessors.

The Great pyramid, like most of the great temples of antiquity, was designed on the basis of hermetic geometry known only to a restricted group of initiates, mere traces of which percolated to the Classical and Alexandrian Greeks.

Like Stonehenge and other megalithic calendars, the Pyramid has been shown to be an almanac by means of which the length of the year, including its awkward .2422 fraction of a day, could be measured as accurately as with a modern telescope. It has been shown to be a theodolite, or instrument for the surveyor, of great precision and simplicity, virtually indestructible. It is still a compass so finely oriented modern compasses are adjusted to it, not vice versa.

It has also been established that the Great Pyramid is a carefully located geodetic marker, or fixed landmark, on which the geography of the ancient world was brilliantly constructed; that it served as a celestial observatory from which maps and tables of the stellar hemisphere could be accurately drawn; and that it incorporates in its size and angles the means for creating a highly sophisticated map projection of the northern Hemisphere. It is, in fact, a scale model of the hemisphere correctly incorporating the geographic degrees of lattitude and longitude.

The Pyramid may well be the repository of an ancient and possibly universal system of weights and measures, the model for the most sensible system of linear and temporal measurements available on earth, based on the polar axis of rotation, a system first postulated in modern times a century ago by the British astronomer Sir John Herschel, whose accuracy is now confirmed by the mensuration of orbiting satellites.

Whoever built the Great Pyramid, it is now quite clear, knew the precise circumference of the planet and the length of the year to several decimals—data which were not rediscovered until the seventeenth century. It's architects may well have known the mean length of the earth's orbit round the sun, the specific density of the planet, the 26,000-year cycle of the equinoxes, the acceleration of gravity, and the speed of light."

Whew, and I thought Mona Lisa's smile held a few secrets!

This morning I was stiff as hell, really hurting. Sometimes I wish I had come to the embrace as a younger man.

I stretched a little, took some pills, and by the time I went for breakfast I felt better. Dozens of Yugoslavians were in the hotel, and getting back up to my room was tough because of a huge crowd at the elevators. Luckily my army buddy Hassan called to me at the back of the crowd. He widened his arms like Moses parting the Red Sea, and the crowd parted to let me through to the elevator he was holding open with his foot.

I was working the front of Khafre when several kids started helping me. They bailed quickly when I said I had no money. One kid stuck it out though, and this guy came up and started asking for money for him.

"Give him some money, he is helping you," he demanded.

"I don't have any money."

"You must have money. Where do you stay, what do you eat?"

"I don't have any money."

"You are a big man. He is just a little boy. Give him some money."

"I don't have any money," I repeated again, getting angry.

"He is just joking," said Bolla from behind me. I didn't know he was there.

He wasn't joking, though, he was being a butt-head. I was pissed off and it put me in a bad mood.

But a few minutes later two security guys came up and thanked me, and helped me a little. One went to get me a cup of tea from the Cave, and I felt a lot better.

It never ceases to amaze me how one incident can change my mood for the worse, and a kind word or action improve it. I guess we should focus on making sure that each day, in all our dealings with people, we try to improve things.

I was working the right side of the entrance to Khafre when Ari Rossner approached me. A photographer from France, Ari is here with his wife and two kids. After a little conversation we discovered his wife lived on the same street and block as we did in Paris. He took my picture, and said he would e-mail it to me.

I sat with some of Rabihr's buddies for a while. One of them had me text a message in English on his cell phone to his Spanish girlfriend.

"Tell her she has strong pussy for me," he said.

"I can't write that," I told him.

Instead I wrote "My love, my love for you is as eternal as the pyramids. It will never grow old. You are my Nefertiti, and I am your slave."

Nefertiti, whose name means "the beautiful one has come" was the wife of Pharaoh Amenhotep IV, who ruled Egypt from 1352 BC to 1336 BC. She had many titles—Heiress, Great of Favors, Exuding Happiness, Beloved One, Soothing the king's heart in his house, Whom he loves, Lady of the Two Lands. Her exact birth date is not known, but a scant 65 BTE stands between us meeting in the flesh.

Nefertiti and Amenhotep started a religious revolution in the fourth year of his reign by worshiping only one god, the sun disc Aten. Perhaps an attempt to unite the people under a single banner, like the biblical Abraham hundreds of years earlier. A year later Amenhotep changed his name to Akhenaten in honor of his new religion, much like Cassius Clay became Mohamed Ali when he converted to Islam.

Nefertiti mysteriously vanishes from the public record in the 14th year of Akhenaten's reign, never to reappear. Some speculate she became the co-ruler Smenkhkare, who appeared at the time Nefertiti disappeared, to rule in concert with the Pharaoh. Some say she fell out of favor with the Pharaoh, who took another lover, Queen Kiya. Others say she simply died.

Though her mortal frame long ago disappeared, a 3300-year-old painted limestone bust of her head and shoulders was discovered in 1912 in sculptor Thutmose's workshop in Amarna, Egypt. It was crafted by Thutmose in 1345 BC. The German expedition that found it, led by Ludwig Borchardt, took it home. Egypt has been fighting for its repatriation ever since, claiming Borchardt tricked them into thinking it was of little value.

"Suddenly we had in our hands the most alive Egyptian artwork," wrote Borchardt in his diary. "You cannot describe it in words. You must see it."

The Egyptians claim that Borchardt described the bust to the Egyptian authorities as "a painted plaster bust of a princess," misleading them so they would let him take it out of the country. Borchardt's diary clearly referred to it as the head of Nefertiti.

"This proves that Borchardt wrote this description so that his country can get the statue," said Dr. Zahi Hawass, who has made countless requests for the return of the bust.

German author Philipp Vandenburg, author of the international bestseller 'The Curse of the Pharaohs,' and a book titled simply 'Nefertiti,' described the theft of the bust as "adventurous and beyond comparison."

Time magazine lists it among the top ten plundered artifacts in the world, second only to Egyptian Frescos at the Louvre, in Paris.

Standing 19 inches tall, and weighing a mere 44 pounds, the Nefertiti bust has become a cultural symbol of Berlin, and appears on German stamps and Berlin postcards.

Nefertiti is credited by some to re-establishing the imperial German national identity after WWI. In 1930 the German press described the Nefertiti bust as the country's new monarch. Adolf Hitler vowed to build a museum to house the bust he described as "a unique masterpiece, an ornament, a true treasure."

"In the middle, this wonder, Nefertiti, will be enthroned," said Hitler.

In 1933 Hermann Goring wanted to return the statue as a gesture of good will toward Egypt, but Hitler killed that idea. He was good at killing.

"I will never relinquish the head of the Queen," he said.

Reason enough to return it now, if you ask me.

The Queen was housed in bunkers all over Germany in WWII, including a salt mine. She was in the possession of the Americans at the war's end, and Egypt again asked for repatriation. The Yanks refused.

Ironically, sitting at number seven of Time's plundered artifacts list is Priam's Treasure, stolen from Germany by Russia at the end of WWII. German archeologist Heinrich Schliemann discovered this treasure, mostly gold and copper shields and weapons, in Anatolia (roughly Turkey) in 1837. He smuggled (those damn German archeologists!) the booty to Berlin and named it after Priam, the king of Troy. He thought the treasure was proof he had discovered that famous city.

Russia kept the theft a secret, until the treasure was put on display in Moscow in 1993. Though bound by a 1990 treaty to restore plundered artifacts to Germany, Russia, like Germany, is refusing to do so.

Nefertiti, "the beautiful one has come" is now prominently displayed in the Nueus Museum in Berlin. I would like to see it 'plundered' back to Egypt.

Today at the pyramids a lot of guys picked up garbage and put it in my bag. Near the end of the day, in front of the Sphinx, I said *shokrun*, thank-you, to a guy putting garbage in my bag.

"No. I say thank you to you," he said. "The laws in this country are shit."

A young man spoke to me near the Valley Temple of Khafre.

"I like to think," he said, "people from other countries say, 'Egyptian people are clean people.' But no," he shook his head, "I think they say they are rubbish people."

When I picked up the trash around the knocked over trash-can at the school in Gimli, it was knocked over again the next day.

When I cleaned White Pine Drive in Hendersonville, it was full of trash weeks later. When I lived in Paris, I could not believe what a trash heap it was! They never cleaned up after their dogs, and it seemed everyone had a dog. To this day my image of a Parisian shopkeeper is a guy leaning against the entrance to his shop, chain-smoking cigarettes while he watches each of his customers step over a pile of dog crap to enter his store, and does nothing about it. If it wasn't for the government literally washing the streets once a week, Paris would be unliveable. The only difference between Paris and Cairo? The government does not do as much in Cairo.

What would an alien race think of us?

I like to think, beings from another planet say, 'Earth people are clean people,' but no, I think they say they are rubbish people.

I plan to grab a cab to the beer store and take in all my empties. Maybe I'll call Amir, maybe not. He offered to help, but he's working three jobs. Then again, one of his jobs *is* tok-tok.

I was stiff and sore this morning, worse than ever. Putting on the tensor, I questioned myself again. I now call it The Doubt. I guess it never ends, when you do something different, out of the box like this. Will the Doubt ever die? Will it win?

Day 22 in the desert—plenty of tea, lesson learned, and security checks me out

"Maybe we should do something like this in Yemen."

Some things forgotten yesterday—I found a one pound note, rare in Egypt. I've kept it. That and the 50 piastres the little boy gave me should be framed.

I had an e-mail yesterday from my son Tiberius.

"Why did you say we should be grounded until you come home?"

I never did, because that would mean my leaving, or being away, means they get punished. Then they hate me for being away. That's just not right.

I had a thought yesterday that to increase the amount our government gives to foreign aid, some magic number rock musician Bono talks about, the government could allow individuals and corporations to make donations where each sees fit. A tax break kicks in, but the donation adds to the government's commitment. Theoretically the people of Canada could make all the payments for the government's commitment to give .07 per cent of GDP or whatever the number is. The people get the tax breaks, and the government meets its commitment. It helps redistribute the wealth of the world, and people feel good about their personal involvement in foreign aid.

Another thought: the Jewish people of the world should know from their own history that continual persecution only breeds strength, not annihilation. They should treat Palestinians accordingly. Perhaps that is the one lesson they were meant to learn from thousands of years of oppression, *and they have not learned it.*

I have always had abstract thoughts when doing something physical and repetitive, particularly outdoors. I think it's due to the blood flow to the brain due to activity, the opportunity to let the mind wander due to the repetition, and fresh air.

Mark Twain liked to write in the morning and hike up to 15 miles through the woods in the afternoon for stimulation. I'm sure he was thinking the whole time.

I have noticed this with my sons. When each turned 13, I decided to take them on a big trip.

I think it's important that fathers and sons do that type of thing, spend that type of time together, and get to know each other. And I think it should be done before the really rebellious years begin.

As Twain said, "When I was 17 my father was the stupidest man on the earth. By the time I turned 21, I was amazed at what the old man had learned in four years."

Young boys dream of adventure, and what could be better than doing a trip with Dad?

Jake and I spent 67 days kayaking the Mississippi River from its headwaters at Lake Itasca, Minnesota, to New Orleans. We spent day after day sitting in our tandem kayak paddling, and he would talk for hours about what he saw in the clouds, or tell me imaginary adventures he would have with his friends.

Day 43 of Jake's journal on the Mississippi River

We paddled for 30 miles and I made up a story about me, Mario and Dylan, and Dad thinks it's awesome. In part of it I, Mario and Dylan fight strange red and black creatures with claws that are impervious to our attacks.

Back at home, with the television, video games, and all the other distractions, his imagination doesn't need to work as hard to keep himself entertained.

I took Ti hiking on the Appalachian Trail, from Springer Mountain, Georgia, to Damascus, Virginia. Born in August, he turned 13 the day after we finished.

One misty morning as we hiked through gently sloping terrain, he suddenly started talking about a book he was going to write.

Day 4 of my journal on the Appalachian Trail

Ti was in great spirits as usual. He reminds me of Jake so much. Today, as we were walking in the mountains and the mist, he came up with an idea for a book, 'Into the Mist.'

It will start with two boys running, the one faster than the other yelling for the slower guy to 'Run Billy, run' but Billy doesn't answer. Johnny returns to find ninjas have slit his throat and there's blood everywhere. Then ninjas start dropping from the trees. I had never heard him so excited, synapses firing away.

It got me wondering—is his imagination fired up by being outdoors, not watching TV or video games, or did I just not take the time to listen to him?

He also told me he plans on selling the movie rights to someone for $2 million, and then maybe go work for Stephen King for a thousand dollars a day as an ideas man. Quite the plan.

Today was wild. I was hurting more than ever. Back hurt, legs hurt, needed to stretch for twenty minutes. I took some pills, acetaminophen for pain, and glucosamine for the knees. I haven't had to wear a knee brace yet, but I have two should I need them.

I started walking through the Sphinx gate but some guy I had never seen before said "ticket over there" and tilted his head toward the ticket counter, indicating I had to buy a ticket. The other guys quickly spoke up and I was let through, with this new guy looking confused. It was a harbinger of things to come.

I worked the front of the Sphinx, and up came Ramadan and Walid. I gave them two bags, and Ramadan was complaining about that, as he thought Walid and he could only fill one bag. I had filled two bags before they showed up to work. *Don't judge, Benson.*

I went to the tiny pit I was shown behind Rabihr the Elder's place, and filled four bags. It got very dusty as I got down about five years worth of rubbish, so I left the rest until tomorrow. I met some new security guys further up the hill, and they invited me for tea in their shack. I spoke French, Arabic and English with the three. One guard spoke passable French, better than mine. With limited knowledge of the three languages we still communicated. I'll probably go for tea there again tomorrow, as, as usual, they showed me an area they would like to see cleaned up.

I walked up to Khafre wanting to work behind the Sphinx, but did not get there. At the tea shop beneath Khafre's Mortuary Temple, the Cave, some new security guys offered me some tea.

"You want Turkish coffee?" asked one, dressed in a pristine uniform with many stars on it.

"What does it taste like?" I asked.

"Very good," he assured me, so I gave it a try.

"Phytooeeey," I said as I spit it out.

He laughed. "I buy you tea, okay?"

As I went to drop off some bags and have some koshery, a man came up and introduced himself, and led me to another fellow sitting on the new boardwalk that Ahmed is overseeing. He is the Supervisor for Antiquities at Khafre, the second pyramid. On the way over my escort put my hand on his arm like I was a woman walking with a man. It made me feel uncomfortable, but it's just a cultural difference. Men walk together like that here. I have seen it many times.

"You should get Mr. Kamal Wahid to give you ten men to supervise," said the Supervisor. "How much you get paid for this?"

"Nothing."

"Oh. Well, you should spend ten days around this pyramid," he said, waving his arm toward Khafre.

I won't. It doesn't need it. Besides, I like to roam around, do a little here, a little there.

I ran into Bolla talking to a South African guy named Froggy who was on a boat and jumped ship, and is looking to get on another one.

"Froggy?" I said quizzically when he told me his name.

"Yeah. French guys always think I'm taking the piss out of them when I tell them my name."

Froggy is staying with Bolla. When I told him I'd be picking garbage for a total of forty days, Froggy talked about the Indians performing given tasks for 100 days in a row.

"It gave them the mind-set to be like that always," said Froggy.

I am determined to write 100 short stories in 100 days before I die. Maybe that will give me the discipline to write every single day of my life. But if I wait until I'm near death, what's the point?

The big party, with five women dancing, is March 5. I may have to go to that, just for the photos.

I saw Rabihr the Younger near the end of the day.

"You forget me," he said, accusingly. I have not seen him since he made the ask.

"No, I have been working."

He made some remark I couldn't quite make out. Clearly I need to distance myself from him.

I cast my eyes over the desert landscape, looking for koshery.

"Have you seen Hassan?" I asked a young vendor.

"Hassan has gone for today," he said.

I was disappointed.

"Look," said the young man, pointing to some young kids near Khufu," they are selling koshery there."

I started in that direction.

"Can you get some for me, too?" he asked, holding out two pounds.

"It's two and a half," I said, but he wasn't paying attention, so I went to get it.

They tried charging me five pounds for one container of koshery, then three pounds.

"Two for five," I said, "Egyptian price."

I took it back and gave the young vendor his koshery. We sat down to eat and immediately he started inviting me somewhere, or himself.

"I walk with you to Siag, okay?" he said.

I asked for the 50 piastres that he owed me for the koshery. Surprised, he gave it to me.

"You need money? I will give you a pound."

"No," I said. "It costs two and a half. You pay me two and a half."

Many times Egyptians have bought me lunch, but I have to be careful. If I give one guy 50 piastres today, a hundred will be asking for it tomorrow.

I was working in front of Khafre later and the guy who was trying to get me to give the boy money called out to me.

"Come, sit here and rest," he said, indicating a spot on his left. "My name is Ashram."

"I have to work," I said.

"All I need is women, food and sleep," said Ashram.

"What about work?" I asked.

"Don't need work," he said.

"I love work," I said.

"Man in Europe, he gets up, and he thinks," he said pointing to his head, "what am I going to do today? Egyptian man wakes up and he goes . . . " and he grabbed his crotch, rubbing vigorously.

I howled with laughter, and got up and started picking up garbage.

"Why you laugh at me?" he asked.

"What makes you think in Canada we don't do the same thing in the morning?"

He laughed, not such a bad guy.

I never did see Maharab, though I said I would go to his house tonight. *Bokra*. Tomorrow.

A man from Yemen, seeing me pick up trash, called out to me.

"You volunteer to do this?"

"Yes."

"That is inspiring," he said. "Maybe we should do something like this in Yemen."

That's always my pay for the day. He was traveling with a very beautiful woman with a hijab. She was absolutely stunning, black eyes like twin ebony moons.

I was nonchalantly leaving, picking up garbage as I went, and some kids helped me. They wanted balloons but I only had one.

"*Bokra*."

Security stopped me, and started asking questions.

"Where are you staying? How long is your visa? Where is your passport?"

The combination of the monthly change of security, and the bombing in Cairo had them very curious about me, and suspicious. They wanted to investigate me.

They took my copy of my passport (I always leave the real passport at my hotel) and gave me a drink that tasted of nectarines.

They were very polite. One older policeman with a bushy moustache said "you are a great man," then sent me on the back of a motorcycle up the road to Khufu. I was then transferred to a horse and carriage and taken around to the west side of Khufu, then walked to security at the Mena House gate.

A tall man in civilian dress, who reminded me of an old partier friend from Toronto named Steve Miller, ordered me to empty my bag. I did. More questions. I had a copy of the Quran, a book about universal ethics titled Bridging the Divide, some copies of the Universal Declaration of Human Rights—items that made them curious, considering what I was doing in Egypt.

They constantly reassured me that there was no problem. They just needed an answer from someone. I was there for an hour before the Steve Miller look-a-like got the call from someone saying, I'm guessing, that I wasn't a threat. His ring tone was "Bad to the Bone," by George Thorogood and the Destroyers.

"Broke a thousand hearts, before I met you. Break a thousand more, baby, before I am through."

Handshakes all around.

"Welcome to Egypt."

"You are a great man," repeated the distinguished-looking older guard with the moustache. How does one respond to that?

One of the guards gave me a ride to Pyramid Road, apologizing all the way for my delay. Me, I was ecstatic that I was good to go, business as usual tomorrow. An unbelievable day, but a good end. Eighteen days to go.

Day 23 in the desert—a day to go out in the woods, rip trees out by the roots and tie them in knots

"You cannot stop the wind!"

What a day!

I felt like my father sounds when he gets up in the morning, joints creaking and groaning, and knees loudly cracking. I had shooting pain down my legs terrifying me, and nausea. This brought on, of course, The Doubt.

I think the ten days from 20 to 30 will be the toughest, mentally. It's not the countdown from ten yet, and the days seem to go slow. Reaching thirty seems to take forever.

I had some fun with Walid today. I was cleaning the front of the Sphinx and along the wall where the vendors sell their wares, when I saw him. He sat with his back to me in front of the Sphinx. I tried yelling his name, but he has hearing problems. A vendor tried tossing a rock near him—or at him, I can't speak for his motives—and it landed close, but still no reaction. Another vendor gave it a try and came very close to actually hitting him so I stopped the entertainment. I didn't want Walid to get hurt.

When he finally came by, I offered him a bag. He refused. I offered again and he finally took it, folded it up and put it in his pocket. I couldn't help myself. I showed him the process of picking up a piece of garbage, then putting it in the bag. He made a gesture like he had to eat first, putting his thumb and first two fingers together and up to his mouth, but I feigned ignorance and did it a few more times.

There were three vendors nearby, and they knew exactly what was happening. We all smiled, and I said "lazy" to the sellers, who chuckled. One of them talked to Walid, I'm sure telling him to get to work. But again, who am I to judge? I shouldn't have done that, and feel bad about it.

I intended to work behind Khafre today, finish my round, and so I walked right there after my fun with Walid. Incidentally, I watched Ramadan for a while today, and have come to the conclusion that those two are about the laziest bastards I have ever known. Not that there's anything wrong with that, as Seinfeld would say.

I said good morning, *Sba al hair*, to maybe 30 people on my way to the back of Khafre, and was at the entrance to the pyramid when I was waylaid by a security guard who spoke little English.

"Mr. Bruce?" he said.

"Yeah?"

"You have ticket?"

"Nooo . . ." I said. *What now?*

He looked flummoxed, like he didn't know what to do, but indicated he wanted me to wait while he made a phone call. The first call wasn't satisfying, so he made more, then waited. I tried to ask questions but it was useless. Finally he said we would go to see Mohamed somebody. Turned out Mohamed somebody was Mohamed Cheoh, the Chief.

"Bruce, how can I help you?" asked Mohamed Cheoh, when he saw me in his doorway.

"I don't know, this guy brought me here," I said, jerking my thumb at my escort.

The Chief questioned him in Arabic, and I noticed the guy started sweating a bit, then he left. I was two hours in the office, and many people came and went.

A professor from Brown's University came in, an archeologist on his way home. Mohamed introduced him to me as a famous archeologist. He said to Mohamed "you would make a good pub . . . pub . . . "

"Publicist," I said.

Mohamed and the professor turned to me.

Mohamed introduced *me* as "a famous, to us at the pyramids, amateur archeologist."

"Really? Do you study the pyramids?" the professor asked.

"I guess, in a way," I chuckled. "I go around and pick up debris, garbage, every day. I've been here for 23 days and I'll be here for another 17."

"So the countdown is going fast," said Mohamed Cheoh, smiling.

"You are lucky to be in Egypt that long," said the professor. "I only had three and a half weeks this time."

An Egyptian woman came in, we knew each other from the last time I was in the office, what I now call my purgatory time, and she and Mohamed were talking and joking in Arabic.

As she got up to leave. Mohamed said "She said if I hurt her, you will be my witness, I said you would be *my* witness."

"I kill you," she said to the Chief.

"I heard *that*," I said.

Two young Egyptian women wearing the hijab came in, and I guessed they are students of journalism wanting to film around the pyramids. A bit of an argument ensued between them and the Chief, but I think they got what they wanted.

The usual suspects shuffled in, many I knew from purgatory. Ever the gracious host, Mohamed Cheoh fed me cake, and falafel.

He said he was waiting for a phone call, and it finally came.

"You can come back tomorrow," said the Chief, "but you must buy a ticket."

Apparently when they asked if I had money yesterday, it was to determine if I could afford the ticket. Seventeen days at 60 pounds comes to just over a thousand pounds, or nearly US $200. I can handle that.

"This silly little bomb has made things crazy," said the Chief. "The day after the bombing *I* was searched."

The Chief of Operations for the Giza plateau was searched by security? Man, I'm lucky to be alive!

I was led by George, a Christian guy quick to tell me that fact, back to Khafre, and there met both Rabihr the Younger and friends, and Ahmed the engineer. Rabihr wanted me to come with him, but I said I couldn't.

I talked with Ahmed, explained what had happened. He was very apologetic for my troubles. But I was cool with it.

I spent a while cleaning the rubbish from under the frame of the walkway Ahmed is building. It will be filled with sand, and then covered with wood, which will last for a long, long time. I wish I had a Canadian Loonie or Toonie I could slip under it. Maybe I'll talk to the consulate.

"Mr. Kamal Wahid told me to tell you that you can have tea with him any time," said Ahmed. "And he sends his apologies for your troubles with security."

I was walking to drop off a few bags when the two journalist girls came by.

"We are proud you are doing this. We feel really proud."

They took my picture, and filmed me working.

I was wondering myself what I was doing, what with my troubles with security, and this was the answer. Very important stuff.

One of the girls works at Sakkara where they have apparently discovered a new pyramid, news to me.

"If you come there, I will show you around."

They both gave me their cell phone numbers. A wonderful part of my day. It makes it all worthwhile.

Coming back from dropping off the bags, Ashram the jokester who pissed me off a few days before, but whom I'm getting to see is not so bad, called out to me.

"You are one man. There are ninety, maybe a hundred million Egyptians. You will never clean it all."

It was windy, and just as he said that a gust of wind sent dozens of pieces of garbage flying in the air. Ashram was sitting on the stone at the foot of Khafre, and he waved his left arm in the air.

"You cannot stop the wind!" he shouted.

I didn't have a response.

"Yes," he continued, "if I picked up the stuff around me, and all Egyptians did it, it would be clean. But that's not how it is."

No, that's not how it is.

Then he asked me to write a message to his friend in Denmark, in English, tomorrow. I had already done some translating that day. I guess I'm becoming the local expert.

Five or ten minutes after Ashram said I was just one man, a young Egyptian came up and asked for my autograph, and then picked garbage with me for at least fifteen minutes. He had two friends with him, not so moved to clean up. It was wonderful. A few minutes after Ashram said it, I was no longer one man, if only briefly.

As I was leaving the site some kids came up and asked for flags, and the three of them went running across the sand waving the flags, shouting "Canada, Canada, Canada." Wonderful. I wonder what tourists from other countries think upon seeing Egyptian children running across the sands of the Giza plateau, waving Canadian flags and yelling "Canada, Canada, Canada."

Homeward bound, I bought some water. There was a little boy saying hi in the water store, and I was going to give him a pin, but a little girl came by. Fearing a swarm, I zipped my bag back up. Standing, I realized it was one of the two little sweethearts who had helped me before. Her sister was with her, and they walked me to the corner, but thankfully not across the very fast and busy Pyramid Road.

When feeling a powerful positive emotion, usually when a child at the school succeeded far beyond expectations, Frank Wiens would snarl, "It makes you want to go out in the woods, rip trees out by the roots and tie them in knots." That's how I felt today.

I can see Frank now, sitting in the Merchants Hotel in Selkirk, two glasses of draft beer in front of him, his pack of Players plain cigarettes resting beside an ashtray. He leans forward, indicating his earnestness. He looks you in the eyes as he speaks, twisting imaginary trees into knots with his hands. His eyes sparkle.

Day 24 in the desert—the desert was cold that day, my friends, a little slow, up late with Joel and Nicholas

"Sing, sing us a song."

I wanted to check my e-mails to see if Joel and Nicholas were coming over, but the internet was down in the hotel, so I went to an internet shop, can't really call it a café, and then came back. Unfortunately, I lost one of the lenses for my glasses. However Rabbob thinks that if I get the prescription, for 20 pounds she can get a pair made. That's less than four dollars, much less than in Canada. I'll call my optometrist in Canada in a few hours.

I had a few beers with the Crete couple, then went upstairs and waited for Nicholas and Joel. They came around eight and left at midnight. We had a great time, and I hope they come by again.

Joel is convinced there is no way humans built the pyramids unaided. They both think what I'm doing is way cool.

"You know where you were working when we met you?" asked Nicholas.

"Yeah, the northeast corner of Khafre, wasn't it?"

"I saw a UFO there a few days later."

I love these guys. We had one of those nights, three Canadians sitting around drinking beer in a far-off country. The conversation ran the gamut. At the end of the night I was reciting poetry, If by Rudyard Kipling, always the sign of good times.

I was a little hung-over this morning. I didn't wear my undershirt because I thought it was warm. Mistake. It was quite cold and windy today.

Ali was at the Sphinx gate.

"I am sorry you must pay," he said. "It is not right." Then he pointed to the ticket, and then his eyes, signaling to me that now I could look security in the eye and tell them to back off. There's freedom in that. There's power in that. I plan to ask to bring a camera the day after tomorrow, as Friday and Saturday are the weekend, and neither Mr. Kamal Wahid nor Mohamed Cheoh are in.

I saw Little Buddy as I walked around Khafre's Valley Temple, curled up on the ground beside his camel for warmth, and shivering.

"*Sba al Hair*," I said to him. He just smiled in return.

I worked the Sphinx as usual, then to the back of Khafre. Time was going slowly, so I just put my head down and went at it. One more day and I'll be done one round of Khafre, then I'll take on Khufu.

I had tea with the boys in the back, quite the cast of characters. The boss has a reddish moustache that looks out of place. Slap a kilt on him and toss some bagpipes his way and he'd pass for a Scotsman. Perhaps his coloring can be traced back to the invasion of Alexander the Great, or maybe the more recent Napolean.

The tea maker asked me for garbage bags again today.

"I will give you one, but I can't give you any more after that," I said, but I suspect he will be asking me again tomorrow. I call him Askman.

I was looking for some koshery, when Hamdy and Samba spotted me. I told them I was hungry, and they led me over to an Egyptian woman, Mahmoudy, another vendor selling food to the Egyptians on the east side of Khafre. They got some bread, cheeses, and falafel. The three of us ate, using the bread to scoop up cheese, leaning against the pyramid. It was very filling.

Cynical as I sometimes am, I was waiting for them to ask for money to pay for it, but they didn't. Instead they offered to buy me a Pepsi as well.

Back to work the far northwest corner of Khafre, a bunch of school kids gathered around me—the future of Egypt. Swarming me, they all wanted to tell me their name. One of them, as is always the case, was a real joker, and had the others laughing. I have no idea what he was saying. Two adults came over and introduced themselves, chaperones or teachers.

"Sing, sing us a song," one kid yelled out, and they cheered.

I don't know if they thought I was some famous singer, but I obliged with a little of Frank Sinatra's 'My Way', belting it out at the top of my lungs.

"For what is a man, what has he got,

If not himself, then he has naught

To say the things he truly feels,

And not the words of one who kneels

The records show, I took the blows,

And did it my way."

Standing beside Khafre, with Menkaure behind me, the Sphinx to my right, and facing Khufu, I sang it my way.

The kids loved it. They all had to shake my hand, much to the consternation of their chaperones who were trying to keep them on schedule.

I saw entrance Ali on my way out.

"What do you think is the problem? Why must you pay?"

"It's just security," I said, shrugging my shoulders.

"It's fuckin' bullshit," he cussed. "You need to see Zahi Hawass, the big boss. He will let you in for free."

Personally, I don't care. It's two hundred bucks until the end, and it gives me the right to have a camera. I'm not going to bring one until I talk to Kamal or Mohamed, but I *will* get my camera in there. There's just too many photos I need of people, places and things.

Ali also asked me if I had some whiskey for him.

"I like whiskey," he said. I will get him some whiskey.

I spoke to Camel Ali first thing this morning.

"Rabihr and I come to you tonight," he said.

"No, not tonight. Tomorrow."

When I was having lunch with Hamdy and Samba, Samba called Rabihr on his cell, and I told him to come for beers tomorrow. I'm going to the expat club tonight with the couple from Crete.

I spoke to Linda yesterday and everything is fine at home. All the kids' report cards have improved.

Note—yesterday I hopped into a currency exchange place, curious, and it seems the exchange rate hasn't changed at all. When Fatih exchanged money for me twelve days ago, he told me the US dollar had gone down. He was burning me a little on the exchange.

Oh, Egypt!

Day 25 in the desert—counting down, and communicating

"So you flew halfway around the world to pick up garbage at the pyramids?"

Last night I went to a different internet place, I guess there's many around here. I took a cab. The cabbie had to ask directions a few times, but he got me there. Four pounds an hour for the internet. The keys were so worn on the first computer that it was impossible to read the letters. I jumped to another one. A kid asked to use the headphones attached to that computer, and when he took them he disconnected my mouse, but he quickly reconnected it. This kid was very computer savvy, and I watched him playing games on the internet for a few minutes. His concentration on the screen reminded me of my own children. Perhaps computer games can bring east and west together.

Kipling wrote;

> *"Oh, East is East and West is West, and never the twain shall meet,*
> *Till Earth and Sky stand presently at God's great Judgement Seat;"*

But that's ridiculous, east is east and west is west, and *always* the two shall meet. We can't get around it, we have to accept it. The sooner the better.

Kipling goes on;

> *But there is neither East nor West, Border, nor Breed, nor Birth,*
> *When two strong men stand face to face, tho' they come from the ends of the earth!"*

I e-mailed a few people, then back to the hotel. Sent Luc from St. Laurent a message to give to Daniel Fortier, my video editor, we'll see if he gets it. Daniel is editing my version of The Gods of the Copybook Headings by Kipling for the Gimli Film Festival.

I met Manolis and Rena at the bar and we went off to the Ace club. It was a nice diversion, but we didn't meet anyone—mainly because we were our own group. It's always better when you go by yourself. You meet so many more people.

The Sudanese boys at the bar said I could work there next week, if I showed up by 5:30. I think it would be fun to tend bar at the Ace club.

We came back and had a nightcap in my room, then to bed. I was a little hung-over in the morning. Ali asked again if I had whiskey, so I'd better get some for him.

I saw Mohawk again. He said his first wife drove him nuts so he sent her away, gave her gold and other stuff.

"I told her I would kill her, if she stayed," he said, clenching his fist. I imagine many husbands have felt that way at one time or another, wives too. Come to think of it, a fair number have acted on that impulse.

"Muslims and Christians can live together," he said, changing the topic, (slightly) "but not the Jew."

He said it with a sad smile on his face and a shake of his head. I believe it's an honest opinion, not a racist statement.

Christianity, Judaism and Islam share a common ancestor, Abraham. What a sad state of affairs for the sons and daughters of Abraham to be in, bickering like spoiled siblings. It reminds me of children fighting.

"It's mine."

"No, It's mine!"

What would Abraham, venerated as the patriarch of Christianity, Islam and Judaism, say?

Perhaps we can look to him for insight in solving religious divisions between his three descendants.

Abraham first appeared in Genesis, the first book of the holy scriptures of Judaism, and the Christian Bible's Old Testament. He later appeared in the Talmud, the New Testament, and frequently in the Quran, the holy book of Islam. Who was this guy?

Most scholars put his birth between 2000-1800 BC. The Pyramids of Giza and the Sphinx were at least five hundred years old by then. To put that in perspective, if Abraham was to appear in America five hundred years after Columbus, he would be 18 years old now, old enough to die as a soldier in Iraq, but not to have a beer in a pub in the United States.

I feel a kinship to this Abraham, as he is most famously known as the founder of monotheism, the belief that there is only one God. Clearly Abraham saw monotheism as a solution to religious strife.

If we all pray to the same God, the one and only God, then we will be like brothers and sisters, he must have thought.

Abraham could not have anticipated the splintering into three religions, all based on monotheism, but disagreeing primarily on the role of Jesus Christ and Mohamed.

I see the embrace as a way of mending the rifts among the three Abrahamic religions—a way to look back at the common ancestor. Further than that, it can bring ALL the religions of the world into agreement. One step further, a person does not need to have a religion to believe in the embrace.

Since his wife Sarah was barren, 86-year-old Abraham had a son with an Egyptian slave girl named Hagar, an acceptable practice at the time. His name was Ishmael, meaning "God has heard." The Quran calls him "an apostle and a prophet."

Lo and behold, the barren Sarah gives birth to Isaac, "he who laughs," 14 years later, when Abraham was 100 years old.

Apparently God then ordered Abraham to banish Hagar and Ishmael, but promised to make a nation for each of the sons.

The Prophet Mohamed and his disciples believed Abraham, through Ishmael, was the founder of their faith. Born in Mecca around 570 AD, Mohamed grew up surrounded by Christians and Jews.

"Abraham was not a Jew nor yet a Christian; but he was true in Faith, and he joined not gods in God," states the Quran.

Jesus was descended from Abraham through Isaac.

The story of Abraham offering his son up to God, as proof of his faith and obedience, is known all over the world. In Jewish and Christian literature it is Isaac who is offered up—in Islam, it is Ishmael. The difference is surely a small matter.

God gave "the promised land" to Abraham's seed, and Christians, Jews and Muslims are all his seed. What's with the constant fighting? Abraham was known as a peacemaker.

"It's not yours, or yours, or yours," I imagine him saying if he was to appear on earth now. "It belongs to all of you. Now shut up and make peace before I sacrifice every last one of you to God!"

Grateful for the Promised Land, Abraham built an altar to God in Hebron, a mere 15 miles from Jerusalem. I found this out weeks after a kid at the YMCA in Hendersonville looked at me and asked, "Didn't I see you on Hebron, picking up garbage?"

Hebron *Street*.

"Yeah."

My Temple to God, to the embrace.

Ya big dummy.

Around to Khafre, I ran into Camel Ali early. He wanted me to go to a party tonight, but he and Rabihr will be here at seven. I don't want to go out after that. I need my sleep. Ali has two guests from South Africa that speak English, I hope he brings them.

The Crete couple leave tomorrow, so I'm sure I'll see them tonight.

Usual suspects today.

"*Ahh, Habibi*," shouted an older man with grey stubble, wearing a white turban and a striped gray calibaya. He held out his arms, and when I approached he grabbed my head and kissed me on both cheeks. *Habibi* means dear one.

Ahmed came by, and we joked about security.

"I guess if I pay 60 pounds a day, I'm not a terrorist," I said.

He brought me the weekly edition of Al-Ahram.

"There is an article in there that will explain Egyptians to you," he said. "You must read it."

We were going to meet at the entrance to Khafre for coffee at two, but when the time came I didn't see him there, so I left. I'll e-mail him later.

A camel rider asked me to text his girlfriend in Norway.

"My dearest Alise,

It is lonely in the desert without you, come to me, my Nefertiti."

Then as I was passing Khufu on my way out, another fellow on a camel asked me to help him write to his friend Steve in the US. I was a little short with him, as he constantly told me what to write.

"Tell him I hope to see him soon. Tell him to write me. Tell him I miss him. Say something smart. Tell him to . . . tell him . . . make sure . . . don't say . . . don't forget . . ."

Texting is not my strong point, in fact I had never texted before I was asked by an Egyptian the other day.

He gave me a dozen orders before I had typed 'Dear Steve.' It would be easier with a full keyboard, but with the abbreviated type, each number has three letters to it. A real pain in the butt.

Then I took a moment to look at him, and see the person he was. He wasn't the pushy type I had initially thought, just a poor camel operator in a very poor country trying to make a living, and cherishing his friendship with this Steve guy. He wanted to make sure Steve sent messages to his phone, not e-mail, because sometimes he doesn't get them from his nephew. I felt bad for being abrupt with him.

When I was finished I held out my hand.

"Ten pounds," I said, joking. He took my hand and shook it.

Leaving the site I had many calls of "Canada" from kids, and I gave away a bunch of balloons. A girl asked for a flag, but I didn't have any. I better call Christian at the embassy for more stuff.

I had lunch today from the woman, Mahmoudy. It was great and only cost 1.75 pounds. I met two guys from New York and ate my lunch with them. One was really curious about me so I

The Causeway that leads from the Sphinx to Khafre is nearly 2000 feet long, and uphill. Khafre's pyramid is built on higher ground than the larger Khufu, so it appears taller.

The big dummy on the second floor of a shop across from the Sphinx Gate. To my left is the oldest and largest pyramid Khufu, behind me is Khafre, and to my right is Menkaure, the smallest of the Great Pyramids. The Spinx is beside my right shoulder.

A couple from Tel Aviv helped me unfurl the flag in Times Square. The concept of the Flag of Humanity resonates with people.

My shadow and I compete for a piece of trash in front of the Sphinx Temple. Perhaps Khufu or Khafre are reaching through time to lend a hand. (Photo by Ken Yushino)

Though I wasn't allowed a camera, there were thousands of tourists with cameras. And like Ken Yushino from Japan, they were happy to send them to me. (Photo by Ken Yushino)

It took five hours to get this area into the state it appears above. The Lady in the Hat made me delete my 'before' pictures of this place. I was working here when Ramadan and Walid came to warn me about snakes.

The only road in the Giza Plateau runs from the right of the Sphinx Gate up to and around Khufu, and then back out of the site and into the city.

The Sphinx Gate. I would buy my ticket from the barred window to the left, then enter through the middle doors and go through a metal detector.

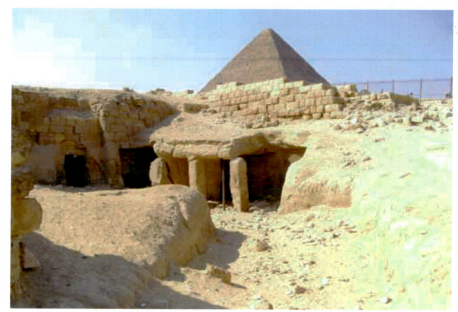

Cleaning this ancient tomb for nobles took many hours over many days. It was full of garbage, and had been used as a bathroom for years. It was here I saw Walid running out, dust chasing him as part of a wall came down. I was careful here, I did not want to die in a 4500 year old tomb.

Saman, the first man I met at the Pyramids. It was a pivotal moment for me, while I debated turning tail and running, The Doubt so strong I could taste it. "Continue what you are doing," he said, unaware of what that meant to me at the time.

I spent perhaps ten hours on this ancient tomb, and took out at least thirty bags of trash. Despite the fact it had been there over four thousand years, I was nervous about the roof caving in and killing me.

Saman took me in here to warn me 'some people are good, some people are bad.' It took time for my eyes to adjust to the dim lighting before I could begin work.

Saman at home with two of his daughters and a nephew. His parents, and brothers and their families all live in the same building. The love of children – another aspect of human nature that binds all people.

The apparently abandoned archeological site in the foreground is where I found a 100-year-old human skull with a hole the size of a lemon in the back of it. A victim of foul play? There is another skull there, in at least three pieces. I know exactly where it is.

Entrance Ali was always a help to me at the Sphinx Gate. "This is your home," he would say. "The Sphinx is lucky to have you."

I never had a conversation with this man, but he would call me habibi, 'dear one' whenever he saw me, and kiss me on both cheeks. My beer belly is prominent in this photo, marching on before me by a quarter of an hour.

A new layer of Phaeronic rock – the true base of the pyramid Menkaure–being unearthed for the first time in perhaps thousands of years. And I was there to see it!

A close-up of the exact spot I found the human skull.
The other skull is tucked under the right side of this rock.
At least it was when I left Egypt. I shall look for it on my return.

This photo of the pyramid Menkaure was taken from the north-east corner of Khafre. There is no garbage drop-off spot at Menkaure, making for a long walk dragging garbage bags between the two pyramids.

Maharab and his wonderful sandwiches! Maharab is very enterprising, and a fine example of minimal packaging. He re-uses everything he can. The only waste he leaves behind is biodegradable eggshells, and the odd pile of manure his donkey produces. He doesn't drive a car to work, he walks leading his donkey that doesn't use gasoline, but runs on fresh, green clover. I'm sure 50 to 100 people are fed by this man each day, and zero non-biodegradable waste is produced from it.

Mahmoudy offering a libation. A poor Egyptian scratching out a living at the pyramids by selling food to her fellow Egyptians, she nevertheless often fed me for free. Perhaps Pepsi would consider paying her for promotion of their product.

Stuffing my face, courtesy of Maharab and his donkey. Maharab should be looked at as an example of how we can greatly reduce our dependance on energy, consumption of natural resources, and packaging waste that clogs our landfills taking decades to decompose. And what does he do it with? A freakin' donkey!

A young man named Ahmed, holding postcards he hopes to sell to the tourists that come from all over the world. Most people don't know that the best price for souvenirs is from the vendors at the Pyramids. Souvenir shops have a high overhead, and usually have to give a kick-back to the tour operators who bring tourists.

Ahmed and I after a long day. "Such effort," he said one day, as I was groaning in pain, and yawning in exhaustion. As Bob Seger put it, "Every ounce of energy, you try to give away."

Nasser the Devout, elevated to such a lofty status when he asked me to watch his stuff while he went to pray. "She think you take Sphinx back to Canada," he joked about The Lady in the Hat, who was so suspicious of me.

Fellow Trashman Mr. Abdutowab leans against the Mortuary Temple of Khafre with a protective arm around my backpack, while the enterprising Hassan serves up tea from beneath the Temple. Off to the left, a policeman comes for tea – to investigate what's going on–or to demand a cut of the proceeds. "The police always want money," is a common lament of the people.

The future of Egypt. Three young vendors take a break to pose for a picture. The young people were quick to approach me, and always had a smile.

Hya-hya , a very good friend at the pyramids. He often inspired me when I needed it the most. Often I would hear his call, "Cooooocaaaa Cola" as he wandered the Giza plateau armed with only a two gallon bucket with drinks and ice, to make his living. Perhaps Coca-Cola can match what Pepsi pays Mahmoudy.

This Egyptian family was having a picnic on what's left of the Mortuary Temple of Khufu. They looked so beautiful, I asked to take their picture. They insisted I pose with them. A man on a camel took the photo.

Reading 'Bridging the Divide, Religious Dialogue and Universal Ethics' with the Sphinx in the background. The book contains a Universal Declaration of Human Responsibility (similar to my Universal Declaration of Human Duties and Responsibilities) that in my opinion capitulates to national sovereignty and lacks the proper order of human responsibilities. It must be; the earth, fellow humans, our offspring, and ourselves.

Two little buddies. Children routinely came to help me, and their enthusiasm was contagious. I often gave them small Canadian flags, and they would run across the sand yelling "Canada, Canada, Canada," waving the flags in the air.

Canadian artist Joel Clark in the King's Chamber of Khufu. According to Joel, the spots on the picture are some type of energy. He says this is "just one tiny aspect of the unseen presences at the Plateau. These spiritual energy forms are only picked up by flash. Sometimes there are none to be seen. At other times they can be quite profuse."

A dirty and dusty Trashman with two days to go.
(Photo by Joel Clark)

Picking trash in the Mortuary Temple of Menkaure, the smallest of the Great Pyramids. In this Temple archeologists found evidence that paid workers, not slaves, built the pyramids. (Photo by Yusif Yusifov)

*Here's the flag flying in front of the United Nations building
in New York City. All the other flags were down that day,
except the United Nations flag itself*

gave him my Center for Civilization card. You never know who can help the cause.

As I was leaving, walking toward the Sphinx, I met a couple of young hippy-looking dudes with dreadlocks to their shoulders from Sacramento, California.

"I used to live in Berkeley," I said.

"Were you part of the hippy movement?"

I wasn't sure if I should be insulted or not. I was born in 1961, and was nine when the sixties ended.

"Do I look old enough to be part of it?" I asked.

The one guy took a discerning look at me, I could tell he was thinking.

"Maybe the tail end."

Ahmed said most people think I'm 30-31 years old, not 47, but these guys pegged me as older. Perhaps it's the ganja I imagine they're into. There's lots of hashish to smoke in Egypt.

"So you flew halfway around the world to pick up garbage at the pyramids?" the taller one asked.

Ya big dummy.

Morning of day 26 in the desert

Feeling a little lonely, miss the family, but only 14 days after today.

I slept for eleven hours last night, and only woke up a few times. I feel good, though my tendons in my ankles and legs are hurting, as is my back. Stiff as hell every morning, but I stretch, shower, stretch, then eat, then back to the room and change, then walk to the site. By then I'm ready to go.

No call from Linda and the kids. I guess they're busy.

Yesterday I wore a hole through the index finger of my right hand. I cursed myself for not bringing two pairs of gloves. I'll try to be ambidextrous today, as I haven't found tape for it yet. It took 25 days to put that hole in the glove, a lot longer than in

Hendersonville. But there the gloves were wet a lot. The Sahara Desert is not as wet as the mountains of Western North Carolina.

Today I will ask about the camera. Now that I'm paying 60 pounds a day, it shouldn't be a problem.

I am really missing the family right now. I'm on automatic, doing what I have to do. This is the hard part, always, the final part.

"It's not the beginning, but the continuing of the same, until it be thoroughly finished . . ." a quote from Sir Frances Drake that Frank Wiens loved.

I have two weeks after today. However, I will be 65% done by nightfall, something no one has ever done before. Must take it easy on my body, make it last. But I have to leave it all in Egypt.

"Every ounce of energy, you try to give away," sang Bob Seger, up on the stage. There's plenty of time to rest at home later.

Last night I got in a tok-tok to go to an internet store, but the guy was taking me way the hell and gone in heavy traffic, so I said "fuck it" and got him to turn around and take me back to Siag. It's tough, because I don't want to walk much more than I have to, fearing injury. I am on the razor's edge, one push too hard and I'll pull something.

Tonight I must find an internet. Hopefully the hotel's computers will be up and running. I don't know how they conduct business in the hotel without it. Fatih said there are only five or six guests in the hotel now. For 100 rooms, that's low.

I read the article in Al-Ahram last night. It's an interview of a psychology professor, Ahmed Okasha, by Sahar El-Bahar. Okasha has written more than 70 books on the subject of psychiatry, and makes many comments about the Egyptian people and their society.

"He says it is a good thing that Egyptians have a sense of humor and are always smiling and joking," writes El-Bahar. "Whatever problems they may face. To a great extent this means they have faith, satisfaction, and are contented. But today, the worse the political and economic situation becomes, the more frustrated and desperate they become, as they are unable to face their problems. Therefore they even give up their only weapon, which is that of jokes."

"Egyptians bear a number of destructive feelings," Okasha is quoted as saying, "disability, hopelessness, indifference, carelessness, and frustration, which consequently result in being aggressive, violent, anxious, depressed and negative. And all these result in ethical and moral deterioration."

"The problem with ethical deterioration is not only poverty as many would imagine, but rather the lack of justice. A person could endure poverty if there were social equality and justice."

The police always want money.

"However, the most notable feature of the character of Egyptians is fear. This emotion is overwhelming. There is a whole atmosphere of fear controlling both leaders and public. Fear dominates when the regime becomes totalitarian and decreases the individual freedoms of the public."

"Okasha's philosophy and advice to us all," writes El-Bahar, "is never feel sorry about the past and never feel anxious about the future, just live in the present."

That's good advice for anybody, not just Egyptians. Looking back, I remember many times in my life when I wish someone had told me that.

"Nothing in life is unsolvable," he goes on to say. "No human being should lose hope in life. And seek to accomplish any kind of achievement."

The next page in Al-Ahram, which means 'the pyramids,' features an article titled "Who won the war?" speaking on the recent pre-Christmas Israeli invasion of Palestine.

"Israeli atrocities in Gaza will live on across generations, giving birth to new waves of resistance. This is the essence of defeat."

The article goes on to state:

"Israel mistakenly believes that by time new generations of Arabs will forget about the occupation of Palestine and Israel will be accepted. But the memory of nations does not forget like the memory of individuals getting older. New Arab and Muslim generations are more determined to fight to end the occupation. Throughout history, no military power defeated a resistance group that had faith. Freedom fighters forced colonial powers to yield and accept defeat, not the opposite. Israel, however, does not want to understand and insists on moving against the tide of history."

After thousands of years of oppression, the likes of which are widely known, the Jewish people, tempered like steel in a blazing furnace, with a strong faith emboldened by their suffering, and a powerful resolve to survive, have forgotten how they became that way. The one lesson they were meant to learn from the millennia of persecution, they have not learned. God has hammered them again and again, but they have not learned. Has anyone? Oppression makes resistance stronger.

But the embrace . . .

I remember a simple parable, the wind and the sun have a bet over who can get a jacket off a man walking down the road. The wind howls and howls, but the man just clings ever tighter to his jacket. The sun shines down on the man, and warm now, he takes his jacket off. He doesn't need it anymore.

Day 26 in the desert—encouragement

"You are the future of Egypt. Make it a great one."

As I said earlier, I was bummed out in the morning. Sleeping eleven hours, and up at five, gave me time to doubt myself. The Doubt was strong, but only 14 days to go.

This morning I was reading "The Inferno," Dante Alighieri's drama of a journey through hell in search of paradise. It's one of several books I brought with me to Egypt. Written about seven centuries ago, the poem describes in great detail an astonishing number of levels of hell, and which sinner belongs to each level.

As Dante passes through the Gate of Hell and enters the Vestibule of Hell, he meets the first of the souls in torment, The Opportunists.

"Those souls who in life were neither for good or evil but only for themselves," writes John Ciardi, who translated The Inferno into English. "Mixed with them are those outcasts who took no sides in the Rebellion of the Angels. They are neither in Hell nor out of it. Eternally unclassified, they race round and round pursuing a wavering banner that runs forever before them through the dirty air; and as they run they are pursued by swarms of wasps and hornets, who sting them and produce a constant flow of blood and putrid matter which trickles down the bodies of the sinners and is feasted upon by loathsome worms and maggots who coat the ground.

"The law of Dante's Hell is the law of symbolic retribution. As they sinned, so are they punished. They took no sides, therefore they are given no place. As they pursued the ever-shifting illusion of their own advantage, changing their courses with every changing wind, so they pursue eternally an elusive banner. As their sin was a darkness, so they move in darkness. As their own guilty conscience pursued them, so they are pursued by swarms of wasps and hornets. And as their actions were a moral filth, so they run eternally through the filth of worms and maggots which they themselves feed."

Dante's Opportunists, looking out only for themselves, commit the sin of omission, and earn a spot in hell. Maybe I am an idiot and wasting my time here, but at least I'm doing *something*. There is some solace in that, in my battles with The Doubt.

I asked Ali at the Sphinx gate what kind of whiskey he wanted.

"Any kind."

To my amazement, the wall where the vendors work was very clean. It has become very easy to clean the area in front of the Sphinx, and even all the way to the middle pyramid, because there is definitely less and less garbage.

A flock of French-speaking tourists were coming by as I reached the end of the tall wall.

"*Est-ce-que tu es de Paris?*" I asked.

"*Non Monsieur, Quebec.*"

"*Ah, je suis Canadien aussi.*"

My fellow Canadians. I talked with them for a while, particularly one woman about my age, who coincidentally was quite attractive.

After they left, Walid came up to me pointing to his ring finger, blowing kisses, hugging himself, and pointing to her. It was quite funny "la, la, la, la," (no, no, no, no) I said which set him off laughing.

He's got a burn on his face. I pointed to it and shrugged, nonverbally asking what happened. He pointed to his face, then the sun, and shrugged his shoulders in return. I had thought he would be impervious to the sun's rays, but apparently not.

Heading up the hill, I worked two bags in front of Khafre, dropped them off, then I went behind the pyramid.

The boys in the back were busy. Every camel was working what must have been a big tour group. Camel Ali had a couple from Florida. Askman had a couple from Calgary.

"Tourist trust tourist," Saman had said, and he was right. The Egyptians would call out to me as they went by, and I would answer back. I could actually see the people relax when they heard me speak English. They would smile more as well, as I believe they felt safer. I would assist in this.

"Show them the whole site," I called out to Ali.

"I will my friend."

Then to the couple from Florida, "You're in good hands."

A tour guide stopped me and took my photo. An Egyptian who lives in Vancouver, he has an office two minutes from Siag.

"I will call you, and take you to lunch," he said.

I met a guy from the Czech Republic traveling alone.

"If I knew I would be allowed, I would have joined you for forty days," he said

I had lunch from Mahmoudy for two pounds, with kids all around me. As she was making me a sandwich, a little boy about ten gave me two thirds of a bottle of Pepsi. I took a little sip and offered it back to him, but he indicated it was all mine.

"How much you pay for watch? How much for this...?" pointing to my gloves, which I must fix tonight. I am a right-handed Trashman, not ambidextrous. I tried but failed miserably.

One kid showed me piles of garbage behind the wall where Mahmoudy was sitting, part of the Mortuary Temple of Khafre. I spent an hour picking it up after I ate.

I was about to pull out a bag and work my way toward Khufu, when I was called over for tea by an Egyptian I had not met before, Josef. I said no, but then he offered me half a cup (in Arabic, thank God for charades) which I accepted. Nice to sit down and relax.

A woman came up to me as I was having my tea with Josef and introduced herself as Marwa.

"I heard you are working on a project in Egypt," she said in good English.

"I am picking up garbage, as my way to embrace Egypt, and the Egyptians."

"That's what I heard," she said."One of my colleagues is a journalist for a magazine, and would like to speak with you."

She will call at four. It is 3:43 now.

I worked the south side of Khufu, out of the way places, when three young guys came up and took my picture for Facebook.

"You are a great man, to show respect for our country."

"You are the future of Egypt," I told them. "Make it a great one."

"We will. We are Egyptians."

I went to see Mr. Mohamed Cheoh who invited me for tea. He introduced me to Dick, an archeologist pushing 80, and his son Spencer. Dick is from Browns University as well. This is his last trip to Egypt. It must be bittersweet, knowing it is the last time in your life you will do something. You want to enjoy it, but the awareness that it is the final time must creep into everything.

"My work can put people to sleep in three sentences at cocktail parties," said the self-deprecating Dick, also dating himself (cocktail parties?) "glazed eyes in only two."

I doubted that, as I found him quite interesting.

I finally asked the Chief about taking photos.

"We can talk about it tomorrow," he said, not soft.

"A tourist pays 60 pounds," I said, "takes a camera, throws rubbish on the ground. I pay 60 pounds, *pick up* the rubbish, but do not have a camera."

"Why do you want a camera?"

"I want to take a picture of the people I have met, including you."

"Then you will write beside our pictures 'I picked up rubbish from these people,'" said the Chief, smiling.

"I would write that I picked up rubbish just from you," I joked, coming dangerously close to 'the line', I'm sure.

There were about five guys there, and we all laughed.

"We'll talk about it tomorrow," said Mohamed with finality. End of discussion.

Ahmed caught up to me as I was walking down to the Sphinx. Always a pleasure to converse with, he walked me out of the Sphinx, talking as we went. I told him about the woman who had a friend that worked for a magazine.

"You must be careful, Bruce," cautioned Ahmed. "The magazine might use the information against the government."

"I didn't get that impression," I said. I assured Ahmed that I would make Mr. Kamal Wahid and the Chief look good.

"I am a journalist, I know how to talk to these people."

Back in my room watching television, there was an interesting show on Fareed Zakaria, discussing Islam. Christopher Hitchens was there. He didn't say much, but he touched on my concept that radical Islam is not Islam at all, but something else. It's like calling skinheads radical Christians. Again, what can we call them?

Day 27 in the desert—morning

The woman or her friend did not call from the magazine, which is probably a good thing.

I'm not sure what will greet me this morning now that I spoke to the Chief yesterday afternoon. Will he think I'm a liability and throw me out for good?

I haven't the whiskey for entrance Ali so I better get on that. Saman wants the prints of the pictures I took of his kids, and I need to call the consulate.

I modified some of my cards to include the *bensonegypt@ hotmail.com* address and the Siag phone number and my room number in case I do meet someone today. I've given out many Center for Civilization cards but have yet to get an e-mail, and I suspect something may be wrong with the website.

I spoke to Linda last night and she said I should just enjoy myself the last few days, as I may never be here again. Maybe I'll go diving in Alexandria, or go see the new pyramid those young women spoke of. But I do miss home. If I was here with several buddies, it would be different. The Canadians will be back Wednesday, so we'll probably have a bunch of beers.

Day 27 in the desert—amazing ups and downs - future unclear

"You are freeing the earth from the rubbish."

I'm getting worse. I had a tough time getting going this morning, really had to stretch and work out the kinks in my body. It was downright painful. I took acetaminophen and felt a little better.

I arrived early, and waited with my Egyptian Gazette for the site to open.

"Do you have my whiskey?" asked entrance Ali.

"Maybe tomorrow."

Camel Ali may come over tonight with a bottle, perhaps I can buy it off of him. I just talked to Bono, a bottle of good whiskey is more than fifty bucks, but for three days after you arrive in Egypt you can buy liquor duty-free if you show your passport. Egyptian whiskey is cheaper.

If I can't get it from Camel Ali, then I'll buy him Egyptian whiskey tomorrow.

Mohawk showed up early, and we chatted. He apologizes for his English all the time, when I'm totally embarrassed about my Arabic.

I didn't see Walid or Hassanan, but I saw Ramadan slacking it as usual. I gave him a bag, and he actually went to work. He had raked the garbage out of the water in one of the boat pits in front of the Sphinx, but was just sitting there. He had nowhere to put the garbage.

As I was working on the right side of the Sphinx, a man from the Czech Republic approached me.

"You are the only one cleaning," he said. "Where are you from?"

"Canada."

"I could tell you are not Egyptian."

He asked the usual questions, and then went into the Sphinx Temple. When he came out he met up with me halfway up the causeway towards Khafre.

"I was impressed by the Sphinx, but more so by you," he said. "I expected to be impressed by the Sphinx, but not to meet someone like you."

Did that ever feel good! The pain in my body diminished considerably. I could tell he meant it, looking in his eyes. He was wearing glasses but I could see he had a tear in the corner of his left eye.

"I promise I will pick up three plastic bottles before I leave here," he said, turning to walk uphill to the middle pyramid.

"I have one already," he shouted down to me moments later. Then he was gone.

The front of the Sphinx was the cleanest I have ever seen it. On my way to Khafre, Mr. Sadek asked for two bags, then went to work. A moment later a kid came up and asked for a bag, "or two or three."

"Are you going to pick up garbage?" I asked him.

"Yes."

"You are? You're going to pick up garbage?"

"Yes. I have just been hired, first day," he said. "I must go to Sphinx."

I looked at him warily, not quite believing him.

"You no trust me?" he said.

"No," I said. "I don't." But giving him the benefit of the doubt, I gave him one bag, and he went skipping down to the Sphinx. I never saw him again.

I saw Camel Ali, who said "I come to you tonight."

"*Settah noss,*" I said, six-thirty.

I was having tea with an Egyptian by the entrance to Khafre when the man in charge of that pyramid came to say hi.

"How long you work at pyramids?"

"Another 13 days."

"I will miss you when you are gone," he said. Then he told me I should spend my time on the front and north side of the pyramid, not the back and the south.

"Do as you wish," he said shrugging his shoulders, "but . . . "

"I will work the back *shwya, shwya,* (little, little) then go to the front."

Most foreign tourists don't bother going to the back and south sides of Khafre, but many Egyptian tourists do, especially couples. It's much more private. There's garbage there, but not nearly as much as the other sides, as the majority of vendors, who produce the garbage, work the front and south sides.

There was an Egyptian couple around my age at the back. I was working toward them when the husband called out to me. His wife was laughing, and trying to grab him to stop him. She tried to put her hand over his mouth. He out wrestled her, and approached me.

"Why you do this?" he asked, in what to the uninitiated would seem an angry tone.

I explained as best I could that I did this for no money, but to show my respect to Egypt, and the Egyptian people, to embrace them. And, this being the cradle of civilization, all the people of the earth.

His English was not good, but after a while he understood, and a smile spread over his face.

"Thank-you. Welcome to Egypt."

A common occurrence. What appears an aggressive demand "why?" changes.

I was taking two bags from the back of Khafre to the garbage when I saw Ahmed.

"I have bad news," he said. "Kamal Wahid said no camera for you."

"Why not?" I asked.

"He is terrified of you," said Ahmed. "They all are."

"...... *the most notable feature of the character of Egyptians is fear.*"

So even though I am paying the 60 pounds every tourist does, because I pick up garbage all day, I cannot have a camera. Every single other tourist from every other nation on earth, who does not pick up anything, can have a camera.

"Not letting me have a camera says more than letting me have one," I said. "He is in effect admitting something is not as it should be, and he is responsible."

No matter, so be it. This will not stop me. I'll just keep coming without a camera, and after March 15, I will return with no bags and gloves, enter at the Mena House gate, and take every picture I want. If they throw me out, then it'll potentially be an international incident, as I won't go easy. But I hope I can just peacefully take my photos. Perhaps the powers that be will lighten up in a few days.

I put the bags away and went to lunch. Mahmoudy was surrounded by men, all hungry. She made me a sandwich with just two cheeses, and I scarfed it down. A little boy bought it for me.

"How much for a seven-up?" I asked.

"Two pounds," someone answered. I'm not sure who.

I took one out of her bucket and another boy took it from me, opened it and gave it back. When I went to pay for it, Mahmoudy waved me off. Again, a free lunch from the people that work the pyramids. These people are very, very poor, and yet so generous to me. Need I say it? It is the embrace.

Would I stop doing what I do because the government says "no camera" to me? Like the Viking said about almost everything in the movie 'The Thirteenth Warrior,' *it is a small matter.*

Slaving away in front of Khafre, I met a young German couple who 'got it,' understood what I was doing and why.

"Someone should let the media know that a Canadian fisherman is trying to clean the pyramids," said the man.

"There are many people hired to do it," I said. "It is just too much."

"Hey, is that camel chewing on your bag?" he suddenly asked, pointing.

Sure enough a camel was gnawing on my bag, grinding those big teeth back and forth. I yelled and ran toward him and he dropped it. It was covered in camel saliva. The three of us went 'eeeugh'? It was the consistency of the slime that covered Bill Murray in the movie Ghostbusters.

"I can't imagine what's in it that attracted the camel," I said, rubbing off as much slime as I could.

"Probably just the orange color," surmised the German.

I was glad the camel dropped the bag when I yelled at it. I didn't want to have to fight the beast. Camels are big, strong animals, capable of easily kicking my butt.

"I have seen a camel grab a man's arm with his teeth, and shake him, and break all his bones," Rabihr told me. "Broke his legs, arms, his head."

"Did it kill him?"

"No, just break bones."

Apparently psychology comes into the raising of camels, to make them docile.

"The camel must think it is small, not big," said Rabihr.

"But they're huge!"

"But camel not know that."

The speed that a camel grows to adult size is determined by the quality of food it eats. According to Rabihr, camels are intentionally fed food that will slow their growth, so they can be trained when they are small, and much easier to handle.

"So camel always think he is small."

I'm sure people are the same. If poorly nourished early in life, they will always think they are small.

As usual, some of the locals saw me talking to the couple and came by to try and sell a camel or horse ride. It usually chases tourists away. They start by pointing at me.

"He good man, he my friend. You like camel ride? Cheap price," and they don't give up. Rabihr and a friend were the first, but they did leave when told no. But another guy I hardly know at all did the same. He was a little unpleasant. The Germans left quickly.

I kept going, and soon found a shiny 50 piastre piece, Egyptian gold that I will treasure. I long ago got over the fatalism that flowed over me when my grandfather died.

Mr. Abdutowab came and asked for a bag, and promptly folded it up and put it in his pocket. I hope he used it to fill with garbage at the pyramids, but I doubt it.

A security guy asked me for a bag as I was eating lunch, and I gave him one.

"Don't give anyone these," said Ali from atop his camel behind me, shaking his head and pointing to my bags with his camel switch. I guess I need to be selective in giving out bags. Most people I have given bags to use them at the pyramids, but some just take them home. They're worth close to 50 piastres each.

I went across to the north side of Khufu, and picked my way to a big vertical shaft about eight feet deep and four feet across.

Yesterday I cleaned out about half the rubbish that had piled up in the shaft for possibly decades. I swear no matter where I work, a curious Egyptian will find me. Deep in this shaft was no exception. It was eight feet deep, so I was not visible from the surface, and yet someone found me, and asked all the usual questions. He stayed up there until it was time for me to go home to Siag.

"*Bokra,*" I said to him. Tomorrow.

Sure enough, I'm down in the same pit today starting to pick, when the guy shows up with his brother.

"You are freeing the earth from the rubbish," he said. "You are a good man, with a good heart."

Walking home minding my own business, I felt something tugging on my backpack. I turned around to see Mr. Abdutowab, smiling. We walked together for several blocks, but had difficulty communicating, as his English is even worse than my Arabic. Then he turned right to go to his home, and I went straight to go to mine. Two Trashmen going home after a day's work, an Arabic-speaking Egyptian muslim, and an English-speaking Canadian embracer. Does that sound silly? Embracer?

I found a stone with some writing on it, behind Khafre. It was jammed under one of the casing stones that had fallen off the pyramid. I can't make out the writing.

Thirteen days of work left.

Day 28 in the desert—four weeks in, twelve days to go, a little film and possible controversy

"I say fuck you in Arabic, you no understand."

Rabihr and his friend Hamdy came by last night. Rabihr had a beer, but not Hamdy. However Rabihr rolled a couple joints, and we went on the deck and they smoked them. Rabihr is getting married in two months, and he still insists nobody knows to whom, except his family and hers. He was complaining about the government quite a bit, apparently he has a fine to pay.

"Fuckin' government," is a common phrase for him.

Police always want money.

I called my optometrist, and there should be a fax and e-mail for me with the prescription for my glasses. I have trouble seeing distances, up close I have perfect sight. I hope the office is open and the internet works, neither was the case yesterday.

I bought potato chips from Fatih last night, and devoured them—never again. I felt terrible this morning. There are no rules on trans-fats here.

I have been wondering what I could leave, and where, at the pyramids, sort of as an offering. I asked Ahmed and his buddy if I could put a Canadian coin under the wooden walkway they are building.

"No problem."

Rabihr read the stone I found behind Khafre.

"It's a heart with a stick through it," said Rabihr, "and the sign of the Jew."

I could see the arrow through the heart and the Star of David plainly after he said that. Who knows who put it there, when, and why?

On my way to work this morning, I came to the conclusion that even though they insist I pay each day, and then insist I don't take a camera, I will embrace the people anyway. Despite everything, no matter what the authorities do or say. That is, essentially, what we need. The people of the world embracing each other, accepting our differences, despite what government rhetoric says, and demanding governments do the same. I will not be deterred.

Working around the vendor area, one of them said, out of the blue, "God bless you for what you do." It is these positive affirmations that keep me going. Linda said I would be looked down upon as an idiot and laughed at for cleaning up the Egyptian's garbage, but that has not been the case.

I walked up toward Khafre and was working around the Mortuary Temple in front when a young man came up to me.

"Everybody wonder why you do this," he said. "They are all talking. Some people say you do this because you have a problem with your heart, you did something not good."

He meant I am repenting for past sins. Because of the language barrier, I didn't dare say anything in that vein. We have all made mistakes, and I certainly wouldn't, and couldn't throw the first stone.

"No," I said, chuckling, "It's not because I have something wrong with my heart. Maybe I have something wrong with my head." But he got me thinking about redemption.

I had a book reading of 'A Season for Skufty' at the American Library in Paris two years ago. The library staff made a poster announcing my reading, and a woman interviewed me about the book. She took one quote out of the interview for the poster, and I loved it.

"The book is about redemption," said Bruce Benson. "I'm a big believer in redemption, being in need of it so much myself."

I worked up to Khafre, and ate with the boys.

As I sat there in front of Mahmoudy, surrounded by Egyptians, many on camels, eating lunch and joking and laughing, it felt so bizarre, and yet so commonplace to me. Forty centuries looking down upon us.

The other day when I was going with Bono to get my glove fixed, we're walking through a normal busy street, then all of a sudden I get bumped by a camel racing by me. It reminded me of the scenes George Lucas puts in his films. This is another world, and yet, not. This is my world, our world.

I went around and had tea with the boys in the back of Khafre. Askman did his ask for a bag, and I finally said no. Then I gave him and the others Canadian pins, which for them I believe is a tool for their trade. If they know tourists are Canadian, they will show them the pins, and say how much they love Canada. Whereas for the children, it is a treasure.

I went in front and had a coke from Hya-hya. Heading to Khufu, Ahmed came over with Mr. Abd El Fattah. He's into Chapter 15 in Skufty, where Susan has gone to see the bad doctor to get Lazarus's files, and Skufty is going to call the Mayo Clinic.

"I think it could be a movie," he said.

Thinking about it really took me back, and to a place far from the pyramids, Goodman's Landing. Another example of the embrace.

I was the only white-man in the fish camp called Goodman's Landing for five seasons, and the native Indians were incredibly good to me.

I was there only twenty minutes when an older man poked his head into the shack I was to make into my camp.

"You don't have a cooler?" he asked. *Ya big dummy.*

"No, I didn't think to bring one."

"Come with me," he said, and waved for me to follow. I did, not knowing what to expect, completely out of my element.

Walter Sinclair was his name, and he lent me a new cooler.

"Give it back to me after the season," he said. He knew me for mere seconds before offering me his cooler.

There's one young man from Goodman's that I consider a personal hero. We were drinking beer in Stubbs' camp, I can't remember Stubbs' real name. We were about three weeks into the spring fishing season, and the boys fishing at McBeth Point, accessible by a one hour boat ride from Goodman's, were in camp blowing off steam. The rush at the start of the season was over, they had caught plenty of fish and could relax for a spell.

The beer was flowing, clouds of tobacco and marijuana smoke drifted in the air, and we were having a good time. I was standing beside Stubbs, seated with his back against the wall, when the crowd parted and this stranger sees me for the first time.

"What the fuck are *you* doing here?" he demanded angrily. My long blond hair was a dead giveaway amongst a sea of black manes.

"That's Benson," said Stubbs, coming to my defense. "He always fishes here."

"Yeah," I said casually, beer bottle in hand. "What's the matter? You're not a racist are you?"

It was like I hit him with a brick. He staggered backward, bending over and looking at the ground.

"Yeah, I guess it works both ways," he said softly to himself, seconds later.

"No, I'm not a racist," he said, raising his head and reaching for my hand. And he became my hero.

He could've said any number of things.

"You white people stole our lands."

"This is our fishing grounds."

"I hate you"

He could've started swinging.

But he didn't.

Stoned and half drunk, with no more than a grade eight education, he did something millions of people the world over seem incapable of doing dead sober. He got over his prejudice.

He was drunk for the next three days, staggering all over camp. Whenever he saw me, he would quickly proffer his hand.

"I'mmmm hnot a rashist."

Though I was the only paleface, I never had any trouble in camp. But I was cautious. Fishermen are similar all over the world, it seems to me—a little rough around the edges. The boys could party pretty hard.

I knew if I walked into a camp and they were drinking beer, I'd probably be all right. If they were drinking beer and smoking dope, it's cool for sure. If I walked in and they were drinking whiskey and smoking dope, I should be all right. But if I walked in and they were drinking whiskey and I couldn't smell pot in the air, I'd get the hell outta there!

I liked to hire people from the nearby Jackhead Indian Reserve, *Kinonjeoshtegon,* in the language of the Saulteaux Indians.

One time I left my man Clyde to dress the fish while I went to town for supplies. When I returned four hours later, he still wasn't finished.

"What's taking so long?" I asked him, pissed off.

"I was hiding," he said, pointing to the attic of the fish station.

A man of few words, it took some time to get the full story out of him. The RCMP (Royal Canadian Mounted Police) came by, and since Clyde was wanted for attempted murder, he had to hide in the attic until they left.

Apparently Clyde was drinking whiskey with the boys the previous fall, when he got mad at the camp's weigh-man, who weighs each fisherman's catch. He grabbed an axe and swung it with full force into the victim's chest. Fortunately, the weigh-man lived.

"Remember when Clyde axed the weigh-man," has been a running joke since.

The weigh-man is an important man at the station. They say a bad weigh-man who also fishes can catch all his fish without leaving the shore by stealing a little from each of the fisherman. He also culls fish for any number of reasons, so it's wise to be on the good side of the weigh-man.

"Always tip the weigh-man," a skipper once told me. Good advice, that. Always tip the weigh-man. Most of us have a 'weigh-man' in our lives.

"I think Mr. Kamal Wahid will change his mind about my camera," I told Ahmed.

"I think he must," said Ahmed, "so he does not look foolish."

Mr. Abd el Fattah said they waited for one hour for me three days ago. I felt bad. If I had my glasses, I would've seen them. I will meet them for tea at one on Thursday, which may be a day after drinking with the Canadians, and if that's the case I could use an early day.

I worked along the perimeter of the parking lot between Khafre and Khufu.

"Can I film you working?" asked a man holding up his cell phone. "I am a tour guide."

"Sure."

He filmed me picking up garbage for a few seconds.

"Why are you here?" he asked, still filming.

"I was here two years ago, and thought they could use some help picking up trash, so I came back to lend a hand. It is my way of showing respect for Egypt, and the Egyptian people. I have been here for 28 days and will be here for another 12, at least."

"On behalf of the Egyptian people I would like to thank you," he said, appearing nervous. "If you don't mind, I will say something in Arabic."

I shrugged my indifference, and he spoke Arabic into his phone. He turned it off, thanked me and left.

"You know, when he speak in Arabic," said a vendor sitting close by.

"Yeah?"

"He said something that was bad, something that might hurt us."

"I thought he said something about cleaning the pyramids," I said.

"Don't let anyone take your picture," said the young man that earlier said some people thought I had something wrong with my heart.

But I have many people take my picture every day, no problem. It's that mentality of fear that is ever-present, that means I can't have a camera. Silly to me, but to the Egyptians? I don't know.

I guess I appeared thickheaded, so one kid tried to explain how I was fooled by the man talking in Arabic.

"I say fuck you in Arabic, you no understand."

Rabihr called to me from across the sand separating Khufu from Khafre, and I called back to him. We met, him on the cliff edge, me on the sand looking up. Just shooting the breeze. Later he came by as I was working my way along the small wall down to the Sphinx.

"The government is talking about you," he said, in a warning tone. "You must be careful."

"The government likes me, Rabihr." We'll see tomorrow.

As I made my way to the road, some men asked me what I was doing with the same quizzical look I have become so familiar with. The change in expression after I told them was equally familiar. One man pulled out his wallet.

"Here's my card, call me any time you want to spend an evening," he said, handing me his card. "At night. I work during the day. You have family here. You are an Egyptian."

I had a few requests from kids for balloons and flags as I was walking the last bit of the way out, so when I got back I wrote here for a while, then had a quick shower and went down to use Bono's phone.

I called Christian at the embassy and he said he'd try to send me some stuff, rather than me going all the way over there. I hope it works out.

Bono charged me ten pounds for using his phone, too much, but what the hell. Two dollars for a local phone call? I went out to get some koshery, but stopped to have tea with some cab drivers that hang around the hotel. One cabbie had a Polish man for a fare, and he gave me a free ride the four blocks to several restaurants where I could get some food.

Instead of koshery I bought three falafels for three pounds.

"Egyptian price," said the young man as he gave me my change from a five-pound note.

"Do you have a taxi?" he asked.

"No," I said, pointing to my legs, "Canadian price."

It's still a steep price as my legs are causing me a lot of pain. I checked the e-mails, and no message from home, but I sent one. I will see Fatih, buy some postcards from him, and send one to my Dad, as my cousin Wray has been pestering me to do. He's 84 years old, and apparently talks about me being in Egypt all the time.

Unbelievable day. I hope they let me continue, but after 28 days, with security and police waving to me constantly and giving me the thumbs up, I still never know what I will get when I show up in the morning.

Hope all is well in Hendersonville.

Day 29 in the desert—a day for Egyptians, and very hot

"To feel the passion to do great things takes years of sacrifice, often painful, often heartbreaking, but always rewarding."

As I was approaching the Sphinx gate, a little boy I see almost every day, maybe five or six years old, who always has a smile and a handshake for me, gave me some sticky, white fudge-like stuff that he had been chewing on. It was bigger than a marble but smaller than a jawbreaker, and had his teeth-marks all over it. Egyptian candy, really sticks to your teeth. He gave me some dried fruit as well.

"See, you believe in the embrace too," I said to him, though I knew he would not understand. What a sweet kid, pun intended.

Speaking of teeth, the public health people need to get on the issue of brushing teeth. I have seen very few white teeth here, particularly amongst the workers on the street and at the pyramids. As I said before, it may be the tea.

In the morning one of the regular vendors came up to me and gave me three pyramids in a box. He said they were broken, but I couldn't see where. They looked perfectly fine to me.

As I made my way to the garbage site near Khafre, I could see a truck with some garbage in it parked close by. The driver indicated to me to put the bags I was carrying into the truck, which I did. Then he climbed the rocks to go get someone to help him load the truck. While he was gone, I carried all the bags over to the truck, and put a few in the back. Then I climbed in to move them closer to the cab, making room for more bags. Another garbage guy showed up and he passed the rest of the bags to me. Mr. Abdutowab came with the driver, and they were happy that the work was done. That ability to see the work. I had no idea what anybody said, it was all in Arabic, but I knew what was going on. Communication without language.

It has become hot again. I was a little late getting going, but the cabbie from several days ago, one with an incredibly cute little girl who points out tourists for her father the driver, picked me up on his way to the Sphinx and drove me most of the way for free. He was going that way anyway. He stopped just short of the newsstand, so I got out, grabbed a paper from my newspaperman Hassan, and went into the site.

The Lady in the Hat came by, such a downer to see her, as she is so suspicious of me. But I do think I've motivated her group to work a little harder. Not that you'd see it in Ramadan. That guy is so cotton-pickin' lazy. I glanced his way from time to time as I was working the wall. Can you say "sloth?"

Walid came to me for bags when I was in the pit, and I gave him two. He came for more as I worked the fence, and with some trepidation I gave him two more. I saw him fold them up neatly.

"Hassanan," he said, but I was worried he was going to take them home. I went up to him aggressively, and he assured me he would pick up garbage. All in pantomime.

I hope they picked up outside the wall, because I did most of their work by then already, but I doubt it. Tourists only go outside the wall on a horse or camel, so they don't worry about it. But I had it clean, and in less than an hour it could be clean again. I'll do it tomorrow, if they haven't.

An Egyptian couple in their late twenties were watching me as I was cleaning the east side of Khafre. They were sitting on the first level of the pyramid. Security allows people to climb up one, two or three levels sometimes, but anyone climbing higher gets a whistle and a warning to climb down immediately.

This is quite the place for young Egyptian lovers, I have seen hundreds. Sometimes there are groups of couples, and many times they have a little picnic.

"What are you doing?" asked the woman.

I tried to explain.

"Do you need help?"

I said no. I had gloves and she didn't. She could cut herself. I picked up a piece of glass to emphasize the point. A moment later she brought me cake, smiling widely. I have to remember these moments to get past my aching body. From the outset I determined I must work as hard as I am physically capable, push myself as much as possible. But it hurts.

I worked the east side of Khafre until after eleven. Then I dumped off a couple bags, and decided to clean the garbage site. Residual garbage that had spilled out of bags had piled up for some time. The fiberglass bags Mr. Abdutowab and the others use and reuse have huge holes, and garbage routinely falls out.

Rabihr wants me to come to his house tonight.

"I will buy five beer for you," he said. "They will be in the fridge, cold."

Mr. Abdutowab took me for tea at the cave, and I chatted with the boys.

"Mr. Abdutowab wants to come to Canada to work for you," one man said. "How much money you pay him?"

"I come to Egypt," I said, smiling, "I work. I get no money." At that I left them laughing.

I filled a bag and went to dump it off at the Khafre garbage site, and two men were sitting beneath the outcropping that leans toward Khufu. We started talking. One had a Pepsi, and opened it and gave it to me. He would not take it back.

I found out he had lost his mother three days earlier. I think the two men were having a heart to heart, as the guy was grieving. The other man looked like he had white powder coming out of his eyes, the salt residue from a lot of crying. Then he started to sing.

"What is he singing?" I asked his friend.

"He is not singing," he said. "He is crying."

He told me words of condolence to say to the crying man, and I repeated them as best I could, then shook his hand.

The conversation lightened up. The grieving man's friend was a witness to the Italian American lady coming on to me. He saw her give me her number.

"Did you go to visit her?" he asked.

"No."

"How long will you be away from your wife with no sex?"

"Forty-five days."

"You no have girlfriend here? Why?"

It seems not having a woman on the side is even more inexplicable than picking garbage for free, even paying for the privilege of picking up garbage, as they all figure out soon enough.

"You buy ticket? Every day? Where you stay? How much you pay? How much to fly from Canada?"

Earlier, Ashram the jokester was saying the same thing with the tea gang.

"Why you no have girlfriend? Your wife is *far* away. Everybody is married, but . . . "

Hilarious.

He reminded me of a magazine article about AIDS in Haiti and how it spreads. Not so hilarious, that.

"Every man has a wife, and every woman has a husband, but they both have many, many friends."

Back to the east of Khafre, five young engineering students from Cairo sitting on the first level of stones on the pyramid asked me what I was doing.

"How old are you?" one asked, an original question.

"Forty-seven."

"You are old. That is how old my father is."

When did I get old?

"When I was your age, I was strong," I said, flexing my biceps, "and all the women came to me." An outright lie.

"Send some women our way."

And I did!

Just down the way, also sitting on the pyramid, were about twelve young women. They, too, were curious about me. I spoke with them for a while. I heard one shout "I love you for what you are doing."

"There's a bunch of good-looking young men just over there," I told them, pointing, "all in college, studying engineering."

Did that get their attention! They jumped up and were stretching their necks trying to get a look. Several girls went to investigate.

The young, looking to meet someone, the same all over the planet, boys and girls, men and women.

On the way out, a young man was pestering me. I was tired and not in the best of moods.

"I don't believe what you say. Why you pick up garbage?"

"I don't care if you believe me or not," I said. "If you don't understand, you never will because your heart has to grow bigger."

He was following me, or walking with me, depending on how you look at it. As I was picking, he was stopping and waiting. At 2:30 I called it quits.

"Why are you nervous?" he asked, walking beside me.

"I am not nervous," I said, and I wasn't. But I *was* starting to get pissed off.

"Yes, you are nervous. Why are you nervous?"

"Don't make me tell you to fuck off," I said, fed up. "Because I will."

He kept pestering me, so finally I told him.

"Fuck off."

He suddenly got a hurt look on his face.

I felt remorse immediately and apologized. But I felt I had to establish that I can tell someone to fuck-off. I'm sure they do it to each other all the time. This was the guy who I believe has been telling people that I have something wrong with my heart, I have done something bad, and that is why I am picking garbage at the pyramids.

I picked some trash on my way out, and he kept following me. He isn't allowed to leave by the tourist exits, so he finally wandered away. We parted not enemies.

I grabbed a cab. One guy wouldn't do it for ten pounds, he wanted 15, but an older fellow with gold front teeth, dark sunglasses and a beret asked him what I had offered.

"*Siag, ashrah*" (Siag, ten)

He went for it. On the trip home he tried guessing my citizenship.

"German? Russian? English? Austria? Australia?"

"I will give you five pounds if you guess," I told him. He smiled. We were making a game of it, with one dollar on the line.

He was struggling, so I gave him a hint.

"Real close to America."

"Canada!"

So he ended up with 15 pounds anyway. He gave me four and a half pounds change, burned me 50 piastres on 20 pounds, but not intentionally.

Checked e-mails, one from Ally, they've had two snow days in a row, and her cousin Kaela is misbehaving. No news there. Be nice if they had time to write, but I guess they're busy with things.

I visited Fatih in his shop and he told me about the bar upstairs on the tenth floor. It seems some women give men the Egyptian equivalent of a lap dance. He and his buddy went up there once.

"A woman rubbed up against my friend," he said, imitating her by swaying his hips toward me. "Then she play with his finger like this," he added, rubbing his finger up and down. "We only had four beer each and it cost over 800 pound."

I wrote a postcard to the old man. I hope he can read it. My writing is so bad. After years of taking notes during interviews I have developed my own style of handwriting. It's not shorthand. More like lazyhand. It's near impossible for anyone else to read. Even when I try my best to make my writing legible, I always slip back into lazyhand.

I have not heard from Linda in some time. I have a feeling she is in no hurry to have me back. I hope everyone is well.

Fatih is saying we will go to Alexandria together, but I don't want to be tied to him. I want to be free to go anywhere I want. If I can't bring a camera in while I'm picking garbage, I may need a few days to just take pictures after my 40 days of work are done.

Evenings can be the loneliest, if I have nowhere to go. I could've gone to see Rabihr, but my legs are just killing me. No matter what, I would have to walk considerably, one always does here. I started to walk the two blocks to get some Egyptian food, but bailed on it because of my legs. I asked Fatih to order some chicken.

Mustafa the room cleaner knocked on my door to say goodby.

"I am going to Libya, to see my father."

I saw him in the street several days ago, walking toward Siag as I was walking to work.

"I not happy," he said, waving his finger at me. "I not happy."

"Me neither," I replied.

Nothing ever did happen about the 400 pounds that went missing. Why, for that kind of money I could've had a finger molested on the tenth floor.

Right now I'm thinking, again, *what on earth am I doing?* But at this point, I'll see it through. Sixteen days and I'm home.

The Doubt. How much damage has The Doubt done to humankind? How much has it prevented from happening? How many people have lived unfulfilled lives because they gave in to that bitch, gnawing away at courage?.

I'm reminded of Frank Wiens, I should send him a postcard tomorrow.

"To feel the passion to do great things takes years of sacrifice," he said in the movie we made of his life, "often painful, often heartbreaking, but always rewarding."

When Frank Wiens started St. John's Cathedral Boys' School, he had seven children and a teaching job in Winnipeg.

"Don't you ever tell anyone I didn't have my doubts," he said to me as we were making the movie, 'Frank, One Man's Life.' "I had huge doubts, overwhelming doubts."

Had Frank let that doubt stop him, my life would have taken another path, and I would be a much different man than I am today. The 'school' as we old-boys refer to it, had a huge affect on me. I believe it was the best thing that could've happened to young adolescent Bruce.

At 13 years old I was walking around with a bag of dope constantly in my sock, emulating my older brother four years my senior. He was good to me, and a lot of fun, though anything but a good role model for a young man. When that older brother was shot trying to rob a store in the middle of the night, my parents decided it was time to do something about me, before I went down that path.

It wasn't that my parents were stupid. On the contrary, my mother was extraordinarily vigilant in watching our behavior. I remember taking some plastic bags from the plastic bags drawer in the kitchen to split up some dope for sale or to give to my friends, I can't remember which. The bags made an ever-so-soft rustling noise. I winced. My mother was in the living room. Sure enough, she came running.

"What are you doing?" she demanded, arms crossed.

"I'm just getting some plastic bags," I said, totally busted.

"What for? All your brother wanted bags for was to split up his marijuana."

"I'm going for a bike ride," I said, uncharacteristically quick-witted. "I'm gonna cut up some oranges and put the pieces in a bag."

I still remember my brother's explanation of what happened that night, when drunk and stoned, and only 18 years old, he was almost killed.

"I thought, that old guy has lots of money and I don't," he said, shaking his head in disbelief at his own thought process. "I'm going to go take some of it, that's only fair."

The 'old guy' was the owner of a country store strangely situated miles from any community, perhaps a victim of some resettlement. The old guy lived in the store. When my brother, unloaded gun in hand, raised his leg to kick down the door, the old guy pulled the trigger on his loaded 12 gauge shotgun, and shot the would-be thief.

Fortunately for my brother, the pellets went through the door-jam first, losing much of their velocity. Nonetheless, he was lifted off his feet from the impact and landed on his back several feet away. His two female companions loaded him into the car and took him to the hospital, where the truth of his actions quickly became known to all. He carries a few of those pellets with him under his skin to this day.

My father was a high school principal, and a big believer in discipline. The toughest boys' school in North America suited him fine.

It was tough, no doubt about it. The best lessons I have learned, the ones that have helped me all my life, no matter how difficult things get, are the tough ones. Life isn't for wimps.

Like the Universal Declaration of Human Duties and Responsibilities, the school was based on four principles in educating boys and young men. Hard work, discipline, high adventure, and spirituality.

"You have to get over the loathing of work, until it becomes a joy to you," said Frank, speaking on the four tenets of the school. "You need discipline from outside first, and then you can develop self-discipline. What young boy doesn't dream of adventure? We didn't proselytize, but we let the students know why we were doing what we were doing. We're Christians."

At the beginning of each school year, new students would arrive at St. John's ten days before classes began, in order to complete a 300-mile canoe trip, an initiation. The journey from Ear Falls, Ontario, to the school on the shore of the Red River three miles north of Selkirk, in the neighboring province of Manitoba could take anywhere from seven to 14 days to complete. It depended on many factors, but mostly the weather. There's a 30-mile stretch of Lake Winnipeg that needs to be negotiated that often strands the canoe brigade because the lake can be so very rough. It's a shallow lake, and can go from dead calm to a full-blown gale in 20 minutes.

Having fished the lake commercially for more than 25 years, I can attest to its volatility, and downright treachery. In the last 100 years, Lake Winnipeg has claimed, on average, two commercial fishermen per year. I have come close to death myself many times.

It's difficult to choose which situation presented the most peril, to choose the 'closest' I have come to death on Lake Winnipeg. In my experience death can pounce at the most benign times. But if I was to choose, I would say it was October 30, 1994.

My brother-in-law Ryan and I were pulling nets five miles out from Arnes, a small harbor 12 miles north of Gimli. Years later I would buy the fish plant there, but at the time I had just moved back from California with $200 to my name, a wife and a baby. I was building my outfit.

We had been drinking the night before, and perhaps that contributed to my carelessness. Perhaps not.

The plan was to pull 20 nets, drop them off at shore, then return for the last 12 nets. There was an offshore wind, so we pulled the nets from the inside, or shore side. The wind blew us down the nets as we filled our tubs with both nets and fish, planning to take the fish out on shore later. This was the last day of the season, and we needed to get our nets out or we could get charged by the Conservation Officers, who loved to harass fishermen.

I was happy to see there was more fish in the nets than I had anticipated, however that meant we ran out of tubs and had to dump the last four nets on the front deck. These last four nets were particularly full of fish, and so we put a lot of weight in the front of the boat.

"That's it," I said to Ryan. "Let's get the hell out of here."

"Let's do it," he answered.

I climbed over the mountain of nets and fish in my small 20 foot fiberglass yawl, and lowered my 75 horse Mercury outboard engine into the water.

"Does it seem a little windier to you?" I asked Ryan. The waves were crashing over the bow.

Ryan was sitting in the bow, waiting for the engine to start. He would then set us loose from the anchor line keeping us in place. My father taught me that years ago.

"Never cast off until the engine starts," he told me. "That way if it won't go, the other fishermen can find you easily when they notice you missing."

"It's just like that because I'm here," said Ryan. "When I come to the back for the ride in, the bow will come up."

"Let us go," I said to Ryan, as I started the engine. Ryan cast off and I let the boat drift back with the wind to get away from the anchor line. Then I turned the steering wheel, heading for shore as Ryan scrambled over the gear to sit beside me. The ride is always smoothest at the back of the boat.

Wham! Five gallons of very cold water hit me in the face. I could see another ten or twenty gallons came in over the bow.

What the hell? I thought. *What's going on?*

I looked at our load. We had way too much weight in the boat for the conditions. The wind had sneaked up on us, pushing us along the nets at a good pace making the pulling easier, but lulling us into a false feeling of security. I quickly realized we were in grave danger, as another five gallons hit my face, and another wave broke over the bow.

"Holy shit!" said Ryan. He looked at me. Then he picked up the bailing bucket, and started bailing water out of the back of the boat. We didn't have a bilge pump, so we often had to use a bucket. Many times before I had to ask Ryan to do it as I drove, and often he would complain about it, but not that day. He turned his back to me, and bailed. He didn't turn around until we entered the harbor.

"I didn't want to look," he said later. "I didn't think we'd make it."

We were screwed. We had tubs with nets and fish at the back of the deck, and loose nets in the front. We couldn't throw out the loose nets, because they would get caught in the propeller, and we'd be without power, five miles out with a thirty knot offshore wind. We couldn't throw out the tubs of fish, because taking weight from the back of the deck would cause the bow to dip even lower into the water. As it was, every wave was cresting over, filling the boat with water. Ryan bailed continuously, tossing two gallons of water out every three seconds or so. Would it be enough?

The water was probably four degrees above freezing. If we ended up in the drink, we were as good as dead. We could maybe last a minute, then hypothermia would get us.

My brother lost a guy in late October once. It blew like hell from the northeast for two days, and we couldn't get to our nets. The third day it calmed, and we raced to the nets in the glow of the sun peaking over the horizon. The nets were loaded with three days catch, and we had a lot of work to do.

Brad was running six boats out of Hnausa, five miles north of my three boats at Arnes.

The night before his men were drinking in the Rollercoaster Lounge in Winnipeg Beach, and a young man, 17 years old, asked if he could come out fishing the following day, just to check it out. Fishermen do this all the time. Knowing their nets were loaded, they welcomed the added pair of hands.

In the morning Brad agreed to let the boy go out with one of his men in a 22-foot aluminum skiff.

"Bring him back to me, okay?" said the boy's father casually, as the boy climbed into Brad's fish truck.

"Sure," said Brad.

It was a good day for fishing, with a light wind to push the boat down the nets as the fishermen pulled out the fish. Brad was on his last gang of six nets when the aluminum skiff pulled up.

"This is the last gang," Brad told his man at the wheel of the aluminum skiff. "Go three nets down, grab on and start lifting."

A few minutes later Brad looked over and confirmed they were on the nets he had sent them to lift. He put his head down and picked fish. Sometime later the other fisherman in his boat went to the back to take a leak off the stern.

"The boat's gone," he said calmly, returning to the front of the boat.

"I thought, 'that's impossible,'" Brad told me later. "'They wouldn't leave without telling me. The only way the boat could be gone is if it sank. *But that's impossible.*'"

So not even believing it could be, but knowing it must be, no matter how unlikely, he threw the net over the bow, ran to the back of the boat, started the engine and raced over to where the boat should have been.

It wasn't blowing hard, but there was still a swell from that two-day northeaster. It was hard to see far ahead.

As he traveled, he saw something in the water. It was a gas can, with a man hanging onto it.

"I hate to admit it, but I hoped it was the kid," said Brad. "All I could think of was what his father had told me in the morning."

Bring him back to me, okay?

It wasn't the kid. Apparently the kid had tried to swim to Brad's boat.

"The kid made it ten strokes," said the survivor in his hospital bed later. "Then turned around with a surprised look on his face, and sank."

Hypothermia had cut off the blood flow to his extremities in an effort to protect the core. Unable to move, he slipped beneath the waves. They were in the water mere minutes.

They found the boy's body the following spring. The boat has never been found.

"I had to tell his father that I wasn't bringing his son back," Brad told me after the accident. "Aaaahhhhhh." Pure anguish.

"Does it get any better?" he asked me, seeking some solace, some light at the end of the pitch black whatever he was in that he prayed might, just might, be a tunnel.

I knew exactly where he was. I wrote a letter to my son Jake, when he was getting his driver's licence.

Dear son,

Yesterday I took you to the Department of Motor Vehicles, and you received your limited learner's permit to drive a car. You can now operate a motor vehicle under supervision. Watching you as you drove us home, I knew I would have to sit down and write this. I have thought of writing it often since you were born, though I wasn't looking forward to it.

Driving comes with a great responsibility, one that some teenagers do not take seriously. I know, because I was one of those who did not give it a second thought until it was too late.

We were drinking beer, not many, since we had very little money, and decided to go party somewhere else. I remember there were nine people in the car, including three children.

Driving down a gravel road, I was swerving from side to side, just for kicks, until a woman yelled from the back seat "There's kids in the car!" Then I stopped swerving and sped up, going for speed instead.

Sitting beside me was my friend Kurt, and beside him, Arthur. They had argued over who would sit by the window, and Arthur had won. We were sixteen years old.

It was dark and raining. I couldn't see the road ahead, and was driving too fast. We hit a bump and flew into the air. When we came down I was out of control of the car. We hit the ditch and the car flipped over completely, coming to rest with the windshield facing the road we had been on, right side up.

Worried about an explosion, I shoved open my door, opened the door behind me and started pulling people out. Kurt was on the other side of the vehicle doing the same, and I quickly saw all the people in the back seat were not seriously injured. But there was a lot of moaning and crying.

"I'll go call an ambulance," I said, and raced off to a farm house I could see down the road. I ran like my life depended on it. Feels funny to put it like that, because maybe someone's life did depend on it, and I wasn't fast enough.

Lungs burning, but adrenaline pumping insanely, I bounded up the steps and burst into the house. The farmer had a startled expression on his face.

"There's been an accident a quarter mile down the road," I said, pointing. "Call an ambulance."

Then I was out the door and running back.

"Is everybody alright?" I asked Kurt.

"Arthur's hurt," he said.

"Where is he?"

"Over there," said Kurt. Then, as I headed to where he pointed, "You probably don't want to go there."

What? How bad is he hurt?

I found him laying on his left side, like he was sleeping. In fact, it sounded like he was snoring. It was that sound that helped me locate him about 50 feet from the car. He had been thrown out the window. He might have been asleep, but the snoring seemed more ominous the closer I came—more like a gasping for breath, a raw, hoarse wrenching of the chest trying to draw air into the lungs.

I put my fingers in his mouth to make sure he wasn't choking on his tongue. He wasn't. But the rasping continued.

I tried to examine his injuries, but it was dark, so I felt around. His arms and legs and body seemed fine, but when I felt his head, warm blood flowed from where his left ear had been. Only a small pulpy piece of cartilage remained. I couldn't detect any other injuries. I placed him on his back, and then thought differently and returned him to his left side, and I held his head in my lap. I put pressure on his ear, trying to stop the bleeding. It was dark, and still raining. The others were all huddled on the other side of the car, not wanting to be near Arthur. I held him and waited for the ambulance.

I remember looking up at the dark night sky, rain pelting my face, praying for Arthur. Praying for the sixteen-year-old boy who was gasping for breath in my arms, and who, at the very least, had lost an ear because of my stupidity. My utter stupidity. The shame and remorse threatened to consume me, but my newfound, too-late found sense of responsibility would not let that happen.

The ambulance came and the paramedics were directed to where we were by the others. Arthur was quickly and professionally loaded up, and taken away.

Back at the hospital it was pandemonium, as nine people needed to be treated for various injuries. I had a cut on my head, and was covered in blood. A nurse tried to wash it off, but I wouldn't let her.

"Look after Arthur first," I said, like an idiot. I looked down at my hands, covered in his blood.

"The blood is scaring the children," she said, and I could see she was right, so I let her wash me up.

Arthur's parents came in, and were told their son had been transferred to the city hospital.

I went up to them and said "He'll be okay, he's a tough guy." How stupid. They just looked at me. I don't think the mother even heard me. She had a horrified look on her face that I will never forget.

I had sat at their dinner table, had sleep-overs, and been to birthday parties at their house, and now I was responsible for the condition of their son. Had they known I would do this to Arthur, I'm sure I would never have been allowed near the house.

It's been more than 30 years, but I think I walked home from the hospital. I'm not sure how that happened. I think my parents were called and were going to come, but I just left. I remember stopping at the steps of a church, rain still coming down, and praying for God to take me instead of Arthur. And even as I prayed, I knew I didn't really want that, didn't really mean it. I wanted to live. The shame of that particular moment has never left me, though it all occurred within my own head. I have never told anyone, until now.

Arthur hung on for a while, I'm not sure now just how long. I didn't sleep that night.

The next day I was walking somewhere, and a good friend picked me up, concerned about me. Stories fly quickly in small towns, and he knew all about the accident.

"But he's going to be okay, isn't he?" he asked me.

"Well, I know he's lost an ear."

He was silent for a moment. "Yeah, but that's not so bad."

I was sleeping in my bed when my mother woke me, crying, to tell me Arthur was dead. I rolled over and went back to sleep. There was peace in sleep.

When I woke up, my mother was in the kitchen. I told her maybe I should leave town. She said I couldn't just run away from my problems. Strangely, I immediately agreed with her, and decided to go to the pool hall, a favorite hangout for kids my age. She said she thought it may be a little early for that, but I went.

A lot of people were angry with me. For months I would go places and someone might yell out Arthur's name. One guy called me a murderer right to my face. That hurt, but I did have to admit, Arthur was dead because of me. I just pretended to ignore him.

For years I would dream that Arthur was alive, that he had been living in a nearby town, and was fine, having a great life. The reason for such an implausible scenario might change from dream to dream, but in all the dreams he had a prosthetic left ear. Even my subconscious couldn't ignore that fact. Every time though, I woke to the nightmare of reality. Arthur was dead. He was not coming back.

Slowly, over the years, I thought about it less and less. The dreams became less frequent, as did the thoughts of Arthur. But to this day if I hear his name, I'm back in that field holding his head as he gasps for breath, cold rain falling as I wait anxiously for an ambulance. If I read about a teenager killed in an accident, I'm back at the steps of the church, lying to God and myself. Or in the hospital, looking at my bloodstained hands.

I asked no mercy from the courts. In fact, I was downright surly to the judge. He commented on it. "At least you're not looking for sympathy."

Sympathy? I deserved whatever they gave me, and I knew it. It wasn't much. I was charged with dangerous driving, as I wasn't drunk, and they took my licence for a year. I can't remember if I was fined. Not a lot, if anything.

I vaguely remember going to see Arthur's mother, to ask forgiveness. Being a good Christian woman she forgave me. At least that's what I remember. I hope that memory is true. There was a lot of crying. I think his father gave me a ride home. He was equally inexplicably kind.

Sixteen years after Arthur died, you were born. It was only after being a parent myself, holding you in my arms, that I realized the true enormity of what I had done. And what it must have taken for his parents to forgive me.

I thought of Arthur being held in his own father's arms. What hopes and dreams might he have had for the newborn boy with his whole life in front of him?

Then I looked at you. Would the sins of the father be visited upon the son? Having taken a son from one family, would mine be taken away from me?

I have known since your birth that I would have to tell you about Arthur, for two reasons.

I don't want you to die in a senseless car accident, and I don't want you to cause one, bringing terrible grief to another family, and having to live with the consequences.

So please, my son, don't be as stupid as me. Drive responsibly, with all that entails, and don't get in a car with someone who doesn't. Please, remember Arthur.

Dad

"Does it get any better?" Brad asked me again, beseechingly.

"Yes it does," I told him, throwing him a lifeline someone had thrown me. "I know it's hard to believe right now, but in time you'll have full days, even weeks, when you don't even think about it."

"Yeah, that is hard to believe," he said, not believing it.

"But it will never go away completely," I added, realistically. "You'll just learn to live with it. But you will . . . you will."

My face was already numb. But I could not take my eyes off the front of the boat, because every once in a while, a rogue wave, bigger than the rest, would threaten to completely swamp us. I had to turn the bow ever so slightly to minimize the damage. One wrong move, one mistake, and we'd be dead.

One of our buoys was to my right. From it I could tell we were traveling less than one mile an hour.

It seemed to take forever, but slowly, ever so slowly, we got closer to shore. The wind being offshore, the waves became smaller and smaller. Gradually I was able to increase our speed, and in two hours we made it into the harbor, a trip that normally takes ten minutes.

I remember passionately recounting this tale to the Government of Canada's Standing Committee on Fisheries and Oceans in Ottawa, trying to emphasize the importance of harbors.

"It wasn't until we were inside the harbor, that I turned to Ryan and said 'We're gonna live, Ryan! We're gonna live!'"

We were both drenched, shivering from the cold, deep in the first stages of hypothermia. We went home to the small house we were renting about four miles from the harbor, and changed clothes and had a hot meal Linda made for us. I played with one-year-old Jake for a while, grateful to be alive.

An hour later we started cleaning out the boat, and took the fish to the fish station to sell.

"What about the other twelve nets?" Ryan asked me.

"Forget it," I said to a visibly relieved Ryan. "We'll get them tomorrow."

Sometimes you just have to say to hell with the conservation officers.

It was very difficult to keep the boat afloat for the ride in, with freezing cold water hitting my face every three seconds or so, for at least an hour. That could easily be a torture the Bush Administration could use on detainees at Guantanamo Bay. Who knows? It was tough as hell, but it was nothing compared to my new-boy canoe trip.

We took a bus to Ear Falls, Ontario, and the first evening we paddled our canoes for perhaps an hour before going to shore to make camp. We were fed some watered down soup, and told to make a shelter. We were given two ten foot by ten foot sheets of plastic and a few pieces of string to accomplish this, with no instructions. Needless to say the shelters we created were as universally diverse as they were universally ineffective in sheltering their creators from rain.

We whispered to each other.

"Are they going to make us paddle like that all day?"

"They couldn't possibly make us."

"Is the food going to get better?"

"I didn't think it would be like this."

The trip was hell, and has been my yardstick for difficulty ever since. The 'masters' made us paddle all day long, and soon my hands were blistered on every crevice and hinge of finger joint. In a few days, sand got into the cuts, and to open or close my hand was excruciating. To survive, I would grip my paddle when I got in the canoe in the morning, and squeeze my hands tightly round the wood. In half a minute the pain would be gone, and I wouldn't let go of the paddle until we went to shore for lunch—two vitaminized hardtack biscuits with a spoonful of jam and peanut butter, and a slice of cheese. Dinner was soup, porridge for breakfast. We drank the water from the river we paddled on, in a cup with a spoon tied to it, wrapped round a belt loop on our pants.

Sometimes I would have to do the paddle-clench several times a day, as we would often have to portage the canoes around rapids and waterfalls, or from one body of water to another. The canoes were big, 22 feet long, and weighing 300 pounds. Four kids would carry it upside down on their shoulders, using life-jackets for padding—two kids in the front, two in the back. Smaller kids would carry the duffel bags and food packs. I was a canoe carrier.

They pushed us hard. Every evening before we made camp I had to fight the urge to cry from the pain in my arms at every stroke of the paddle. Others lost that battle. (I remember thinking of how I used to complain about taking out the garbage at home—what a whiner I was!) Discipline was a stick across your butt. They called it beats, or swats. My first swats came for loose gear. I tied my raincoat to a duffel bag, then helped carry a canoe over a portage.

"Who's 905?" Mr. Clark yelled out as we began loading the canoes after the portage. He was holding a raincoat, my raincoat. It had fallen off the duffel bag.

"I am," I said.

"Come with me."

He took me into the woods a few yards, out of sight of the others. He grabbed a fallen tree limb.

"This'll do," he said to himself.

"Bend over," he said to me.

He swatted me three times on the butt. I barely noticed it, which I attributed to his choice of stick.

"Don't let it happen again," he said, as he passed my raincoat to me.

Any number of transgressions could result in swats. Planting, a Chinese-American kid from Chicago was swatted for not 'feathering' his paddle. Feathering, turning the paddle so the blade slices the wind when reaching forward, reduces the impact of paddling into the wind.

"Planting, feather your paddle!" yelled Mr. Clark.

"I'm trying sir. I'm trying."

This went on all morning.

"If I catch you not feathering your paddle three more times, I'm going to take you to shore," said Mr. Clark after lunch. We all knew what that meant.

"That's one."

"That's two."

"That's it!"

Mr. Clark steered the canoe to shore, and he and Planting got out and went into the woods. I knew what was going on. I was in a different canoe, and we stopped paddling, waiting. We couldn't see the action, but we could hear.

Snap. Snap. Mr. Clark was breaking fallen branches over his knee, looking for one strong enough to deliver the reinforced learning he felt Planting was so sorely in need of.

"Ugggghhhh," grunted Mr. Clark in near unison with the 'thunk' of a branch not breaking on his knee.

"Okay Planting, bend over."

"Why, sir?" Planting couldn't possibly have been that dumb.

"Just do it."

Whack! Clearly Mr. Clark had picked a winner.

"Ahhhhh!" screamed Planting. "Don't hit me in the same spot! Don't hit me in the same spot!"

Whack!

"Ahhhhh! You hit me in the same spot! You hit me in the same spot."

Whack!

"Ahhhhh! You did it again! You did it again!"

Our caloric intake was hugely insufficient for what we were doing, and most of us experienced real hunger for the first time on that trip. I remember sitting next to Goodwin, a kid from Toronto, as we ate lunch. Some of my jam had fallen off my hardtack, and landed on the muddy cuff of my jeans.

"Aren't you going to eat that?" asked Goodwin, wonder in his eyes.

"No."

"Can I have it?"

"Sure."

He took his spoon and scooped the jam with an equal part of mud off my pants and stuck it in his mouth.

We were all hungry, some more than others, as everybody has a different metabolism, and some people were paddling harder than others. I knew I didn't want to miss a meal.

"Too many of you guys have been losing your cups," said our leader Mr. Voss, on what was to be the last day of the trip for the brigade. "From now on, anyone who loses their cup doesn't get to eat."

We paddled across Traverse Bay, and prepared for the Victoria Beach portage to the shore of Lake Winnipeg. As we lifted the canoe to our shoulders, my spoon slipped out of my belt loop, and both my spoon and cup fell to the ground. I was about to ask someone to give it to me, when Mr. Clark yelled at us.

"Get going, get going."

My three canoe carrying partners were eager to go, so I left my cup and spoon behind. We were the first canoe across the portage, and the rule was that whoever gets over first goes back to help the people who are last. We headed back, and I saw Mr. Clark underneath a canoe, helping the kids with the heavy weight.

"Mr. Clark, can I go back and get my cup? It fell off when I picked up the canoe."

"What? Oh, yeah, I guess so," he said, clearly distracted.

I ran back as fast as I could, but I couldn't find it. Worried I'd be in trouble, I ran back up the portage to rejoin the others.

I went straight instead of taking a turn in the road, and ended up way off course. I hit the shore, then went left for a half a mile. I returned and went in the other direction. I had no idea where they were. I was utterly lost.

After an hour of running one way along the shore, and then the other, I came across an old man sitting on a bench, looking out at the lake.

"Have you seen any canoes around here?" I asked him.

"I saw some big yellow canoes paddling that way," he said, pointing out into the lake. "Maybe an hour ago."

I sat down on the bench beside him. "I was supposed to be with them," I sighed.

We talked for a while, and he told me he was a retired fisherman.

"Did you know my grandfather, Gisli Benson?" It was a longshot, but what the hell.

"Yes, I did," he answered, surprised. "I fished with him and his boy Harvey."

"Harvey's my Dad!"

"Well, what a small world we live in. What's Harvey doing now?"

"He's a high school principal."

"They must be really hard up for high school principals," he said, gently laughing.

He drove me to Selkirk, and gave me money and strict instructions to take the bus to Gimli.

I called home and told them I was coming.

"We'll see you when you get here," said my Mom.

I was worried I would be in big trouble from my parents for getting lost, but they were glad to see me. I must have been quite the sight. My Dad took one look at my hands, swollen and infected cuts on every crease, and took me to see Dr. Scribner, who worked out of his house.

"He shouldn't be paddling for at least two weeks," Doctor Scribner said to my Dad, as he washed the cuts and bandaged them up. "I can't see how he was able to do it at all."

"Do you think he should stay home or go back?" my father asked the doctor, unsure of what to do.

"*I* wouldn't send him back."

We drove home.

I remember sitting in the kitchen, both my parents looming over me.

"You don't have to go back if you don't want to," my mother said.

"That's right," said my father. "It's your choice."

I tell my children often that the decisions they make now, even at such a young age, can have huge ramifications in their future.

"I want to go back," I said, surprising even myself.

What part of me could possibly have wanted to go back? Going back meant hunger, hard work the likes of which I had never known, strict discipline enforced with a stick on the backside, and pain. What part of my Id, in pure self-preservation, chose to go back, and save me from a life of quitting, a life of sloth and laziness? I'm not that smart.

I am perplexed still, though I know that may have been the single most important decision I have made in my life.

"I want to go back," I said. I was 14 years old.

I went back, and was put in another brigade that had just reached the Victoria Beach portage. Lake Winnipeg showed her penchant for rough water and we were three days finishing the trip. My original brigade reached the school eleven hours after I got lost.

I graduated four years later, and returned to teach at the school for two years. For years after graduation every fall I would quit whatever job I had to steer a canoe on the new-boy canoe trip, and every spring I would go on one of the end-of-year canoe trips.

The school believed in the true meaning of education, 'Educor— to bring forth that which is within.' We were challenged mentally as much as physically. It was many years later I learned the purpose of the school was to teach the ability to reason. Everything we did there was just a lesson in that. But there was so much more.

I think of the school as my foundation, the fundamental principles on which I am founded. I plan to write a book about it some day, if I can get Frank's blessing. I'll call it 'My name is 905,' with the subtitle 'and I've just become alive,' after the song by The Who. I believe it was at the school I came alive, first stood on that foundation. My laundry number at the school was 905, stitched to every article of my clothing.

My first job at the school was in the laundry room. It was an easy job, therefore desirable. But it was always warm and humid, and made me tired. When playing sports I didn't have the energy my classmates did. I kept up with my studies easily enough, and stayed below the radar, but something was wrong.

Every Sunday we were allowed off the property for ten hours. Most students went to Winnipeg to catch a movie or go roller-skating. Since I lived so close, my parents would come and get me and I'd visit friends and family in Gimli.

When we returned to the school Sunday night, Frank would give us a lecture in the chapel. The Sunday Sermon. He was a captivating speaker, and he always spoke on relevant issues of interest to the students.

"I want to talk to you about doing your best," he said one Sunday, as we sat down to listen. He spoke at length about students who just do enough to get by, who do not challenge themselves.

"They rob themselves of a real life by not stepping up to the plate and swinging hard."

I felt he was talking directly to me. I swear I saw him look at me, and felt him see clear through to my soul.

The next day I spoke to the master in charge of the laundry room, John Corkett.

I have been given two great compliments in my life, and the first was from this man, John Corkett. I had returned to the school to teach and work, and Corkett and I were drinking beer with the intent of getting drunk. Corkett was 36, I was 20. We were talking about canoe trips.

"Benson," he said to me, "I wouldn't trust you with a bottle of booze or a woman, (very astute of him) but I'd trust you with the lives of those kids in that canoe."

The second, and greater compliment came from fellow student, Michael Rowe, in two parts. A writer of some re-known now, he was a gay kid at the toughest boys' school in North America, a year younger than me. The school was tough enough on the rest of us, but to be gay added a new dimension of difficulty to be overcome.

I had not seen Rowe for some twenty years when a letter appeared in the mail. It was three pages long.

In the letter he describes a snowshoe run we were on. We would walk in a line, keeping in stride with each other.

"It was dark, and you came back to check on us, just to make sure we were alright. Watching you as you walked away I was filled with a sense of complete admiration. I knew then that I was going to be alright in this world. I would be alright in this world because there are people like you in it, people who can throw the ball far, and do all the things men are supposed to be able to do.... but most importantly, people who have the strength to be cruel, and choose not to."

This bowled me over, and even as I type this my vision is blurred.

The second half of the compliment came in an inscription in a copy of his book Enter, Night that he gave me.

"To my great friend Bruce, a man's man who always had the strength to be kind, even when it was just as easy to be cruel."

To go to what some called the toughest boys school in North America and be remembered by at least someone, not for toughness, but kindness... this has been the greatest compliment ever bestowed upon me.

"Mr. Corkett, can I get transferred to the meat room?" I asked him. Corkett was in charge of the meat room as well, where the students made thousands of pounds of pork sausages each week to be sold door to door in Winnipeg—an effort to lower student tuition fees.

"What?"

I repeated the request.

"You do know the laundry is the easiest crew in the school?"

"Yes, sir."

"And you do know the meat room is probably the hardest?"

"Yes, sir." Everybody knew that.

He looked at me, bewildered and chuckling. "Okay then, I shouldn't have a problem finding someone who wants to get out of the meat room and into the laundry room." I'm sure he thought I'd deeply regret it.

A year after I graduated, a friend of mine in grade 12 told me of a Sunday Sermon Frank had given.

"Do you remember Benson?" Frank asked. "I know you new-boys never met him, but the rest of you do. He was a big man around here. He ran the meat room, and was on the Interschool snowshoe team. He was given the award for leadership in work last year, at Open House. An important guy."

"Do you know what he's doing now? Do you know what kind of work he was able to get?" He paused for effect.

"He's a *garbage-man*," he said, with mock derision. "He goes around picking up other people's garbage."

He paused again.

"But I'll bet you he's the best garbage-man that he can be."

Made me want to rip trees out by the roots, and tie them in knots.

In making the movie about Frank's life, I discovered this foundation I mentioned earlier goes back to the Reverend Harry Cartlige. It was Harry Cartlige that introduced the simple farm boy Frank to great literature, by letting him into his library. It was Harry Cartlige that pushed Frank into going to University. Without Harry Cartlige influencing Frank as he did, St. John's Cathedral Boys' School would never have existed. So in a very direct way, Harry Cartlige has had a positive impact on my life, and the thousands of boys who attended the school.

I would not be here at the pyramids picking garbage if it were not for Harry Cartlige, a man long dead before I was born. I don't believe I would know the embrace. How far back in time does that foundation go? Who influenced Cartlige? Who influenced that person? What butterfly flapped its wings? What chain of events over millennia had to occur, for me to be here now? Or to make it home off the lake in such perilous conditions, half frozen?

I believe we all lay a foundation of some kind, something that will reverberate into the future, for good or bad. The theme for the sequel to Skufty, (The Wave-almost finished) is that kindness and meanness are waves we send out to distant shores. These waves will affect everyone in their path. What kind of waves do we want to send out?

Enough reflection.

My path to work has changed much over the time I have been here. The dirt road was first replaced with fresh gravel, and was paved yesterday. Asphalt. Quite the metamorphosis.

I am going to bed lonely, wondering and thinking, and as always, wrestling The Doubt. Hope for the best.

Day 30 in the desert—a day of discovery

"Corruption."

I'm always a little down in the morning, as I'm physically hurting, and far from home. This morning was no exception. I rolled out of bed at six, and performed my usual routine. I stretched, showered, shaved, stretched some more, checked my bag, dressed and went for breakfast. Today I ate with two guys from Milan. They went to Alexandria today. They were a little bummed out about the Egyptians fleecing them a bit, asking for more and more money all day.

Yesterday they enjoyed a six-hour horse ride to Sakkara and back, and were walking normally. Something I could never do.

One of them is taking Human Rights in university or college, so I gave him my card.

"Maybe you can translate the Universal Declaration of Human Duties and Responsibilities into Italian."

"And Portuguese," he said. "We were raised in Brazil."

Ali asked about his gift again, but he's cool that I'll get it to him. Not really a gift if you ask for it. Or is it?

I saw Mr. Meek as I went in, and we shook hands. He talks to me whenever I see him, and I have no idea what he says, but he's always smiling. I always imagine what he might be saying.

How are you today? *Ya big dummy!*

I was determined not to do inside of the wall, just leave it to the incredibly lazy Walid and Ramadan. I was cleaning outside of the wall, when Walid came up and in his gesticulations, and his Arabic which I did not understand, said I should clean inside, not outside of the wall.

"That is your job," I said, pointing to him.

He said something in Arabic, then threw an empty water bottle at the wall, clearly upset.

That made me want to say 'you do it you lazy shit.' But he left, and went to the other side of the front of the Sphinx, slacking it with Ramadan.

Screw it, I thought. I'll do it for the vendors, not for Walid or Ramadan.

As I was working, lost in thought, Hassanan said something to me from up on the wall, and scared the hell out of me. We laughed. I told him Ramadan and Walid were doing nothing, by sitting down, and saying "Ramadan and Walid." He got it, and went to motivate them.

I finished the area, then went around to walk up to Khufu and Khafre on the left side of the Sphinx. Looking back I saw Walid waving angrily, clearly pissed at me. Hassanan was standing over him, arms crossed.

"I love you, Walid," I yelled out to him.

I filled a bag on my way up from the Sphinx and headed over to where all the bags are still sitting so many days later, with some ripped open. As I finished today, Rabihr the Elder's buddy Mohamed said it would cost 100 to 1000 pounds to get rid of the bags. No way . . . I'll get to it, though it will be difficult with my injured legs. The constant pain is really getting to me.

I had to meet Ahmed and his friends by one, so I walked over to the area with the French-speaking guard and had a good talk. We actually had a religious discussion in French, both of us struggling, me more than him. I tried to answer why I am here, picking garbage.

I spent a good half hour cleaning a tomb entrance that had been sealed with concrete by the authorities. I removed five bags of garbage, a crushed 45 gallon drum too full of sand to move very far, about eight two or three gallon gas cans, some wire grating, and two of the rubber containers made from old car tires and used to haul debris away from archeological digs. Looks much better now. However, I put the bags on the pile that nobody wants to take away. The Eternal Pile.

Then off I went to meet Ahmed and his friends for tea. One of the boys on a camel wanted me to meet him tomorrow and go see Maharab, but I wouldn't promise.

I found a pair of sunglasses as I was walking the east side of Khafre, planning to meet Ahmed on the north side where he has the boardwalk project. One of the arms was bent, so I straightened it the best I could. I saw a security guy, a good guy who looks out for me, and I showed him. He put them on.

"Where did you find those?" asked a vendor to my right. "Over there?" He pointed to roughly where I had found them.

"Yes," I said.

"Then they are mine."

He spoke to the security guy in Arabic, who shook his head.

"Take them from him and give them to me," the vendor said to me.

I wasn't sure what to do. Just then Ahmed showed up, and was able to translate. On his advice I ended up giving the vendor the glasses.

"He is probably lying," said Ahmed. "But they are cheap glasses anyway."

To his credit the vendor was willing to go to the head of security to argue his case, but maybe he was bluffing.

"The government has been keeping journalists away from you," Ahmed told me on the way to the car. He also said that a guy at the office of Kamal Wahid and Mohamed Cheoh said that I do as much work as the company that has been hired to clean the pyramids. Interesting.

Ahmed is discovering Skufty and tells me about it, which takes me back so much. I still remember when the idea hit me. Goodman's Landing, so far from the pyramids of Giza, and yet so close. I am willing to bet nobody from Goodman's Landing has been to the pyramids, and nobody from the pyramids has been to Goodman's Landing, and yet the people have treated this weary Trashman in the same fine manner.

Ahmed told me the company that has the job to clean the garbage at the pyramids gets paid 50,000 pounds each month, nearly ten thousand dollars. Each month! Un-bloody-believable. Ahmed has told me in the past, and I know from my own curiosity, 500 pounds a month is the most garbage pickers are paid. At that rate, the company could hire 40 people for 20,000 pounds and still pocket 30,000 pounds. But there is no more than eight or ten people picking, and some supervisors that do nothing. What a rip!

"Corruption," said Ahmed.

He said it is understood that if you want to join the police academy, it costs 80,000 pounds.

"No," corrected his buddy, Mr. Abd el Fattah, "it is more like 150,000 pounds."

If you want to be a crown prosecutor, it costs more, and to be a judge, lots of dough. So the corruption is so endemic, it will take a long time to rid the society of it.

"A police officer might be paid 200 pounds per month to be a police officer," said Ahmed, "but will receive 2000 pounds in bribes."

So who is he working for?

"Many people in Egypt do not feel a part of the country," said Ahmed, "because they are on the outside of these bribes." The disenfranchised, in need of the embrace.

A person could endure poverty if there were social equality and justice.

They offered to give me a ride home to Siag, but I decided to work a little more, and went back in through the Sphinx gate. The guy who got 40 pounds out of me long ago, my 'guide,' said I should be there early tomorrow, as they are expecting many people. How many could they be expecting? Already some 5,000 people a day visit the pyramids.

I worked the front and around to the wall. I cleaned until I filled a bag, and left. One of the young girls, perhaps 13-15, helped me. Then she sold some bookmarks to a Finnish woman for two euros, a good price for her.

"This young lady works very hard," I told the Finnish woman, who then tipped the girl. Grateful for my intercession, the girl helped me some more. I wish I had permission to have a camera, as I would like a picture of her.

Day 31 in the desert—When will it end?
Nine days I know, but now comes,
the work, to stick it out

"You no good. You always say Bokra, Bokra."

Nagua and another woman are cleaning my room right now. Nagua is making my bed and singing, while the other one is doing the bathroom. I asked them to clean when I got up to my floor, as I'm sure it was Mustafa who took my money, and he has gone to Libya. I trust these women.

I feel sorry for them, as my feet have got to be making it bad for Nagua. I'm embarrassed about my stinky feet, so I'm writing feverishly.

Now Nagua is vacuuming the carpet. It's been at least two weeks since I had the room cleaned, so they're earning their pay. I was just a little leery of Mustafa getting back into my room.

Yesterday Rabbob returned my glasses with new, but much heavier lenses. She paid for it, or the hotel.

"A small *cadeau* (gift)," she said, smiling. Being in the tourism industry, she speaks a little of so many languages.

Saman speaks a little German, Russian, French, Japanese and several other languages.

"For my business," he said, meaning only enough to negotiate a deal on a camel ride.

I was on my way to Menkaure today, thinking I had not found a horseshoe for days, and immediately found two, and on the way back, a third. A needed boost.

Ali asked about his gift again.

"It is expensive," I told him.

"You bring, or you not bring?" he asked.

"I bring."

I ran into Saman again, and he asked about the pictures I took of his children when I had dinner with him. I'll try to get them done today, take them to him tomorrow. I should probably call Rabihr as well, maybe go have a few beers, but the Canadian guys may be back looking for some drinks, Nicholas anyway.

It was a regular day, not much traffic on the way to work as it's a holiday. I did the front of the Sphinx and all the way up one side and then the other. I was waiting for Maharab to show up because I hadn't seen him for a long time, and I was hungry. He seemed to take forever, so I worked my way up to Khafre and had a falafel and a drink from Mahmoudy.

Hamdy, who came here with Rabihr last time, came to get a drink from Mahmoudy.

"I am eating the desert today," I told him. There were gale force winds, just howling, and my falafel was indeed grittier than usual. Everyone was doing what they could to avoid the wind, using the ruins of ancient Egypt for shelter.

I have been here for a month and still at one point today a security person wouldn't let me hop over the wall to the back of the Sphinx. I had done it countless times before. Usually another guard is around to tell the new guy it's okay, but not today.

I was walking around Khafre to go to the Mortuary Temple in front of Menkaure, when I noticed that even with all the wind, there was no trash flying around. I was at the corner of the east and north sides of Khafre.

(The girls are finished cleaning my room and are outside the door laughing and giggling.)

I credited some degree of this lack of trash to my doing.

"You cannot stop the wind," Ashram had said, as trash was blowing all over the place.

Perhaps we can't stop the wind, but we can stop the trash. I was so enamored of myself that I wanted a witness. There was a tourist nearby being pestered by a guy on a camel.

I asked him if he was Egyptian. No, he was from Azerbaijan, Head of the Department of Industry, Transport and Communication Statistics (I'm copying from his card).

"I want a witness," I said. "Look here." I pointed down the east side of the pyramid. "And here." I pointed down the north side.

"Do you see any garbage?"

"No," said Yusif.

It was incredible to me, but I'm sure Yusif Yusifov was not so moved.

We walked together against the wind to the Mortuary Temple in front of the third pyramid, Menkaure. We were talking about languages.

"Most people speak English in Canada, but we have two official languages, English and French."

"After 80 years of domination by Russia," said Yusif, "people in Azerbaijan all speak Russian."

Never one to miss an opportunity, I gave him a Center for Civilization card. He gave me his, which blew away in the wind. I chased it for a while, but no luck.

"Come back, I have another." *Ya big dummy.*

I explained what we at the CFC were trying to do.

"Do you think you could translate the Universal Declaration of Human Duties and Responsibilities into Russian?"

"Yes," he said simply.

We would then have it in English, French, Arabic, Russian, and Icelandic. All we would need to be in the six United Nations languages, would be Chinese and Spanish.

A guard started asking Yusif questions as we stood just outside the temple, after money I thought.

Police always want money.

"He is my friend," I told the guard. "He does not speak English or Arabic."

"Okay," said the guard, and walked away.

I looked at his card. It says Yusif X Yusifov.

"What is the X for?"

"It was my father's name."

I showed him my card. Benson meant 'son of Ben' in the past. In Arabic, Ahmed bin Walid, would mean 'Ahmed, son of Walid.' We are all so similar.

We went into the Temple and I started picking garbage.

"Can I watch you work?" asked Yusif.

"Sure. Can you take some pictures and email them to me? I'm not allowed to have a camera."

He took my picture, and we talked while I worked, but when I moved to another room he said "Okay Bruce, I will go now" and we shook hands and he left. Good timing too, as that part of the Temple had clearly been used as a bathroom for years.

Here we are in the year 2009, and the only way to prevent terrorists planting bombs is to have no bathrooms. People are forced to urinate and defecate all over the ancient Temples, even on the pyramids themselves. No garbage cans means garbage piles up everywhere. Such backward thinking.

When Hillary Clinton was in Egypt recently, at the seaside resort of Sharm el-Sheik for the International Conference in Support of the Palestinian Economy for the Reconstruction of Gaza, did she have to find a rock to crap behind? Ridiculous, someone should rattle this cage, wake the leaders up.

What am I saying? The first rule of being a Trashman is DO NOT JUDGE!

Ya big dummy!

Somewhere in the Mortuary temple of Menkaure archeologists found the names of competing gangs of workmen, evidence they say, that paid workers built the pyramids, not slaves.

The Greek Herodotus, the first chronicler of the pyramids, estimated upwards of 100,000 slaves would be needed to do the work. But he arrived twenty-seven hundred years after the pyramids were built. Modern archeologists believe a workforce of 20,000 could have done it.

The latest belief is that Egyptians from all over Egypt took their turn working in Giza, about two years each. The religious belief at the time was that each person's eternal life depended on his or her Pharaoh having eternal life. For the Pharaoh to live eternally he needed a proper tomb, so the construction of a pyramid was of concern to everyone. As an Egyptian, your eternal soul was on the line. That's motivation!

Perhaps we need that level of commitment for our planet. If everyone believed their eternal life depended on passing a healthy, diverse, peaceful earth on to following generations, maybe we could do it. That is the embrace, the one commonality of all religions, and beyond that—all peoples. We may have been 'born to be wild,' but also to 'take the world in a love embrace.'

"The human condition comes with a flaw," a teacher once told me. "We cannot rise above our primitive instincts unless . . . "

The bastard didn't finish, but I wondered how we could change our nature, our condition. I think the first step would be to acknowledge what we are. There should be a class in grade school that explains our nature to us early on, and then more detailed in senior year, a required credit to graduate high school. Human Nature.

I told my two sons that one of the biggest problems they would have in life would be with women, and their desire for them. But there are many other problems to be confronted in dealing with our baser side. In that vein, I wrote a newspaper column on shaken baby syndrome.

On August 20, a Bryson City man was sentenced to three years in prison for severely beating his four month old twin sons, even breaking their legs. Apparently they would cry "and get on his nerves." A heinous crime, no doubt perpetrated by some lowlife psychotic scumbag. After all, how many reasonable people would ever want to hit such young children for crying?

Plenty. I will admit my children's cries "got on my nerves." I didn't beat them, but the impulse was there. And I think most men know that impulse, if honest with themselves. We can deny the human condition, but that won't change it. It's like we're hardwired to leave the cave and go kill a woolly mammoth when we hear a child crying. For me, I learned to check to ensure the child was fine, and then just leave the room. Maybe crank the stereo a bit, or run around the block.

Ten years ago my wife and I were running a commercial fishing business in Canada. We had a young couple from Newfoundland working for us. The couple became pregnant and decided to move home to Newfoundland to be with as they awaited their first child. We threw them a going-away party.

A father for many years, I wanted to give the young man some advice. After several drinks and much laughter, I turned to Billy.

"Billy, I've got some advice for you. If the baby is crying and driving you crazy, just check to make sure the kid's okay, doesn't have a wet diaper, isn't hungry, is safe in the crib. Then get out of the room."

Billy just nodded, looked a little quizzical, but seemed to get the message. I hoped he would remember it should such a moment arise. I thought it was the best advice I could give him based on my own experiences, and the all-too frequent stories in the media of people, mostly men, hurting children of all ages. The shaken baby syndrome. I do not believe all these people are evil incarnate because I have wanted to silence my own children's cries. Nobody told me I could just leave the room, just get away.

My wife overheard what I said to Billy and was aghast. How could I say such things to a soon-to-be father? How negative could I be? And to advise him to leave the child alone?

A week later I related all this to my psychiatrist cousin Wray. He told me a story.

Like the Bryson City man, Wray had twin sons, who are now in their early thirties. He was working as a psychiatrist in Cleveland, as was his psychiatrist wife. Way's wife left the house for work at seven a.m., Way left at eight, when the nanny would arrive. Way was responsible for the infant boys for only one hour each morning.

"One of the boys woke up and started crying," said Way. "Just one. And I wanted to throw that fucking kid out the window."

"And I'm a trained psychiatrist," he added.

Way explained to me that he had no money troubles, no mortgage worries, no employment issues, and had a good relationship with his wife. And a nanny coming in one hour.

"And yet I wanted to throw the kid out the window," he said. "What about the poor guy who dropped out of high school, can't find work or money to pay the rent, and hasn't anyone coming to relieve him in the foreseeable future? How bad must it be for him?"

I don't know anything about the Bryson City man going to jail for three years, but I'm sure everyone would agree it would have been better for all involved if he had just left the room. Whether the kids had dirty diapers or not.

I have long wished for public service ads on television, radio or print to carry this message to new parents and care-givers. If the kid is driving you nuts, or "getting on your nerves" get out of the situation. Make sure the kid is safe, and then . . .

GET OUT OF THE ROOM!

Aleksander Solzhenitsyn asked the question, "who is this wolf?" that preys on his fellow man, imprisoning and torturing people in the Gulag. Then he answered his own question—"it is us."

I believe we are all capable of monstrous acts, and of noble ones as well. Never have we been in a better situation to educate the children of the world on what it means to be human, and how we must act in order to preserve our race. And more important, how we *must not* act, no matter the desire.

"The man has not been born who can write honestly about himself," said Mark Twain, and I agree with him. I cringe at the very idea of anyone being able to read my thoughts. Everyone does. But we have to shine a light on ourselves to understand and to prevent past atrocities on ourselves and our environment from being repeated. This is who we are, good and bad. These are the thoughts you will probably have, good and bad, petty and profound, cruel and kind.

The human condition comes with many flaws, but I have hope. Perhaps that is the message of the pyramids, a sign, built of rock in massive proportions to survive the ages. A sign to tell us that we, humankind, working together, can achieve anything. How else could such a message of hope be sent through time?

I walked back and dumped two bags at Khafre, then cleaned up the garbage area a bit. I started working back to Menkaure, but the wind was gale force, ridiculously strong. I found a little crevasse filled with garbage that a mean-looking donkey was taking refuge in, and a smaller one with no donkey, and not out of the wind as much. I decided to start on that one. I carefully pulled the bags out of my backpack, and separated one to work with. Then I carefully put the rest back.

I started to open the bag but the wind ripped it out of my hands, and it was gone. For a moment I thought I had a chance to get it back as it hit the side of the Mortuary Temple, but as I moved toward it, whoosh, it was out of sight. I hoped it didn't hit anyone.

I decided to pull the pin. I had been sandblasted enough. I still had grit in my teeth from lunch, and a thin layer of sand all over me.

My 'guide' said yesterday it would be busy, an understatement. It was the busiest I have ever seen it, must be an Egyptian holiday. There were tens of thousands of people on the Giza plateau.

As I left, I gathered garbage as usual. The two little darlings came up and asked for flags and I gave them my last four. Well, up comes this boy who has been asking for balloons for days, and I have always said *bokra,* tomorrow. He wanted a flag. But I had given my last flags to the girls.

"*Bokra,*" I said once more.

"Ohhhhh, you no good," he said, wagging his finger at me. "You always say *bokra, bokra.*"

He's right. The embassy has not sent anything like Christian had inferred. I'll have to call. It's a pain in the neck not having a phone in my room. I have to go to Bono for everything.

I sat and watched the people for a while before exiting, trying to smell the roses. I have always had a hard time stopping whatever I was doing, to look around me.

I caught a cab down the road. My laundry from this morning was done, but they couldn't find the laundry from three days ago.

Bono and I went down to the laundry in the basement to look, and is this hotel ever on its last legs! Everything is breaking down, old and dirty. A man was fixing one of the elevators. It did not look like a professional job. I hope the elevator doesn't plummet me to earth one day. But then again, the guy who fixed my glove would not have looked professional beside a North American sewing shop, but his work was first rate.

Only floors two, four and six are fully operational in this hotel. If a guy could get it for nothing, sink half a million into it, it would be phenomenal, with more than 300 rooms.

Day 32 in the desert—The sand was howling that day my friend, or, how to sandblast your face in one easy step

"What is my name?"

Hung-over like a coon dog. Went to the Ace club last night, the Germans were there, with another guy, and a Canadian guy named Daryl, married to a much younger Egyptian woman, good looking and no accent when speaking English. He's from Calgary. He said he has a blog, and will put me in it. He asked for my journal, said he'd put it on the net after he edited it. I said *I* had to edit it first. He had a hard time understanding what I was doing, like he was waiting to discover the real reason. It's tough to fathom, I guess. I'm no pyramid nut. I did explain the embrace to him, and I think he got it.

I got back late, had a beer and went to sleep. I didn't think I drank that much, but when I left the pyramids today I was beat. It might have had something to do with the 50 mile an hour winds blasting sand all over the place.

I cleaned the Sphinx area, and then went up to Khafre. I was lucky enough that the kid who said I was a bad man, always saying '*bokra, bokra*,' approached me and I gave him my last two Canada pins, putting my finger to my lips and whispering "shhhh" conspiratorially to him, cautiously looking left and right.

Then another kid came up to me.

"What is my name?" he asked me.

It took me a moment, but I remembered it.

"Islam."

"What is my name?" asked the kid I gave the pins to.

"Ahmed."

Both kids were very happy, smiling broadly. All it took to bring happiness and joy, was for me to remember their name. Once again, that's a power that must come with some level of responsibility. There's a lesson in that. Simple acknowledgment. Uncle Ben's lesson to Peter Parker—with great power comes great responsibility.

I grabbed two bags from The Eternal Pile—also called the "pile that will always be unless I do something"—and took it up to the Khafre garbage area. By the time I was contemplating going to Menkaure, the sand in the wind was already ripping my eyes out. I saw a little pit with garbage in it, (every little pit has garbage in it) and I decided to clean it instead of braving the desert between the pyramids.

Strangely, Walid came by, way out of his jurisdiction. I have never seen him so far away from the Sphinx. We exchanged greetings, and he walked to the back of Khafre. I wonder what he was doing?

I took a few bags to the dump area with the wind just whistling, threatening to rip the bags out of my hands, or knock all 200 pounds of me to the ground. I met Froggy, and then the jokester Ashram who I am beginning to really like. We discussed my troubles with security.

"I work here my whole life and I meet you once," said Ashram. "Or I not meet you. They don't know what to do. You are different."

Around 11:30 the wind became just too much, and I said to hell with it. Standing next to one pyramid, you could not see another. I felt sorry for the tourists who had designated one day of their vacation to the pyramids, and had to be there regardless of the wind. It reminded me of the windstorm in the movie Laurence of Arabia.

Walking home, someone yelled out my name from a café. I looked in, but didn't recognize anybody, and nobody was waving. Then further on Ahmed's buddy Mr. Abd el Fattah called out to me, and I went to join him and his friends for tea. They bought some food but I was absolutely beat, yawning away, and was able to excuse myself without insulting anyone. I think. The cigarette smoke made me nauseous.

People are so friendly here, and I don't think anybody resents me picking garbage. I do make sure not to judge, and not to say anything negative. I try, anyway. As I told Daryl last night, nobody asked me to come here.

I bought six waters on my way out, and took a cab back. I gave the cabbie a twenty-pound note. He had agreed to ten, but he tentatively gave me a fiver back. He watched me closely as he offered it to me, gauging my reaction to see if he could get away with it. I let him keep 15, what the hell, the difference of one dollar.

I bought some whiskey today for 70 pounds. When I got it back to the hotel last night I showed it to Fatih, who then very expertly flipped it upside down quickly and examined the bottom.

"It's gooood," he said. The label was confusing, made in Scotland, by Egyptians? I don't think so.

Day 33 in the desert—tired, need sleep, wasting away

"I say nothing, because nobody asked me to come here."

I called home this morning. I hadn't received an e-mail or phone call for some time. Linda's brother Laurence answered and said everybody was sleeping. He woke Linda and she called me back, half-asleep. The last e-mail was "I love you, come home," but she told me this morning that she alternates between missing me, and being angry with me. She still doesn't get it!

But then again, a Trashman shouldn't judge.

On the way to the Sphinx I tried to drop off my memory card at a photo shop to get the pictures developed for Saman, but the store clerk indicated he couldn't do it. He spoke no English. When I left the area to go back to Siag at the end of my day, I popped in again, and an English-speaking guy was there. They can do it after all. However they need my camera, so I have set it up that I can drop off my camera each day there, and pick it up on the way back. Now I can take pictures to and from work, just not on site.

I was talking to an Australian woman in line to get in this morning, when I looked up and saw Joel, without Nicholas. I assumed Nicholas was back at their hotel, sleeping off the night before.

"Is she with you?" asked Joel, tilting his head toward the Australian woman.

"Yup. Picked her up last night," I said.

"News to me," said the woman.

"I'm going in to take some more pictures before I go home," he said, smiling. I assumed Nicholas was back at their hotel, sleeping off the night before.

I gave entrance Ali the whiskey I picked up yesterday.

"Keeping the troops happy?" Joel asked, as I handed Ali the brown bag.

"Whiskey," I said.

"That should keep them happy for a week," he said.

Which is all I have left.

I took photos of Joel as he asked, and then had him take some photos of me that he'll send to me later.

Mohawk walked by just then and I introduced them to each other, then Mohawk and I walked down to the front of the Sphinx area so I could begin work.

I saw Walid, and he just waved to me. I don't think he likes the flak he is probably getting for not doing his job. Then I saw the Lady in the Hat, always a bummer. I decided not to do the wall, leave it to the Lady in the Hat and her crew. Walid came up and asked for a bag, which I gave him, the Lady in the Hat watching from a distance.

I worked my way up the side of the Sphinx and back again, and left two bags behind security. There's a litter of puppies at that garbage site. I've tried to pet them, but they're afraid of people. I'm sure nobody feeds them, but they don't look like they're starving.

I've seen many dogs in the time I have been here, but I have yet to hear one bark. Perhaps barking dogs get eaten faster, Darwin's theory of natural selection at work.

I do know the Lady in the Hat is absolutely terrified of dogs. If one comes close to her, she recoils like a vampire from sunlight. This is her kryptonite.

Then over to Menkaure, I worked the temples, and took two bags and put them away by Khafre.

I sat with Bolla and Mahmoudy and had a coke.

"You look tired," said Bolla, looking concerned. "Your eyes fell."

Ali came up on his camel, and also expressed concern over my health.

"When you come here, you strong man," he said, striking a body-builder pose, "but you look weak now."

"I *am* tired," I admitted.

"I'm worried about you. You friend now, you not tourist."

I know I've lost weight, but didn't know I looked that bad. I have been feeling rundown lately, and the sandstorm yesterday was a killer. Also, I haven't been eating like I should. I miss Maharab and his wonderful food.

Two more bags from the temples and I saw Ali again. He again invited me to his house. I said maybe tomorrow or the day after.

"My mother wants to meet you," he said.

Then he leaned over his camel, and with a grin that would make the Cheshire Cat jealous, said "Promise?" I had to laugh at that.

I went to see Mohamed Cheoh, who offered me tea.

"Can I bring a camera with me to work?" I asked him.

"You will have to talk to Kamal Wahid."

Two young women came in. One was the daughter of the Ambassador from Canada. They were from Montreal. I gave them my CFC card to give to the Ambassador. They were wholly unimpressed by me, and probably threw the card away.

Then I went outside and met several Egyptian archeologists.

"Where is your dig?" asked a female archeologist named Sawsan. I guess I looked like I had been digging.

"All over," I said.

"Mr. Bruce is making a statement about what Egyptians should be doing for themselves," chimed in Egyptian archeologist Hassan.

Sawsan and Hassan both seemed a little defensive about the rubbish issue.

"I say nothing," I said, "because nobody asked me to come here."

"Mr. Wahid has some plans in place," said Sawsan, "including a sign to tell people not to litter, and a fine for littering."

I hope 'fine for littering' doesn't mean the poor vendors will be subject to more abuse. I have many ideas that could help, having been here for so long on the front lines of garbage. I would love it if they asked my advice.

Hassan grabbed my hand and Sawsan's hand, and put them together.

"I now pronounce you man and wife," he said, laughing. I guess he noticed some chemistry between us, as I had. I'm sure every husband and every wife has felt it with someone other than their spouse. Ignore it, and it may haunt you. Give in to it, and you go down a slippery slope. The curse of being an animal, I guess. It has happened many times in my life. Most times I ignore it, or if it's stronger I fight it. But not always. I wasn't always married.

Once, drunk in the French Quarter of New Orleans with two college buddies, Billy and Darren, I left them in a bar and went for a walk for some fresh air. I saw a voodoo shop on Canal Street. Curious, I went in. A beautiful black woman was standing behind the counter, and the electricity between us was palpable. I was drawn to her!

We spoke maybe two sentences to each other, and then spent five minutes kissing and groping each other. I disengaged, said goodby with a lingering look, and went back to the bar, never to see her again.

I saw Billy standing outside.

"Darren's past out," he said, laughing. "The tourists are taking turns getting their picture taken with him."

Looking inside, I could see Darren slumped down in his chair, his chin resting on his chest, glasses askew. A young man had his arm across Darren's shoulder, as his buddy took a picture.

"Our friend in New Orleans," said the photographer.

"We better go wake him up," I said to Billy.

I asked Mr. Kamal Wahid if I could bring a camera.

"What for?" he asked tersely.

"To take pictures of the people I have met," I said.

He said something that ended in 'journalist.'

"It's all good," I said.

"Not now, we'll see," he said with finality. I'm hoping that he will come to understand, quickly, that I mean absolutely no harm.

I made my way out by the Sphinx. A security guy came up and introduced himself.

"Do you remember me," he asked?

"Yes."

"Do you need anything?"

"*La shokrun. Quice. Quice.*" No, thank you. I'm fine. I'm fine.

"*Shokrun,*" he said, shaking my hand. He had been talking to the Lady in the Hat.

I was carrying a bunch of litter in my hands near the exit, and I heard "Canada" in the distance. Looking toward the Sphinx I saw two young girls in bright clothing, wearing the hijab. Perhaps in their early teens, they are vendors selling postcards and pyramids.

They were waving goodby to me enthusiastically, with wide-open smiles and sparkling eyes. What an embrace!

I waved back. *"Bokra, enshallah,"* I yelled out. Tomorrow, God willing.

"Bokra," they replied in unison. Tomorrow.

Out I went and was approached by a cabbie. I didn't recognize him at first. It was the guy who guessed my nationality for five pounds, Guessman, all smiles. He waited for me while I dealt with the photo issue.

Day 34 in the desert—tired and hot, friendships

"Write something from your heart."

What a day. I finally spoke with Linda at 5:30. She had trouble getting through since four. Great talk, everybody is well and I'll be home soon. These phones are right screwed up. I was sitting here drinking beer and watching television and I got a phone call.

"There is a message for you."

"Is it from the Canadian Embassy?" I asked.

"Yes."

So they sent it up, and it was from Ahmed El Nagger.

'Call me as soon as you can, about an interview.'

I called down for Egypt-Israeli war vet Hassan, and he brought me his cell phone. I have an interview at five today with Ahmed's father. I sent my clothes to be washed in case he wants a picture on site tomorrow. First interview, after day 34. If I had quit at day 31 . . . ?

I waved to Ali as I approached the entrance. More and more people are recognizing me and saying hi. Cars are honking on my route. I get asked at least twenty times a day, still, about what I am doing and why, and today was no exception.

"What, are you going to pick up garbage?" a guard asked as I pulled a garbage bag out of my backpack.

"Yes."

I cleaned the Sphinx area, and then went up to Khafre via the left side of the Sphinx. Egyptians just seem to love it when they see me working. One father with three young kids picked up a few pieces of paper and a pop can and put it in my bag, smiling broadly, and giving me the thumbs up. I wonder what he will tell his children. He spoke not a word to me.

I went to Menkaure and filled two bags, some of the guards said hi. One didn't.

"What is in your bag?" he demanded, but the others set him straight.

I went back to dump off the bags, and a young guy sitting down called me over to text a message to his girlfriend. I did, a wonderful break. Hassan the koshery man came running by.

"Bruce, koshery."

"Two minutes, Hassan."

But the kid wanted a long message. I felt myself getting a little miffed by his demands, but pushed it away, and did my best. Was I glad!

The kid called Hassan over and bought me koshery and a Pepsi, even though I said I didn't need a Pepsi.

The day he met his girlfriend that I was texting, Andrea from Spain, was the day he bought his first camel. On the day she left him to go back to Spain, his camel died, *with him on it.* Camel and Egyptian hit the dirt and the Egyptian broke his back. He showed me his brace, and said he has some pins in his spine. I can understand back problems.

I guess when it comes to buying camels, it's *Caveat emptor—* Let the buyer beware.

"The doctor told me not to work for a year," he said. "But I must work."

He has to work to survive. He works with his Dad at the pyramids, but I'm not sure I have ever met his Dad.

"Write something from your heart," he told me as I began the text message.

"Don't worry. I'll write something romantic."

"Tell her I miss her pussy."

"That's *not* romantic," I told him.

"What do you do in Canada?" he asked me as I was getting up to go back to work.

"I'm a fisherman."

"You must be a good swimmer."

"Yes, I am," I said, though that's merely a coincidence. I know many fishermen who can't swim at all. "I swim like a fish."

"I swim like a camel," he said.

Ali is insistent I see his mother tomorrow, which I have promised to do. I'll probably have to go see Rabihr tonight, big party. As long as I can be in bed by ten, I'm laughing.

"When you came here, you were strong," Ali said to me. "Now you are weak. It hurts me to see you like that."

"You must take two days off," he added, holding up the peace sign.

But that's not my plan.

As I was working across the parking lot up top, a security guy stopped me, wanted me to stop doing what I was doing, and go with him to see his supervisor. I was tired and not into that, but thankfully the old Egyptian vendors who call me *habibi,* 'dear one' were waving to me. I called one over, and he came on his camel to straighten the guy out.

I continued on my way, and heard a guy from England behind me explaining to someone that I was picking up garbage, and not getting paid for it. How on earth he knew that, I'll never know.

Then he caught up to me. He had a cute little two-year-old boy on his shoulders.

"Why do you do this?" he asked.

I had trouble answering why, not for the first time.

"It is my way to show my respect for Egypt and the Egyptians," I said. "To embrace them, and being at the pyramids, man's first great civilization, to embrace the people of the world."

It has come to mean so many things. Every day I work here, it's a little better, and that's symbolic of when we do something to make the world a little better place, it becomes a little better place. Every day we don't, it doesn't.

On my way out, one of the morning guys, I call him Smiley as he is always smiling at me and shaking my hand, met me with another guy and two kids. The other guy is a photographer at the Sphinx, taking photos of tourists.

"Before you come here, when I want to take photo, I have to . . ." he bent over and pretended to pick up a piece of trash. "Now it's clean when I get here."

It was tough to describe 'why?' today, so I better have a good answer for this interview. This has been plaguing me all day. I must prepare.

Ahmed called from downstairs.

I thought his father would be in the lobby and we'd do the interview in the bar, but instead we walked to Pyramid Road and took a microbus several miles to the newspaper building. His office is on the eighth floor with quite a view of the bustling city of Cairo.

I was worried that the story may take a bad turn. I did not want to criticize anyone. Ahmed was saying in the microbus that after the article was printed Kamal Wahid, Mohamed Cheoh and Dr. Zahi would be really angry.

"Some people need to be punished," he said with conviction.

This scared the be-geebers out of me, so I started the interview with a disclaimer.

"I'm not here to hurt anyone."

They seemed to get it. Ahmed translated for Al-Sayed, his father. A real nice guy, I can see where Ahmed gets it from.

"All of Egypt should be proud of the work done at the pyramids," I said.

"What!" exclaimed Ahmed, jumping out of his seat. "Do you really think *all of Egypt* should be proud? What are you saying?"

"Well . . ." I guess I overdid it.

Ahmed translated for his Dad, who raised his eyebrows and smiled at me.

Al Sayed asked me many questions and took about ten pages of notes. I think I conveyed myself well.

I thought about telling the story of 'rubbish people' but decided against it. He invited me to dinner on Friday, and I'm looking forward to it. He had a photographer come in and take many photos of us talking together.

The building looked like it had seen better days—the lift a little beat up, walls dingy in the halls—but a great atmosphere for an Arabic journalist. Somehow appropriate. A shiny new building would seem empty of life. This place was lived and worked in.

"We want to spend as much time with you as we can," said Ahmed. "We can watch a movie," he added, pointing to a television in his Dad's office.

But I was beat. It was eight o'clock and I wanted to get home. (home?)

Ahmed tried to get me to say something about Walid and Ramadan but I wouldn't. At the end of the day, they are such a small part of it all, hardly worth mentioning.

"It will be best story," Al-Sayed said when he shook my hand as we left. I could tell he really appreciated what I was trying to do. Like his son Ahmed, he 'got it.'

Back to the hotel at 8:30, I offered to pay for the taxi, but Ahmed would have none of it.

"My father says anything you have forgotten today, you can tell him on Friday when you come for dinner," said Ahmed.

I have clean clothes for tomorrow as Ahmed will meet me at noon at the wooden walkway to take photos of me in action.

Day 35 in the desert—hot and tired,
        showed Ahmed the skull

"No, gift."

A few things I forgot to tell Al-Sayed last night, George Bush and his belief in a pre-emptive strike, versus the pre-emptive embrace. And if ever there was a time for the great Embrace, it's now, during the worst economic disaster in two generations, with headlines in The Economist 'The End of Cheap Food.'

Last night, talking about Bashir in Sudan with Ahmed, I mentioned George W. Bush, and how he should be judged. Ahmed said this is what they call 'white man's justice.' It is my belief that most people in the west do not know how two-faced they appear to those in the Middle East.

"We know Bashir is a bad man, and should be charged by the International Court," said Ahmed. "But how can we agree to that, when George Bush and the United States went against the United

Nations and invaded Iraq? If Bashir should be charged, so should Bush. How many people are dead because he invaded Iraq?"

Getting Bush charged by the International Court should be an easy matter, as I can't see who would oppose it. Those who think he's innocent should welcome the chance for exoneration as much as those who think he's guilty would welcome a conviction. Only those who consider him guilty yet still approve of his war crimes would be against charges being laid. Who will admit to that?

I saw Mohawk early.

"I think I will go to work in Libya," he said. "I will make more money there."

He'll leave his wife and child for three months, then come back for 15 days.

"Maybe someday I move my family to Libya."

That put things in perspective for me. Linda is angry at me for leaving for a month and a half, and she wants for nothing. Mohawk will leave for three months at a time without batting an eye, leaving his wife and child with his parents in Egypt, not the affluent community of Hendersonville where, did I mention, Linda wants for nothing.

Yesterday a camel operator I call 'Saman 2', my friend since I convinced a Canadian to take a ride on his camel, told me the Australian girl I met at the Sphinx gate with Joel went for a camel ride with him.

"Tried to buy me. She wanted sex," he said. "Her husband died long time ago."

"Did you . . .?"

"Why? You have sex, and she have AIDS, you kill yourself," he said, shrugging.

"You buy ticket to get in?" he asked, changing the subject.

"Yeah."

"First he say you no need ticket. Then he change his mind, huh?"

"Yeah."

"Egyptian way," he said, shrugging his shoulders again.

Later that day a horseman said he had a Polish woman stay with him for a month once.

"Fuck every day. Every day eat, drink, and fuck."

I guess not all Egyptians are the same.

Today I ran into the same guy.

"I get married in one month," he said. "Then I will never leave my wife like you. I will have sex every night."

I was cleaning and Ramadan was doing his lazy gig. I offered him a bag and he finally came over and took it. I had pretty much finished the Sphinx area by that time.

A man on a camel called to me, and told me some bags left on the horse path to the Sphinx needed to be removed because the horses would trample them, spreading the garbage on the sand.

"They wanted to go home at the end of the day," he told me, "so they left it."

I assumed, making an ass out of me, for sure, that 'they' meant Ramadan and Walid.

"Tell Ramadan to move it," said the camel man.

I tried, but he speaks no English, so the camel man went and told him that he would call the boss and complain if he didn't move it. Ramadan went and moved the bags out of the path of the horses, but didn't take it to the pit where it should go.

As I was working uphill, Walid yelled out to me from the pit, and crossed his hands like they were tied, and then flattened them and ran one over the other, in a 'that's it, it's over' signal. I filled a bag and went down to the pit to see what he was on about.

It turns out they thought I left the bags there, and I thought they did, but it was somebody else. (The only answer to come to my mind was a Japanese tour group, with masks and tweezers.)

We figured it out and departed as friends again. Such a small misunderstanding. We have to work on that universal communicator, a universal Rosetta Stone.

Created in 196 BC, the Rosetta Stone was discovered by the French in 1799 at Rosetta, Egypt. The stone had a single passage in three different languages, Egyptian Hieroglyphs, Egyptian Demotic (letter writing) and classical Greek. From this stone the languages of ancient Egypt were finally decipherable.

The text of the stone is as mundane as its find was not. It is a government decree giving temple priests a break on their taxes.

In 1814, Thomas Young of England translated the demotic text, and started on the hieroglyphic portion of the stone. Many scholars worked on the translation, most notably Jean-Francois Champollion.

According to Wikipedia:

"From 1822 to 1824 the French scholar Jean-Francois Champollion greatly expanded on this (Thomas Young's) work and is credited as the principal translator of the Rosetta Stone. Champollion could read both Greek and Coptic, and figured out what the seven Demotic signs in Coptic were. By looking at how these signs were used in Coptic, he worked out what they meant. Then he traced the Demotic signs back to hieroglyphic signs. By working out what some hierpoglyphs stood for, he transliterated the text from Demotic (or older Coptic) and Greek to hieroglyphs by first translating Greek names which were originally in Greek, then working toward ancient names that had never been written in any other language. Champollion then created an alphabet to decipher the remaining text."

"In 1858, (nearly sixty years after discovery) the Philomathean Society of the University of Pennsylvania published the first complete translation of the Rosetta Stone."

At 45 inches high, 28 inches wide and 11 inches thick, the granite (actually pinkish-grey granodiorite, an igneous rock similar to granite) Rosetta Stone weighs about 1,700 pounds. It has been on display in the British Museum since 1802. In 2003 Dr. Zahi Hawass asked for the Rosetta Stone to be returned because "it is the icon of our Egyptian identity." In 2005 the Brits sent a replica to Egypt. Assuaged somewhat, Zahi Hawass said he would stop asking for a permanent return in exchange for a loan of the stone for three months. The Brits didn't fall for it. (Where are the German archeologists in all this?)

Three people today complained to me about the police wanting money. One vendor said he was getting kicked out because he did not pay the government yesterday.

"Government want money every day," he said.

Then two young brothers in their early teens came up and complained as well.

"Police always want money," one brother said in a disgusted tone—a now familiar refrain.

As he was saying it, I looked up and saw two men, well-dressed but not in uniform, harassing Nasser the Devout. One stood on either side of him, and Nasser's pockets were turned inside out. It would have been comical if it wasn't so tragic.

"Are *they* the police?" I asked the brothers, pointing to Nasser's antagonists.

"Yes."

It seems a shame, shaking down these poor people who barely make enough to live on. Oppressive. Rabihr has complained about the government every day, "fucking government," to the extent that I could see him being part of a plot to overthrow the current regime. It made me think of what Ahmed had said about some Egyptians not feeling like they are part of the country, being outside of the bribes and corruption. And we in the West whine about taxes.

I made a mental note to watch for those guys. I've been here over a month, and that's the first time I witnessed the extortion of the vendors, though I'm told it happens every day. I do remember my first day here, Nasser the Horseman, and his argument with a policeman.

The police always want money.

I planned on going to Menkaure, but I was filling a bag and worked on the rock wall beside the parking lot until I reached the garbage at Khafre. On my way, four policemen eating off the back of their truck offered me some food. The usual, pita bread, hot peppers, and many plastic bags of sauces and cheeses to dip it in, or scoop up. As I was eating the man who runs the Cave invited me for tea. So after I ate, I went for tea.

Not the usual suspects today at the Cave, but new guys. I didn't need to explain who or what I was, but they still had lots of questions. One is, of course, "Do you buy a ticket every day?" I cop to it, even though I know it makes many people think I'm rich, stupid, or both. *Ya big dummy!*

I finished the tea and was working toward the Khafre garbage site when a security man said the 'captain' wanted to see me. Another captain.

The captain was sitting in the back of a police car. He looked about 50 years old with a gray moustache and gray hair. He had an 'I'm the boss' attitude and I was worried I was in for another trip to see the Chief.

There are always four or five police vehicles in the big parking lot between Khufu and Khafre, usually with four people in the front, and four or five in the covered box of the truck. They all have automatic weapons.

"What is your name?" demanded the Captain.

"Bruce Benson."

"What country?"

"Canada."

"Where you stay?"

"Siag."

He waved his hand holding his almost finished cigarette with an inch of ash dismissively, shook his head and said "No Siag."

He didn't believe me!

"I have been here for five weeks," I said, and pulled out my room key that says 'Siag Pyramids Hotel.'

"*Tesah kamsah* (95) Sakkara Road," I said.

He talked with the man sitting next to him for a minute.

"Okay," he said, and shook my hand.

I picked trash along the front of Khafre until close to noon when I was to meet Ahmed. An Egyptian girl, maybe 18-20, came up and gave me a piece of strawberry shortcake in a wrapper. At first I thought she had some garbage, and opened my bag.

"No, gift," she said with a beautiful smile.

I ate it later at the coffee shop with Ahmed and Mr. Abd el Fattah.

Ahmed was right on time today, but he didn't have a camera. I understood that he would have a camera today, and was disappointed, but tomorrow he will have mine. I showed him many of the places I had cleaned, the two big piles of garbage, the bad place where I got into it with Ramadan, the tombs behind that, and especially the skull I found. We stepped over the barbed wire to get into that site, and soon realized there were four puppies trapped in there. They looked like the puppies I had seen at the garbage dump site behind the guardhouse to the left of the Sphinx.

"They weren't here the last time I was here," I said.

"The mother must have carried them here," said Ahmed, "in her mouth."

There is no water, and they are too small to get out. I wonder if the mother can carry them out, as they look heavy now. Three were really cowering, and one was growling.

"Be careful, it might bite you," said Ahmed.

Not wanting to have a dog bite in Egypt, we walked around to the other side and Ahmed jumped in. Then I followed. The growling puppy was now hiding on the side opposite the skull, so I reached in and pulled it out. I put it on top of the structure we had climbed over to get in.

The hole in the back of the head was the size of a lime. I had initially thought the person must have been murdered, or fallen and struck his head. When King Tutankhamen's skull was first examined, he had a similar hole in the back of his head. Like me, scientists speculated he was murdered, until a CT scan in 2005 found the hole was most likely from the mummification process. Had I found the head of a mummy?

"Can you take a picture of it tomorrow?" I asked Ahmed, again wishing he had brought a camera today.

"Why don't you put it in your bag?"

"I might damage it," I said.

Ahmed reached down to grab a small plastic bag, debris that had blown in since Mr. Sadek and I had cleaned the area.

"I can wrap it in one of my big bags," I said.

"I will put it in Mr. Abd el Fattah's car," said Ahmed. "I won't tell anyone about it until you are back in Canada."

He left and I went to Menkaure.

Picking up garbage at Menkaure, I started to worry that there must be a seriously hefty penalty for smuggling skulls out of the site, and grew very concerned bad things might happen to Ahmed or myself. Images of Ahmed and I chained to a wall in a dungeon came to mind. I thought I would e-mail Ahmed to take it back.

I needn't have worried, as when I saw him for tea, he said his colleagues asked him right away what he had.

"I said 'a skull,' and gave it to Kamal Wahid," said Ahmed. "He gave it to someone else and said 'examine it.'"

Ahmed told them *he* had found it, but I think the question will arise 'where?' and if he tells them, they will ask 'what were you doing there?' I have a reason—picking garbage—but Ahmed does not.

I'll e-mail him to come up with a good story. Ahmed said he would give me credit for the find after I leave Egypt.

"I can see it now," I kidded him, "the headline in the National Geographic Magazine—'The Ahmed Skull, biggest discovery in 500 years!'"

"You know what I'll say then?" I added. "Those damn Egyptians!"

Working around Menkaure, a group of people came by, asking questions. I think the policeman here, an older fellow with grey hair and a moustache, had told them what I was doing.

"It is wonderful to see you doing this. We were just commenting on how much garbage is around."

They are from Kenya, except one woman from France whom, we discovered in discussion, was one restaurant away from me the night Nicholas Sarkozy got elected President of France, and I got tear-gassed. Such a small world.

Linda and our friend Irena had gone to London for the weekend of the election. After I put the kids to bed, I wandered down to my favorite Irish pub in *Le Place de la Bastille*. There had been dire warnings of possible riots, and I was curious.

As I got closer to the pub, my eyes started to itch. It gradually worsened.

"Man, are your eyes bothering you?" I asked the guy next to me as I sat at the bar, rubbing my eyes.

"That's tear-gas," he said. "They're doing all the streets."

I had seen hundreds of people milling about as I approached the pub, so after a few pints I went for a walk around *La Bastille* to gawk at the rioters. It was hugely disappointing, as curiosity-seekers far outnumbered rioters. I saw the odd punk toss a brick at the odd window, but that was all. However, the police tear-gassed all the streets leading to *La Bastille*, one at a time, and then started over. I managed to quickly get back in the pub and close the doors before the gas hit us. Still, a lot of gas leaked in, making for a foggy, teary-eyed night.

On the way down to the Sphinx I said hello and goodbye to the regulars that work the road, and I encountered the biggest group of ten-year-olds yet. They saw me picking up garbage and heard me speak English, and were all over me. Then they heard me speak Arabic and things went wild. Every one of them had to high-five me, and tell me their name. I had to be loud to be heard. The teacher took some pictures of me with all forty or so kids. The future of Egypt.

Out the gate I went, and saw Walid, the young man who befriended me what seems years ago. He came up to me and started a guilt trip.

"You have forgotten me," he pouted.

"No, I haven't."

I largely ignored him as I was taking photos of the Sphinx gate, with the Sphinx and pyramids in back.

"Come with me," said Walid, when he saw what I was doing. "You get good photo of Sphinx from the roof."

I followed him to the roof of a gift shop across the street, where there was a good view, but I think the sun was wrong.

I had arranged to meet Ali at the KFC and then ride his camel to his place, so I went back down to the entrance and sat on the curb of the sidewalk to wait for him. An old Egyptian man next to me offered a sip of his tea.

"*Quice*," I said. Excellent.

Day 36 in the desert—This is the embrace, the commonality of all religions, and my way of expressing it

"You must share."

I dropped my camera off this morning at Konica, and had Saman 2 translate for me.

"Why don't you just take camera into pyramids?" Saman 2 asked me. "Be strong in your heart," he said softly, clenching his fist. "Don't be afraid."

I didn't want to tell him I was getting Ahmed to take photos for me. However, Ahmed didn't show up. I hope he's not in trouble for the skull, already rotting in an Egyptian jail. I'll check my e-mails later.

I avoided the area by the wall that is Walid and Ramadan's responsibility, and when I left at the end of my day I walked by, and sure enough it was a mess. The two of them were sitting in the shade, relaxing. I will not go there tomorrow, then maybe the next day see what it looks like. The guy in the Sphinx Temple does a good job, but then the tourists do not make the mess, it's the Egyptians.

I'm winding down now, feeling really tired. I think it's the food I've been eating. It does not agree with my stomach. I remember an English couple some time ago saying that I must be used to it by now, but somehow I don't think so.

A man on a camel approached me as I was picking up garbage.

"I have an idea," he said in good English. "If they charge everyone who works here five or ten pounds each day, they can hire enough people to clean it up.".

"But government doesn't listen to me," he added, raising his arms up, shrugging his shoulders. *It's hopeless,* said the gesture.

"I'll pass it on and say it was my idea," I said laughing.

"No, no, no, that's okay," he assured me.

Ronald Reagan has a famous quote, "It's amazing what you can get done when you don't care who gets the credit."

I met a Canadian from Ponoka, Alberta moments later. John Van Doesburg is an expert on water management systems, in Egypt to speak at a conference on that very subject.

"We in the West have bleached our water so much that we now need to drink bottled water," said John, "whereas the Egyptian's stomachs are so hardened to the bacteria in the water, it doesn't bother them."

That might explain my digestive problems.

We talked of many things, including the oil boom in Alberta. John is probably a conservative, as he talked about "the conspiracy of the east." I avoided mentioning politics.

"So you're picking up garbage," said John.

"Yeah," I said looking around me, "it's a lot better than it was when I first got here."

"I don't know, it looks about the same as it did last year."

"Go ahead, make my day."

"No, maybe there *is* less," he backtracked slightly. "Perhaps the wind has taken it away."

The camel man rode past as we were talking, and I told my fellow Canuck about his idea to clean the Giza Plateau.

"But the government doesn't listen to me," the Egyptian said again.

"The story of my life," I said, thinking of the Universal Declaration of Human Duties and Responsibilities. I've been pushing it and pushing it. I've sent both French and English versions to Canada's Standing Committee on Foreign Affairs and International Trade, met with many of the Members of Parliament on that committee. I've personally handed bilingual copies to two leaders of the Liberal Party, and even traveled to New York to meet Iceland's Ambassador to the United Nations, Hjalmar Hanneson, all in an effort to have the Declaration on the table at the United Nations. People listen, but that's about all.

My 'guide' from my early days was talking to me at the end of the first little wall near Khufu.

"As soon as you go, there will be lots of rubbish," he said.

Maybe, who knows? But The Doubt was feeding.

Later I saw the 'guide' and another weasel that works the front, both hassling a tourist. They were hounding him for money as he hurried to get away. It was bad. That type of behavior should not be tolerated, and I will mention it to Al-Sayed on Friday.

Soon after a truck drove by with an Egyptian standing in the box and yelling, thumbs up, chasing The Doubt away.

I saw Rabihr, who once again invited me over anytime.

"I think you have something in your mind, but *don't* have something in your mind."

He was referring to the time he asked me for money. I have almost forgotten it. I should forget it. I've borrowed money many times from countless people in a myriad of circumstances. Perhaps I should have just given him the money, I don't know. I might see him tonight.

Years ago when I was living on Albert Street, in the red-light district of Winnipeg, I asked a friend to lend me two dollars to buy breakfast at the Royal Albert Hotel.

"You don't have any money?"

"No, I'm broke."

"Jesus Christ!" he said in disgust. He threw two dollars onto the floor of my apartment and walked out the door.

Hungry, I bent down and picked it up.

On the way to Menkaure I saw some men digging a trench. Well, there was maybe one guy digging a trench, and thirty, I am not kidding, pretending they were digging. About eight guys were in the process of making tea on three small fires.

Just past the entrance to Menkaure, I saw they were excavating right next to the pyramid. I was curious so I went closer to watch. This youngish, well-dressed Egyptian in sunglasses approached me.

"You!" he yelled. "Step back! Go away!"

So I stepped back. He came at me.

"Step back! Go away!" he said angrily, putting his hand on my shoulder and giving me a rough shove.

This infuriated me, but confused me as well. Egyptians can be loud and sometimes verbally aggressive, but I have never been shoved by one, except when Ramadan wanted me to do his work. And that was more of a nudge.

"Don't shove!" I said, raising my voice.

I was thinking of my options, when he started laughing.

"You don't remember me?" he asked. It was Hassan, an archaeologist I had met at the head office of the big boys, Kamal Wahid and Mohamed Cheoh. He was the one who put my hand and the beautiful Egyptian archaeologist's hands together and declared us married.

I got punk'd.

Hassan explained they had just discovered another layer of phaeronic rock, meaning Menkaure had one more level hidden beneath the sand, being unearthed for the first time.

Looking down into the excavation I could see workers slowly removing the sand. The layer of newly exposed rock had a reddish hue, unlike the rest of the pyramid that was yellowish grey. How many thousands of years had the base layer of the pyramid been hidden in the sands of the Sahara? And there I was watching it being exposed.

"Do you think there could be even more layers?" I asked Hassan.

"I doubt it," he said. "This is the last one."

I went around the corner to work another side of Menkaure, and Hassan came by later and helped me.

"I like what you are doing," he said. "I tried to do something about the rubbish before. You get some support, but most people don't care."

I was invited for tea again by the tea guy at the Cave. His name is also Hassan.

"Can I have a bag?" asked Samba, one of Rabihr's friends, as I sat enjoying my tea.

"It's for garbage, not for home?" I asked.

"Yes, for garbage."

When I gave it to him, he folded it up and tucked it in his pocket. I picked up some empty tea cups that were strewn all about, and motioned to him to put it in the bag I had just given him.

"No, it's for my home," he said, completely contradicting what he'd said earlier.

"I don't want to give you a bag for home," I patiently explained, "because then everyone will want one."

"Can I have a bag?" asked a woman to my left, as if on cue.

"She wants a bag, give her a bag," said another guy.

Samba saw my words were true, and immediately gave me the bag back. Then another guy told me to have a nice day, and motioned for me to leave, as an argument ensued amongst the others. I imagine between those who wanted to get something from me, and those who didn't.

I left and started picking rubbish around the corner, when who should appear to help, but the Coca Cola man, Hya-hya. He silently helped me for a while.

I was not happy with the way the scene had played out at the Cave, so it was wonderful to get this show of support from Hya-hya. Immediately I thought of Tomato, the old Indian in A Season for Skufty. Hya-hya and Tomato have something in common. They both came over without a word and started helping. There is something noble there.

Snowshoeing side by side with a friend one day, we both walked through the deep snow, each leaving the thin trail for the other to take. I didn't notice it until my buddy pointed it out.

"It's like there's some unwritten code we both understand," he said

I filled a bag and dropped it off at the Khafre garbage site. Mr. Abdutowab was washing his arms, getting ready to leave for the day. I hadn't seen him all day, and have no idea where he was cleaning, if he was. (Don't judge, Bruce.)

I worked my way along the causeway down to the Sphinx. A guard sitting on the edge of a pit motioned me over. We both climbed down fifteen feet and cleaned it up. He made sure we left the pop cans the guards use for heating tea, and the cardboard they burn for warmth. I guess this pit's a good place to hang in the middle of the night if you're a guard.

Further down I came to another pit. There were four people on the wall surrounding it.

"Can you watch my backpack?" I asked them, and climbed in.

When I came up there were many more people gathered around.

"What are you doing?" asked an Egyptian guide with a German couple. "Are you a believer in the phaeronic religion?"

"This is the embrace, the commonality of all religions, and my way of expressing it."

The German man was making motions indicating that I pick up what the Egyptians throw down. He showed me how he puts trash in his bag around his waist, and pointed to his head, I believe to show the Egyptians are crazy, or he is smart. I was starting to think he thought *I* was crazy.

As he left, he said something in German to his guide.

"What did he say?" I asked.

"He said 'don't let people laugh at you for what you are doing.'"

Nobody has laughed at me yet, as far as I know.

Down to the Sphinx, and there I saw Saman.

"Where's my picture?" he yelled at me from a few hundred yards. As I walked toward him I thought of asking him why he doesn't say "how are you?" instead, but forgot. It reminded me of the joke 'where's my cookie' in Sharp-eyes, the book I wrote about aboriginal entitlements.

My friend's Dad told him this joke when he was in grade four, and wanted an increase in his allowance.

There's this guy, goes to the doctor. He says to the doctor, "I don't know what's wrong with me, but I'm getting skinnier every day."

The doctor says, "You got a tapeworm, come back tomorrow with an apple and a cookie."

The guy leaves, and comes back the next day with an apple and a cookie. The doctor says "Okay, now pull down your pants and bend over." The guy pulls down his pants and bends over. The doctor shoves the apple up his butt. He waits a few minutes. Then he shoves the cookie up his butt.

This goes on for two weeks. Every day it's the same. The doctor shoves the apple up his butt, waits a few minutes, then shoves the cookie up his butt. Finally, the doctor says "Okay. Tomorrow bring an apple and a hammer."

The guy's a little nervous about the hammer, but he brings the apple and the hammer the next day anyway. The doctor says "Pull down your pants and bend over." So the guy pulls down his pants and bends over.

The doctor shoves the apple up his butt, waits a few minutes, waits a few more minutes, waits a few *more* minutes. . .

The tapeworm sticks his head out of the guy's butt and shouts "Where's my fucking cookie!"

Wham! The doctor hits the tapeworm on the head with the hammer.

Human nature in a nutshell. Once you get something for even a little while, some treat or privilege, it's not long before you start to think it's your absolute right. Usually a hammer of some sort comes down to put things back in perspective.

I walked around and saw the lazy Ramadan and Walid had done nothing, and I talked with Saman.

"Are you hungry?" he asked.

"No," I replied, but then I saw someone waving to me from a distance.

"Is that Maharab?" I asked, and started walking toward him.

"Yes," said Saman.

Maharab had only a few scraps of bread left, but he mixed some of his strong cheese and tomatoes together, gave me the scraps to work with, and peeled two eggs. Delicious, but the bowl he mixed it all up in looked very unsanitary. I was thinking of what the Canadian had said earlier in the day about bleaching water, wondering what my insides would think of this.

"I ask if you are hungry and you say no," said Saman, smiling. "But when you see Maharab, you are hungry."

I bought a small bottle of water, took a sip, and four kids hanging around all asked for some at the same time. I took another sip and gave it to them.

"You must share," I told them. They must have been thirsty as it was gone in no time, but they did share.

"See. You believe in the embrace too."

Day 37 in the desert—tougher every day

"I am Muslim. I am good Muslim."

I really felt down this morning, downright depressed. I'm feeling alone, missing the family, and doubting myself again.

Then I saw a show on TV about American wrestlers in Iran.

"The people here are nothing like we were made to believe back in the States," said one of the wrestlers, looking somewhat mystified. "They are wonderful people."

It brought tears to my eyes. The wrestler's experience must be like the East Germans visiting West Germany and discovering that all the rumors that their government said were false, were in fact true.

I remember a story of an old East German woman, allowed to travel because of her extreme age. She stood in a West German supermarket, weeping at the abundance denied to her family in the East.

My digestive system is still acting up, but I only have three more days to go.

I was in bed by eight last night, and slept off and on until six this morning. I needed all of it.

As I left Siag this morning, I saw this hefty woman dressed up like a hooker, leaving in a car with two guys. She must be one of the women who do the lap dance stuff upstairs. It reminded me of strippers in Canada, traveling with security.

I have to admire the morals of this Muslim society. I have felt safe my entire stay here in this very populous city. Would I feel so safe in Detroit? Or Chicago? And while most women wear the hijab, and some wear the veil, they also appear to feel safe wherever they go.

I'm reminded of a woman I met on the overnight train from Aswan to Cairo when I was here two years ago with Jake. She had both American and Egyptian citizenship, and was the principal of an American school in Cairo.

"I may wear the hijab, but I can go anywhere I like in Egypt, at any time of day," she said. "I am safe in Egypt, but not in America."

I avoided the wall again, left it to the boys, and saw Walid. He headed uphill, and I saw him arguing with someone later. I spotted an area near Khufu that needed some TLC, then dropped two bags off at Khafre. I had a late breakfast from Mahmoudy.

Camel Ali asked "today?" and I said yes. So I will go to Rabihr's and then to Ali's. Perfect. I can still be home by ten.

I saw Mohamed Cheoh and Hassan the archaeologist with many other people at Menkaure. Hassan saw me and smiled and waved.

"Don't touch," he said with a grin.

I filled two bags and was taking them back when the boys digging a trench called me over to have tea. Delightful, wished I had a camera.

One old-timer looking about 70 years old spoke to me in Arabic.

"He say you are the loveliest man in Egypt," interpreted the man who invited me for tea. Fifty-six years old, with a little English, he has worked the pyramids since he was six. Fifty years. What did this place look like in 1959, the year Castro marched on Havana?

"What do you think of Obama?" he asked me.

"What do you think?"

"Bush bad, Obama good."

I was walking back to Khafre to dump the bags when a guy on a camel came up to me. We had spoken many times in passing, always him on a camel, me on the sand.

"My son, Caron, he likes you," he said, though I don't remember meeting the boy. But then there are so many children on the Giza plateau.

"Muslim is good," he said. "Maybe you become Muslim. Many people become Muslim. It is not hard to be Muslim." Trying to gently convert me, I guess.

I had a coke after dumping the bags, and talked with Mr. Abdutowab and another cleaner.

"Bring your sister to Cairo," said the other man. "I want to marry her."

"Dude, you don't know my sister."

Back to Menkaure and a guard asked me to clean the entrance to one of the Queen's temples behind the pyramid. I was walking to where I thought he was talking about when he shouted out, and came scrambling down the rock, to show me where he really meant. I could tell by his gesticulations he wanted me to clean an area I had cleaned yesterday, so I waited until he got close enough to see it was already clean.

"Ho-ho," he exclaimed, surprised. He smiled and gave me the thumbs up.

It reminded me of my sister-in-law asking me to clean her street in Hendersonville.

"Do you take requests?" she asked.

"Of course!"

I went back to Khafre to dump off some bags and grab a coke from Hya-hya. A group of 50 or so ten-year-olds gathered all around me. I was the center of attention once more. It took the teacher ten minutes to get them all moving, they were so excited to be there with me. Though there were many tourists milling about, I was the only one they seemed interested in.

I confidently spoke what little Arabic I could, and smiled and laughed. The Egyptians love to laugh.

It is a good thing that Egyptians have a sense of humor, and are always smiling and joking . . .

I met Maharab again on my way down to the Sphinx, had another super falafel, and then went to meet Saman and give him the photos.

I then went back up the hill toward Khafre to look for Ali. Just another day almost over . . . kind of boring . . . and then . . .

I saw these three kids, a boy and two girls—probably a brother and two sisters. They have known me for weeks.

"Are you Muslim?" the little girl asked.

I hesitated.

"*Shwya, shwya,*" said the boy, (little, little) which is probably a better description than I could have come up with.

"Are *you* Muslim?" I asked the little girl.

"I am Muslim," she said with an Arabic accent, shaking my hand softly and firmly. "I am good Muslim."

She looked not at me, but down to the sand, and then, off into the distance. *She meant it.*

Her jet black hair was tied in a pony tail, and she wore a clean red sweater over a yellow shirt, and jeans. Like almost everybody I have seen in Egypt, she was well groomed.

The conviction of her words, from one so young, surprised me. I pegged her age at eight, maybe ten years old.

I've always felt that the delivery of words, the tone of the voice, the timbre, can speak so much more than the actual words. If a picture can be worth a thousand words, then the *sound* of words must be worth a few hundred.

I knew, when I heard her say "I am good Muslim," that she wanted to be the best person she could possibly be, for her parents, presumably, and for her God. I knew she was full of love and kindness for everybody and everything, that she wanted peace on this earth, and for everyone to live a long happy life. She wanted fairness, and truth, and all that is good, like so many children all over the planet, like my own little girl Ally, who was a little whimpery when I left, yesterday and an eternity ago. I also knew that being born into relative poverty in Egypt, this little girl was unlikely to get it.

If the world that is prejudiced against Muslims could have seen her face, and heard her speak, I think it would have produced marvelous consequences. There was absolutely nothing but the goodness of childhood in that look, and that earnest voice. If only I could have filmed the little girl say "I am Muslim. I am good Muslim."

The hair on my arms stood on end, I was so moved. From the mouths of babes, they say. Any parent in the world would be proud.

The older boy and girl with her assured me that they were also good Muslims.

When I went up to Khafre, I couldn't see Ali so when I saw Mr. Abdutowab leaving, I left with him.

I grabbed my camera, and a cabbie who said he was a friend of Guessman caught me coming out of Konica and drove me 'home.'

I've been thinking about home a lot lately. Where the heart is?

"I do not like Egypt," said the cabbie. "The government is against the people."

He stopped short of Siag, so I could pay him out of sight of the police, because they would want a commission. The ever-present shakedown of the disenfranchised.

A person could endure poverty if there was social equality and justice.

Day 38 in the desert—a day of urine and feces, and beautiful children smiling

"He said you have already eaten stuff that I couldn't eat."

I went to Rabihr's last night. The cabbie dropped me off at the corner, and man, was it busy. Apparently they closed Pyramid Road because some famous Egyptian football player was going to see the Sound and Light Show at the pyramids.

I bumped into Ahmed, the guy I told to fuck off. He called Rabihr on his cell phone, who came to get me, thankfully on foot, not a motorcycle. Ahmed waited with me, then he showed up at Rabihr's later. Turns out he's a fine young man. He invited me to his sister's engagement party on Tuesday.

One thing I noticed walking to Rabihr's, camels seem to have a bounce in their step on the pavement or stone, but not in the sand.

I had wicked diarrhea this morning, and I finally took a few pills for it.

I gave my newspaper guy, Hassan, his photo today. He was happy to get it. Rabihr was happy to get his last night too.

Yesterday I asked if I could clean in the Sphinx area between the bars and the stone.

"Kamal Wahid say no."

As I left today, I could see it had been cleaned. It had not been cleaned any time prior that I'm aware of.

Going through Checkpoint Charlie this morning, day 38, a policeman called me over to his desk.

"Where is your passport?" he demanded.

"I leave it at my hotel in case I lose it."

He didn't seem convinced, but Mr. Smiles spoke up for me. I've seen that policeman many times before. He must know me.

I cleaned in front of the Sphinx and then along part of the wall. I kept looking for Mohawk, and had to keep reminding myself he had the day off. I sat down to write some notes, feeling depressed about the garbage, being away from home, and exhausted from a lack of nutrients due to my digestive problems.

Then three kids came up, brothers Islam and Ahmed, and friend Mohamed, all selling bookmarks. They all wanted to shake my hand, and say hi. Their smiles and happiness were contagious, and I cheered up.

I met a Japanese fellow named Kentura, and asked him to take my photo and send it to my e-mail. Mohamed, Rabihr the Elder's friend, offered to take a photo of the two of us together, but we both ignored him. I ignored him because I was asking Kentura for a favor, and didn't want Mohamed to ask him for money, making me an accomplice. I imagine Kentura ignored him because I did. Perhaps I made an ass of myself again.

I saw one of the men that cleans inside the Sphinx take out his penis, and with his back three feet from an older tourist woman, he urinated on the Valley Temple of Khafre, making no attempt to hide it. To the rest of the world this place is sacred, but for the Egyptian government, (because they are the ones who do not provide bathrooms and garbage cans) it is a trash-can and a toilet.

Which brings into question America's US $200 million donation for civil works this year alone. Is that money spent like the ten grand spent per month to keep the pyramids clean? In 2008, the Canadian government gave more than $17 million. As a Canadian taxpayer, I have my concerns. Does it all go to shakedowns, bribes and corruption? We must look into that.

Does the Minister of Culture in Egypt, responsible for the greatest heritage site in the world being full of garbage, human urine and feces, really deserve to be the chair of UNESCO? Ahmed the engineer told me Farouk Hosni is campaigning for just that position.

Seems every nook and cranny a person could fit into, is a toilet, every crevice a trash can for the 500 or so people who work at the pyramids. It's not their fault though, when you gotta go, you gotta go.

I constantly have to remind myself of the first rule of a Trashman.

Working my way up to Khafre, I heard a hissing sound. I looked up to see a stream of urine ten feet in front of me, coming out between two rocks of the Mortuary Temple of Khafre, about eight feet high. It appeared the person was going for distance. Trying to set a record? Had I been walking five seconds faster, maybe not stopped to pick up one piece of garbage, it would have hit me in the head! When I worked my way inside the temple, I saw there was a teenager with a young man, and two young women. I suspect the teenager. Egyptian tourists, not vendors.

I was despondent. What next? I felt really down, demoralized, like I was wasting my time.

Twenty seconds later a German woman, with no English, came up and shook my hand. She gave me the thumbs up, and two euros. She had no idea how much that meant to me at that time. There's the embrace again, it can mean so much more than it costs us. I do not mean the two euros. She didn't need to pay any attention to me at all! Her husband came up and gave me two more euros, I tried to refuse but he insisted.

"For ice cream," I think he said.

I filled a couple bags in the temples in front of Khafre, and while I was just finishing a plainclothes cop came up to me, identifying himself as a policeman. He showed me his gun on his hip, and gave me the thumbs up. He didn't ask for money.

Today must have been the busiest day I have ever seen, thousands and thousands and thousands of people.

A hundred feet from the exit an old man named Mohamed confronted me.

"Why? Why?" he kept on asking, loudly and aggressively, pointing at the garbage bag in my hand. But that is just their way, loud. In a minute he was giving me the rest of his tea, wanting to come to Canada, and pointing to his God, who approved of what I was doing.

It's 9:05 p.m., and I just got back from dinner at Ahmed's. I ate with Ahmed and his father. His mother Olphat and aunt Medea who prepared the food, ate elsewhere. They joined us later watching television. The food was great, but way too much. They must have pulled out all the stops, as I recognized some famous

Egyptian foods. You name it, they had it, including rabbit and duck. What a feast! I ate all I could, and then they coerced me into eating more.

They have a nice flat, but it's on the fifth floor with no elevator. My overworked and heavily abused legs were shrieking at me when we got there.

I looked at some photos on the mantel, Sayed identifying the people for me. There was a picture of a very beautiful Olphat, his wife, as a young woman. It reminded me of the picture Frank Wiens keeps in his wallet of his wife as a young woman, some sixty years ago. It's how they still see their wives, I imagine. Behind the eyes the person has not changed.

My stomach was beginning to bother me again, and I blamed it on the Pepsi we had before dinner. I vowed not to do that again. I told Ahmed I had experienced some digestive problems.

"It might be the concoction Maharab mixed up for me the other day," I said

"I told him to be careful, because your stomach is not like ours."

"What did he say to that?" I asked.

"He said you have already eaten stuff that I couldn't eat."

What has Maharab been feeding me?

I checked my e-mails, one from Ti and one from Jake. Ti got in a fight and has three days of some punishment, Jake figures he can beat me in basketball. Nothing from Linda or Ally.

Ahmed came home with me, and took my camera. I'll meet him at noon at the boardwalk and he'll follow me and take pictures. I'm glad, because I have decided I am not going against the wishes of Kamal Wahid. I have yet to bring a camera in when I am picking garbage. This may be splitting hairs, as Ahmed is bringing *my* camera in, but I can rationalize it away.

Ahmed, a romantic I discovered, told me he wanted Skufty to marry Susan. I didn't give away the ending.

He counted the empty beer bottles in my room one by one, though they are arranged in groups of five, which I showed him.

"Wow!" he exclaimed, pointing to the corner of the room, "There's even more cans."

"Forty-two beers for 38 nights isn't so bad," I said, misleading him. Little does he know the vast amounts of beer that has flowed through this place.

Sayed said he hopes to have the newspaper story about me printed before I leave for home. He also said he'd try to arrange a ride to the airport for me. Not practical, as I need to be at the airport at five a.m. or so.

I told Sayed about the garbage collector urinating one meter from the tourists, and the teenager (allegedly) going for distance at Khafre, barely missing my head.

Day 39 in the desert—unbelievable to be here, secret photos and secret police

"I know them. They are bad."

The coffee this morning was pathetic, cold *and* crappy. (what a whiner I am)

This morning I was early, and entrance Ali invited me for tea at one of the small tea houses outside the Sphinx gate while we waited for the gate to open. We were joined by Saman 2. *Be brave in your heart.*

"I invite you, don't let him charge you," said Ali, referring to the waiter.

I saw Mohawk early, and got his address. He said he has gifts for the kids, and agua for me. It's supposed to be Egyptian Viagra.

"We will all miss you, even the Sphinx," he said.

As I was working along the wall up to the pyramids, I saw Walid and Ramadan behind me. They were heading into the area of the Sphinx that I was barred from entering a few days ago. They had no bags so Walid asked me for some, in his way, saying something in Arabic, and pretending to hold a garbage bag. I gave one to each of them.

I'm not allowed in the area, only the official cleaners. However, they have no bags to put the garbage in, and must use mine that I paid for. Fifty thousand pounds a month is not enough to buy garbage bags at nine pounds a kilo.

(Rule number one, Benson)

I met a couple from Oklahoma leaning against the wall leading up to Khufu. The man was holding the camera at arms length, trying to take a picture of both of them with the Sphinx in the background.

"I can take a photo if you like," I said.

"No thanks," said Billy, but Britain said "I'd love it if you would."

I think Billy was just so used to saying no that it was an automatic response.

I met them later as I was working a deep ditch in front of Khufu. Billy looked down at me from the edge of the pit.

"Can I put this can in your bag?" he asked, holding up an empty pop can.

We talked for a while. They took some photos of me and agreed to send them to my e-mail address.

Still walking up, I saw an Egyptian man hassling two women for money, really shameful. I have to report it. The women sloughed him off quickly, but one looked at me with an exasperated look that cut me to the bone. I think that many people who come to the pyramids leave with a very negative impression of Egyptians. This hassling should not be allowed. Why was this guy let in? Somebody please explain it to me.

Still walking up the hill, I bent down to pick up a piece of candy wrapper, and I saw a small snake, about a foot long, raise its oblong head, then lower it and go into a hole in the wall. It made me think.

I have put my hands deep into crevasses, and many times jumped into pits full of garbage that nobody has been in for years. Until today, I had yet to see a snake. I thought there weren't any, despite what Walid and Hassanan had said so long ago. But now . . .

Not being one to really learn anything, I jumped about six feet down into a pit in front of Khufu, and discovered bags of garbage. At first I thought they were mine, but I didn't remember leaving them there. Sure enough, they were much larger than mine, monster bags. Someone had discovered it was easier to just throw the bags into the pit than take them away.

I took two of the monster bags to drop off at Khafre, and Ahmed and Mr. Abd el Fattah were waiting for me. Some kids came by and Ahmed took photos with my camera, and—it ran out of juice right away!

We went to The Eternal Pile and used Mr. Abd el Fattah's cell phone to take some pictures, then we took his car to Konica, and charged the battery for my camera. They had tea at a local tea shop, waiting for it to charge, while I went back inside to work.

While in the car waiting to go to Konica, I observed Camel Ali at work. He approached a tourist couple, struck a pose, his arm with his camel whip raised high, pointing to the sky. He had a big grin on his face.

"Take my picture?"

They weren't interested, and his smile ran away from his face. It must be a tough job, being in sales at the pyramids. It must be tough on a man's pride to do that. I understand it is what they have to do, but still, it must be difficult. Some of the guys that work the site deserve respect, and some don't. Ali and his kind deserve respect. To anyone reading this, if you go to the pyramids, take a ride on a camel, buy some trinkets. And don't be a cheapskate!

As I went through security to re-enter the site, the man checking my bag figured out who I was when he saw my gloves and garbage bags.

"Ahh, Mr. Bruce," he said, smiling at me. I had never seen him before, and it made me proud to be recognized by the tools of my trade, gloves and garbage bags.

Ahmed and Mr. Abd el Fatah showed up at the perfect time to see Maharab. We found him between two camels, feeding the riders. One of the riders had been after me for some time to eat with him from Maharab, so it was serendipity.

We took some photos, and Ahmed and Mr. Abd el Fatah got pictures of the piles of garbage bags. Mr. Abd el Fatah offered me my camera, then dropped it as I reached for it. I clutched for it, but he had the string around his finger and it didn't fall—a joke. It was very funny, and we all laughed.

Then two plainclothes police appeared, and any trace of mirth vanished in thin air. Tension was palpable.

"No photos now," whispered Mr. Abd el Fatah. "Five minutes. I know them. They are bad."

It was nearly two and we decided to leave the site. Ahmed and Mr. Abd el Fatah went for tea. I went to Konica and had the photos put on a disc, which I gave to Ahmed to give to his father. Then I joined them for tea.

I discovered Mr. Abd el Fatah can draw quite well.

"Like Picasso," he said, smiling. He drew a smile for me, and signed it.

I asked Ahmed to call my wife Linda for me.

"This is Ahmed Allah Akbar Mohammed Naggar, we have your husband. If you give us five thousand dollars, *we will kill him for you*! ALLAH AKBAR!"

"Whew, time for me to go," I said, yawning. "I need some sleep."

"Such effort," said Ahmed, looking at me and shaking his head.

Day 40 in the desert—unbelievable

"Everybody is talking about you, asking 'why does he do that?'"

Last night I went down for some beers with the boys in the bar, but they didn't have any cold ones. Mohamed promised to have five for me today, cold and ready. I went and got my own cold beer from my room.

I was bored last night, sitting in my room drinking beer, waiting for it to get late enough to go to sleep.

What on earth am I doing? I thought, once more. Even now, the eve of day 40, still wondering. The Doubt.

I had wicked diarrhea again this morning, and a horrible feeling in my gut. Despite the flow I felt I had a blockage, a hot area in my stomach. I took more pills and went down for breakfast.

The coffee was the best I have had here, tasted great. The waiter took a photo of me, for his records I guess. Big smiles, made me feel good.

There was a group of Egyptians sitting at the table next to me that obviously had been up on the tenth floor all night. Two guys and three girls. The girls were giggling, at my expense I'm sure, but not in a bad way.

I met Amer on my walk to work.

"Why you not call me?" he asked.

At the newsstand a guy on a motorcycle offered me a ride the rest of the way to the Sphinx gate, a sign of things to come. I bought a ticket, and then because Konica wasn't open yet, I dropped my camera off at the grocery store next door. The grocer assured me they would give it to the man at Konica as soon as he arrived. I was hesitant to leave it with him but needn't have worried. It was there at the end of my work day.

It was an amazing start to the morning. Every Egyptian that went by had a smile, and most of them shook my hand.

The tour guide that was with the Quebecers weeks ago came up behind me and tapped me on the shoulder.

"I have Americans today," he said,

Then he put his arm around my shoulder.

"Listen up, everybody," he shouted to his group. "This is a great man."

"Tell them," he said to me. "Tell them what you are doing."

Moments later another tour guide touched his heart, pressed his hands together and looked to the sky.

"Thank-you, thank-you."

I gave Mr. Meek a kilo of bags. The Lady in the Hat came by and it looked like she was asking him to give her the bags.

"I have some for Ramadan and Walid, too," I told her. Then she backed off Mr. Meek.

I met the tour guide with the Americans again at the vendor's wall, and he asked me for more business cards. I wrote the bensonusa e-mail on the back. I talked with a professor, Peter Cohen, from Clemson University in South Carolina, and he took my card.

" I could easily get people to come here to clean the pyramids," said the professor. "It would be a great trip."

"I could get people too," said the guide.

Maybe it could be an annual thing, with this the inaugural trip.

Mohamed, the tall lanky guy who works with the Lady in the Hat, appeared. I hadn't seen him in weeks. I gave him bags for the boys, Walid and Ramadan. The Lady in the Hat took them from him. I thought she was getting ready to pack them up to take home, so when I saw Walid moments later, I told him I had 'sacks' for him that I had given to the Lady in the Hat. I hope he gets them from her.

I walked past the entrance to the Sphinx Temple, and the guard and two other guys called me over. Typical male conversation.

"Are you married?"

"Yes," I said. "*Talata* babies." Three babies.

"Strong," he said, curling his arm. "Three wives."

"No, no, no. Three *children*," I said, holding my hand flat at waist height.

He moved his hips in a thrusting motion, big smile on his face. He stopped, made a motion back and forth with his hand, like he was parting a woman's legs, then back to the hip action.

"How long?" he asked me. "A minute? Two minutes? Five minutes? Half a minute?"

"Half a minute?" I exclaimed. "Half a day!"

"I don't believe you."

Working my way up to the big pyramid, two Japanese girls stopped me.

"So, you pick up the garbage," one said, a statement.

"Yes," I said.

"What are you?" asked their Egyptian guide.

"A man," I said.

We laughed together.

"You are a great man," said the guide.

It never ends. Three guys in the Sphinx area saw me going by.

"*Sba Alhair*," good morning, they said, thumbs up.

A guy in a police car said "very clean" as I went by.

I went to see Kamal Wahid but he wasn't in his office. However, Mohamed Cheoh invited me in and ordered tea.

"If you come back as a tourist you can take as many photos as you like," he said.

As I was leaving I saw Sawsan, the archeologist I had met before, talking to another woman.

"Good news, Bruce," said Sawsan, "we have signed a contract with a new company that will have thirty to sixty people picking garbage. We have divided the area into ten regions."

"You should make the regions flexible," I suggested. "Once you see where the garbage accumulates, you'll have a better idea on how to divide up the area."

"About 30 lightweight garbage cans could be placed in areas not impeding photos," I added, "but in high garbage areas."

I also told her that vendors need to be taught not to litter, and of course, bathrooms are necessary.

"There are hundreds of bags filled with garbage waiting to be taken away right now," I told her.

"I want to see," she said, so I led her to the Eternal Pile.

At the ledge in front of the Eternal Pile, we rested. She smoked a cigarette and I ate two fig newtons she gave me. She started rubbing her right eye with her finger.

"Can you look in my eye and see if something is there?"

"I have trouble *not* looking in your eyes," I told her. Egyptian women have such incredibly beautiful dark eyes. A man could easily fall into them.

"What?" she asked "Did you say . . . ?"

"Yes, sorry. Egyptian women have lovely eyes."

"I thought maybe I didn't understand," she said, blushing.

After the Eternal Pile, I showed her the tomb that produced 28 bags. Someone had taken a crap in the middle of the tomb only days before, demonstrating the need for bathrooms better than any of my protestations. The place really stank. Then I took her around the back to the other pile of bags.

"I will go see Kamal Wahid now and get a truck to take it away," she said firmly, impressed by the need to get rid of all this garbage before the bags broke down in the hot sun and the contents started blowing around.

Yeah, sure, I thought.

She went back to the office and I went to Menkaure and loaded up a couple bags from the small pyramids in the back.

I was talking to Josef by Menkaure when the wind picked up suddenly and blew the sand around us so hard I had trouble breathing. I had heard of dust devils before, but never experienced one. It was about ten feet wide. Josef and I were the only ones affected by it. The wind must have been thirty miles an hour in our tiny tornado of sand. It had me thinking again about the lethal dust storm in Laurence of Arabia. People die in sandstorms. I was beginning to panic about my next breath when the storm died as suddenly as it had sprung to life.

"What was *that*?" I asked Josef.

He just shrugged his shoulders and dusted himself off.

How quickly things can come upon us. It reminded me of a near-death experience I had on the Mississippi with my son Jake.

There were many trying experiences on our trip. We had to contend with a drought, low water conditions, an incredible heat wave, and later heavy traffic on the river, plus a host of other difficulties. But it was on our thirteenth day that one of the strangest things happened to us. It could have been deadly, and it came out of absolutely nowhere. It really rattled me.

We were paddling merrily along on a sunny day, with wind at our backs for once, when we stopped for a weigh-up, a rest. There was a little current, and we had already gone 17 miles by late morning.

Jake had taken to sitting up on top of the kayak on weigh-ups to stretch his legs. He just lifts himself up from his cockpit and moves his butt back about one foot, his legs still in the cockpit.

Since the wind was with us, he suggested I do the same.

"We'll make better time that way, Dad," he said.

I agreed with him, and since the river was relatively calm, I saw no harm in doing so. But when I got on top of our craft, it became really tippy, so I quickly sat down. In doing so, I banged my left knee on the side of the cockpit.

I must have hit it in just the wrong fashion, as the pain was immense. I felt extremely nauseous, and red and grey flashed before my eyes.

I said to Jake, "Man, that hurts. I hope I don't pass out." And then I passed out.

I had never passed out from pain before. I used to think that passing out would be a slower process, you would feel yourself losing consciousness, somehow have time to think 'I'm passing out,' but it was instant. As soon as I finished speaking, I was out.

Then we had a problem. I'm passed out in the back, and Jake is on top of the kayak. If I were awake, I could keep the balance of the boat easily by staying in the center of my cockpit. But I'm unconscious.

I don't know how the kayak rolled, I just know that it did. I assume I fell to one side or the other, and since the boat was tippy already because Jake was out of his cockpit, it rolled over. What happened next was really freaky.

I must have woken up as soon as I hit the water. I just remember thinking that I had to get somewhere, and pulling my arms through the water like I was doing the breaststroke. I had no idea who I was, no idea I was on a kayak trip, that I was with Jake, or even that I was in water. I just felt I had to get somewhere.

Getting out of an upside-down kayak can be difficult. In fact the technique is to roll yourself forward, a somewhat unnatural motion, and something one needs to learn to do. Getting out of an overturned kayak when you do not even know you are in one, is even more difficult.

I wasn't wearing my life-jacket, a fact that may have saved my life. If I had it on, it would've kept me floating up against the kayak, and I would've had to fight that buoyancy as well. As it was, it took me a while to reach the surface. I had no idea I wanted to go to the surface, only one thought, 'I gotta get there', not knowing where 'there' was.

Jake, with his 13-year-old imagination, said later he thought I was fighting a giant fish. I guess he could see me thrashing about. He said he was about to dive down to look for me when I finally surfaced.

I hit the air before I panicked. I could feel panic coming, but it wasn't there yet. I still had no idea who or what I was when I took my first breath of air. It was only when I turned my head and saw the upside-down kayak, and Jake's smiling face on the other side of the hull, that it came back to me.

I remembered who I was, who I was with, and where I was. Strangely, the memories came back slower than they left. I passed out instantaneously, but recovered my wits a little slower. And the pain in my knee was completely gone!

"What happened?" I asked Jake.

"I don't know."

"I must have passed out," I said.

It could have been a terrible mess. Jake could easily have found himself 15 miles from civilization, floating down the river with a dead Dad and an upside-down kayak. Me, I could've been dead so suddenly I never saw it coming. This happened on a sunny day in calm waters.

We then used our bilge pump for the first and last time, and were on our way in ten minutes. It was the only time we rolled the kayak on the Mississippi, but the memory sticks. I gave Jake strict instructions not to tell his mother about Dad passing out in the kayak until we were finished the trip.

A few hours later as we were paddling into Brainerd, Minnesota, we met Dave and Penny, a Christian couple traveling with some friends on a houseboat. They invited us for lunch at their place, which was on the river, and three houses over from the Potlatch Dam that we had to portage. We happily accepted, were well fed, and I even had a shower. They were full of questions, and we told them of our dumping experience. I couldn't help but think of baptism, or being born-again.

Jake wasn't quite so affected by it, though.

Jake's journal—day 13:

I remember when we were paddling and had a weigh-up, I said to Dad, "Sit up like me and we'll catch more wind so we'll go faster." And he did, but the boat got wobbly, so he quickly slid down and banged his knee on the side and said, "Oh, I hope I don't pass out," and he passed out right after and caused us to tip, but the water woke him up.

Clearly not a big deal to Jake.

I met a Canadian guy traveling with his father. He said he'd take some photos of garbage for me.

"What do you do?" I asked him.

"I work in neuroscience, focusing on how the brain interprets images from the eyes."

I carried some bags over to Khafre, then cleaned up the garbage area.

Out of curiosity I went back to the Eternal Pile, and lo and behold, there was a big tandem truck, loaded up with the bags.

Do my eyes deceive me? Is my brain interpreting images from my eyes correctly?

As I approached, I could see six or seven men, and Sawsan.

"We got it all," she said proudly.

Wow.

"Boy, you sure are the go-to girl," I said, impressed.

"We will be back tomorrow to clean up the rest," she said, pointing to a small amount of debris that had fallen out of some bags.

The truck pulled away, and the one man left who works the guardhouse down the hill invited me for tea, but since it was my last day picking garbage, I wanted to clean up the remainder of the Eternal Pile—eternal no more—before any wind came. I filled two bags then dumped them at Khafre and met Mr. Abdutowab. I gave him one bag and he promptly put it in his pocket and went home.

I filled two bags at Khufu, dumped them at the Khafre garbage site, and went and gave Sawsan the kilo of bags I would have given Mr. Abdutowab, had he not failed the test.

Then off to wait for Ali, who did not show again. Egyptian time, I guess.

I was sitting on the curb, beat, when a man sitting on one horse and holding the bridle of another, approached me.

"Why do you do this?"

I told him.

"I am here fifteen years," he said, "and I never see anybody like you. Everybody is talking about you, asking why does he do that?"

"Maybe my brain is too small," I said, "or my heart is too big."

They all know I pay 60 pounds to go in every day, so it's difficult in such a poor country to understand the expense.

This led me to thinking about the difficulties I have faced in getting here, and the notion that I will perform the embrace no matter who or what opposes me. That is what we need to do as peoples, perform the embrace anyway. In Sudan, for instance. To hell with the governments and bureaucracy. Just do it. Perhaps we could end up being bigger than governments. Hell, all the people of the world together are. What if we all stood up, united, and said NO to war, NO to hunger, NO to violence, NO to nuclear weapons, NO to the pollution of the earth, the poisoning of the oceans and the air? What if we just bloody well told those who would do harm to this planet and the people on it, NO!

I first had thoughts of people coming together to stop war when my son Jake was born. As I held him in my arms, I thought, among other things, what a tragedy it is that this wonderful little baby, if he's *lucky*, will grow old and die. And equally tragic, in not so many years he will come to realize his own mortality. Worse yet, would be for him to get killed in some preventable war. What parent could possibly want their child to go to war? What if all the parents in the world refused to let their children go? War declared and nobody shows up. Can we do that? John Lennon thought so. Certainly never in the history of humankind has there been the capacity for communication amongst the peoples of the earth as we have now.

The fierce urgency of now. If *we* don't do it, who will? If not *now*, when?

Some of the site kids came by, three on a donkey, waving enthusiastically, teeth shining.

"Hey Canada!"

I love it.

Day 41 in the desert—hellos and goodbyes, and photos, to hell with security, I'm a tourist

"He's not taking my camera."

On the way to work today I saw a herd of goats sifting through the garbage. I asked the herdsman leaning on a wooden staff if I could take a photo, and without batting an eye or moving much at all, he said "give me money" rubbing the fingers of his left hand together.

"Well, fuck you too," I said, and walked on. I regretted it almost instantly, turned and looked back. He had not moved—

completely unaffected. But in my heart of hearts, I knew I behaved badly.

Security didn't find my camera at Checkpoint Charlie, so I had no explaining to do. I felt a little nervous going through. I didn't want a big scene.

Be strong in your heart.

Once through I started taking pictures.

A drink seller came up to me, kissed his hand, then shook mine.

"You very good," he said.

Mr. Abdutowab came by and I took his photo, though he looked uncomfortable about it.

I saw a tourist trying to take a picture of himself with the Sphinx in the background, and offered to help. He was from England. He was heading toward the entrance to the Sphinx Temple, when my 'guide,' locked step with his. It was amazing, he fell right in as if they were lifelong buddies on a trip to Egypt together. Then he started to go to work, and I took some photos of him in action, ingratiating himself to the Englishman, a precursor to the demand for money for services rendered. It's really extortion.

"I'll quit bothering you, if you give me money."

I was going to intercede on the Englishman's behalf, but fortunately security caught the 'guide' and chased him away. The Englishman was oblivious to what was going on, and slipped peacefully through the entrance to the Temple of the Sphinx.

I was about to take a picture of the guard with the hip moves at the Sphinx Temple when we heard what sounded like an explosion. He headed for the door and was looking off to his left. I followed suit. Many people were running in that direction.

Terrorists?

I went up the hill and saw a truck that had jumped the two-foot rock wall, and was hung up, gas tank pinned against the wall. It was lucky it didn't explode. There were people milling about further up the hill. I went back down, but the extortionist, my 'guide' who had returned, said the real problem was further up, so I went up again.

There were many injured men laying on the ground being tended to in one fashion or another. One man had a blood-soaked cloth held to his head. Another was laying flat with a man comforting him. Sitting across the road from me was another man holding his head in his hands. He didn't look to be badly hurt, possibly in shock.

The Englishman came by.

"I saw the whole thing," he said. "It was horrific. The truck was going uphill, when it suddenly stopped moving, and started rolling backwards. It hit the curb, flung the men from the back, flipped over and back again, and then rolled downhill."

We stood there watching helplessly as an ambulance came and the men were loaded in and taken away. I was tempted to take photos, that's what a professional photographer would do, but no, it would be too insensitive. Besides, I'm not a professional photographer any more than an Egyptian or a cowboy. I wanted to help, but thought I would just get in the way.

I walked with the Englishman up the hill, talking. He's been traveling through the Middle-east for 3-4 weeks, and will stay one week in Egypt, then head home. Things have been more expensive than he thought they would be, so he's cutting his trip short.

"This is the first place I have been where they always want money," he said. But he is at the pyramids, that's what they do.

I went up to Khafre and took a picture of an old guy who frequently calls me *habibi* and kisses me on the cheeks. I laid down to rest for a while next to the pyramid. I covered my head with my newspaper as I forgot my hat today.

"Cooocaaaa-Cola," sang out Hya-hya, waking me up. I asked him to write his name in Arabic in my notebook, but he pointed to his thumb and pressed it on the paper. I guess he can't write.

I headed over to Menkaure, and had tea with the boys working the trench. The supervisor gave me a guide book.

"Thanks, for what you have done."

I checked out the dig at Menkaure, and went round to the back. I wanted to climb one of the smaller Pyramids of Queens, but Ramadan the watcher wanted money to climb, so I said forget it.

"I need to pay security," he explained. That's Egypt. Nobody can climb the pyramids . . . unless they pay the security guy whose job it is to make sure nobody climbs the pyramids.

Back to Khafre, I sat with Hya-hya, people watching. This young woman, really a girl, walked by dressed in impossibly short shorts.

"Very nice," said Hya-hya, and we chuckled.

Some people dress much too provocatively when visiting Egypt. It is predominantly Muslim, and very conservative. Out of respect for their culture, people should dress appropriately. That's my opinion. Though Hya-hya didn't seem to have a problem with scantily clad women.

I went to see Kamal Wahid, and said goodby. Mohamed Cheoh and Sawsan weren't there.

"When are you coming back?" he asked.

"I might come back next year, with people from many countries," I said. He just nodded.

He gave me his e-mail address. I plan to keep up some sort of correspondence.

I was sitting on the east side of Khufu, thinking of Ozymandias, and what the black granodiorite I was sitting on might have looked like in its glory, when I spotted an Egyptian family having a picnic. I walked over to them.

"Can I take your picture?" I asked the group.

"What do you want?" asked one of the men, in the deceptive tone that seems threatening or aggressive, but is not.

"I'm from Canada," I said. "I looked over here and I saw such a happy family. It looks beautiful. Do you mind if I take a picture?"

What a response! They quickly shuffled into position and I took several pictures. They insisted on a picture with me, and made a spot for me in the midst of them. I gave the camera to a man on a camel and he took a few. I was looking at the photos, and showing them around, when I heard "are you married?" from someone.

"Yes, I'm married," I said, and we all laughed. I had never met those people before.

They shook my hand, and I said goodby, but one young woman came up to me twice, with two different camera phones, to take my picture.

"What is your nationality?" she asked.

In all the time I've been here, I have probably said Canada thousands of times.

"Canada," I said, wondering for not the first time what the repercussions may be, possibly years down the line, of my being here. Who knows?

How people respond. The French have a reputation for being rude and difficult. I was in a bar in Paris once, (after a fight with my wife) a sole tourist surrounded by Parisians.

"What do you think of the French?" the man to my right asked.

"I think they're great," I said. "Wonderful people."

The response was phenomenal. The question was asked in a slightly menacing tone, but after the answer I had friends for life. The people in that pub that night were great, wonderful people. Sometimes you get what you expect, good . . . or bad.

I was approached by a man on a camel as I walked by the Mortuary Temple of Khafre.

"What is this coin worth?" he asked, handing me a Toonie, a two-dollar Canadian coin.

The Toonie is so named because it rhymes with Loonie, which is the common name for the one dollar coin because it has a picture of a loon on it. A person would have to know the history of the two coins to understand the term Toonie.

An extreme example of strange nicknames is the Australian term for an American, 'Seppo.'

I was fishing on the 62-foot Kristina out of Eden, south of Sydney, Australia many years ago. We were poling for striped tuna.

Poling is a method of catching tuna rapidly being replaced by more efficient means. Six or seven men sit right beside each other on one side near the bow of the boat. These are the 'polers.' They hold a ten foot fishing rod with an eight-foot line on it. A rubber 'squid' with a barb-less hook dangles on the end of the line.

The man in the crow's-nest, thirty feet above the deck, looks for schools of striped tuna surfacing to eat. When he spots the fish, he yells to the captain and points. The captain steers the boat over to the school of fish. He turns a tap to run water through a hose that winds beneath the feet of the polers, and splashes out into the water. This is an attempt to simulate rain, and hide the shadow of the boat so as not to scare the fish.

Another man scoops live bait from the bait tank. The bait tank is refilled at night by shining lights into the water, luring fish into a purse-seine net—a net that encircles the fish, with the bottom closing up tight like a purse. The top of the net is gradually pulled into the boat until very little remains overboard, and the fish is ladled into the bait tank.

The bait man throws the bait into the school of fish, to induce a feeding frenzy. The poler flicks his line into the water, and immediately pulls it back. In theory, a fish will be on the hook. The poler pulls his line back at the perfect trajectory, then jerks it forward again. The barb-less hook comes out of the fish's mouth, and the fish lands on the deck. The line hits the water again, and the scene is repeated. Many times a fish will fly over the boat to land in the ocean on the other side. Sometimes the hook will get caught in another poler's ear, or in his clothing.

They say a good poler can have three fish on the go at once—one on the hook, one in the air, and one just hitting the deck.

I was on the Kristina for three weeks, for a total catch of seven tons, selling for $300 per ton. The other fishermen pointed out larger boats with huge nets, working in tandem with airplanes, and hauling in 100 tons at a time. This was more than 15 years ago, and I suspect poling may be a way of the past already.

My career as a poler was cut short when we pulled into Sydney Harbor to avoid bad weather. We had a few days off, so I had a buddy row me to shore in a small dinghy and I went home to my apartment in Rushcutter's Bay. The next day my brother-in-law Laurence and I were in King's Cross heading I can't remember where. I had to go to the bathroom, so I ducked into the Bourbon and Beef, a steakhouse, and went downstairs to the head.

When I came out Laurence was standing alone by the bar, holding a big bottle of Jack Daniels by the neck between his thumb and two fingers, waving it at me.

"Bruuuuuuce," he said, taunting.

No more words were necessary. Laurence was wearing a tank top, and couldn't possibly sneak the bottle out. But I had a short-sleeved dress shirt on.

We went across the street, looking both ways so as not to forget which way to look, and spent several hours sitting on a bench drinking whiskey and coke. When the bottle was done, we decided to walk back across the street and get another one—clearly flawed logic. Surely the set of circumstances that enabled us to liberate the first bottle would not be repeated. But, flawed or not, that was the plan.

I was the first to cross the street. Unfortunately, I forgot to look both ways, and only looked to my left.

Wham! I flew up in the air, did an unintentional somersault, and crashed back to the pavement. I wasn't hit head on, instead I had walked into the car as it was going past. The car did not stop. I discovered later the driver was a recent immigrant, afraid of being deported for speeding and hitting a pedestrian.

A hooker rushed to my side. I don't know what it's like now, but at the time Kings Cross was full of hookers, pimps, strip clubs and junkies, with hypodermic needles all over the place. At first glance I thought it had a pleasant family-friendly atmosphere. But after three weeks I started seeing the cracks. It usually takes three weeks in a new place to see the cracks.

"You can sue him," she said. "I know somebody who got hit by a car and got $25,000."

"Holy," said Laurence, staggering a little, "Why'djou do zhat?"

I went to the hospital because I couldn't move my right arm. Luckily it wasn't broken, but I couldn't use it. I lost my job on the Kristina.

Just days before I showed a picture of my girlfriend to some of my fellow crew.

"Where is she from?" asked crewman Clive.

"The states," I said.

"Oh, a Seppo," said one of the guys.

"What's a Seppo?" I asked, innocently.

"You know, Seppo, septic tank."

"What did you call my girlfriend?" I asked, incredulous, but ready to fight. "Did you just call her a *septic tank?*" I really couldn't believe my ears!

"Bruce, Bruce," soothed Clive, "It's just a nickname for all Americans. If you fight him, you'll have to fight the whole country."

I called Linda on the phone later, and told her about it.

"Oh yeah, they call us Seppos," she said, indifferently.

The Aussies like cute little rhyming nicknames, and endeavoring to find a word suitable to match with 'Yank' all they could come up with was 'septic tank.' It was later shortened to 'Seppo.' That is the history of 'Seppo.'

Standing on the Giza plateau, with millennia looking down, I thought about the history of all humankind, and was dizzy.

"It's worth eight pounds," I told the Egyptian with the Toonie. "I'll give you five."

"Okay."

I went to the wooden walkway and carefully stashed it under the boards, reaching as far as I could in an attempt to make it irretrievable.

One of my little buddies came up with a Canadian tourist, keen to introduce us. The woman's husband was in Khafre's pyramid. The boy had attached himself to her to be her 'guide' and wanted money for his work—acceptable from a charming little boy, but not from an aggressive full-grown man.

"How much should I give him?" she asked me.

"Ten pounds would be nice, (two dollars) but if you wanted to give him more, he's a hardworking little guy," I replied, rubbing the top of his head.

I tried to take his photo but the battery was dead. Aarrgghh!!

I went out and charged it at Konica. On my way back in, past the security desk but not yet out of the security building, a security man reached for my camera.

"NO!" I yelled, clutching it to me. "Kamal Wahid say camera good. Mohamed Cheoh say camera good."

My voice was nowhere near its capacity, but louder than they have ever heard. He waved for me to go in. Rabihr's lesson once more.

I have been blessed, or cursed, with a loud voice. My sons have not inherited it, but my daughter has. Many times I have been at a conference partying in a hotel room, and someone will knock on the door.

"I didn't know what room you guys were in, so I just followed Bruce's voice."

On a portage down a road one day I saw one kid drop the canoe off his shoulder and into his arms. This put strain on the other three kids, and I thought the canoe would be hitting the ground soon. They were almost a quarter of a mile away from me, so I couldn't physically help the kid get the canoe back on his shoulder. So I yelled.

"DESMARAIS, GET THAT CANOE UP!" I put everything I had into it, and could feel it coming right from my feet all the way up my body and out my mouth.

Zip, the canoe was back on his shoulder. I was impressed with myself.

However, spending the night in an airport in Tahiti drinking vodka with a Norwegian, I constantly heard "keep it down, be quiet, some people are trying to sleep, shut-up, etcetera."

I took pictures on my way into the Sphinx, along the wall, outside the wall—following my usual routine. Then I ran into

Saman, who's keen on those boots he wants me to bring the next time I come to Egypt. We had someone take a photo of the two of us in front of the Sphinx.

Walking into the Sphinx Temple, another security guy approached me.

"Excuse me, excuse me," he said, while talking on his phone and gesturing for me to come to him.

That's it.

"NO, I WILL NOT," I yelled again.

"Don't worry, don't worry, he works here," said his sidekick, placatingly.

"I DON'T CARE," I yelled. "HE'S NOT TAKING MY CAMERA!"

"Go in, go in," said the man with the cell phone. I started to, but came back out.

"I PAID SIXTY POUNDS LIKE EVERYBODY ELSE . . .," I yelled louder still, and was really feeling like taking the piss out of the bastard.

"No problem, no problem, go in," he quickly said.

Saman and the others, who have known me for all this time, were surprised at my outburst.

Later I talked with Saman about it.

"When you are here picking up garbage they have you . . .," he pointed to his foot, raised it a little, then lowered and twisted it " . . . underneath. If you come as tourist they are underneath."

As well said as anybody on earth could say it.

"Today I am here as a tourist."

"You pay ticket?"

"Yes."

"That's good," he said, smiling.

The little darling girls came up for photos, gotta love 'em. One gave me a bookmark, the other gave me the cardboard covering of the bookmark package. Beautiful girls.

I headed for the back of Khafre, looking for couples. I wanted to get some pictures of young lovers, the same everywhere. A guy at the walkway stopped me, and tried to call Ahmed on his cell. I guess Ahmed told him to, but there was no answer. I did meet an officious, elderly white-haired portly fellow who explained who he was. The description went on and on. Lord of all he surveys, I thought. Clearly quite proud of his position.

I left, and said goodby to many people. Michael, the cab driver I see often, said from behind me as I left the site "camera good," and laughed. I turned around.

"That was good," he said, smiling. I guess I struck one for the little guy who always gets harassed by security, or police.

Day 42 in the desert—time on my hands

'Greatest find since . . . '

When I got back to Siag yesterday, Ahmed was there with his cousin and his cousin's wife.

"The skull is human, roughly 100 years old," said Ahmed.

Probably not a mummy then, I thought.

"Do you think I could have it?" I asked, knowing the answer.

"I don't think so," laughed Ahmed.

It really did look like the body was the victim of foul play with the big hole in the back of the skull. There was no mummification process 100 years ago.

I told Ahmed about Sawsan's beautiful eyes.

"I thought men liked *blue* eyes," said Ahmed's cousin's wife.

"Oh no," I said, looking in her dark eyes, careful not to look too long and raise the ire of her husband. "Egyptian women have the most beautiful black eyes in the world."

She blushed slightly at that, but sat a little straighter, prouder I thought, knowing the windows to her soul are appealing to men.

I was up late for the first time since I have been here. Breakfast at eight, off to get a paper and photos from Konica. A store owner pointed to his watch as I walked by, as did a few other people I met along the way. I guess I have been like clockwork. *White-man walks by at 7:45 a.m.*

Or would it be *big dummy?*

I took a cab back and got caught in a traffic jam. Just as my driver was turning around to go another way, I saw Hassanan crossing the road. I rolled down my window and shook his hand. He kissed me on the cheek, and I got his photograph.

I went to an internet shop, ate some falafels, then went back to my room for a nap. Housekeeping woke me up, and I went down to the lobby and read my paper while they did their thing. I'm really feeling at a loss as to what to do. Everything feels anticlimactic. Fatih wants me to go to Alexandria, but I really haven't the time if I'm going to buy nice things for everybody back home.

Ahmed said he'll take me to the El Khalili market for some good shopping on Wednesday. That is where the bomb exploded, killing the young French woman and injuring 24 other people.

A couple from Sweden were discussing splitting the cost of a car to Alexandria with me. But I can't. Besides, I would like to take a few more photos, maybe get a photo of me with the skull. Will I get credit for the find? Imagine, the front of National Geographic, 'greatest find since . . .' I wonder if they can determine cause of death? Or if there's a 100-year-old missing persons case waiting to be solved. Missing persons, plural, as I know there is another skull where I found the first, but in three pieces.

The internet was still down at Siag so I went back to the internet café, and the French photographer, Ari Rossner, had responded to my e-mail and will send photos soon. Curiously, when I tried to send something to the woman from UNESCO, there was a problem. I wonder if the government stops that somehow. Is it possible to prevent Egyptians from contacting the UN via e-mail? I wonder why I'm doing so much wondering today?

Nicholas had responded as well, they'll send pictures. I should get quite a few in the next while.

I'm back in my room sipping on a few beers. I'm feeling very emotional, and have tears in my eyes. I feel great that I had the idea to spend my 40 days in the desert, and by God I did it! I want to get into the bush and start ripping trees out by their roots and tying them in knots.

The Canadian embassy was great at first, but a disappointment in the end. But again, they didn't ask me to come here any more than the Egyptians did.

Morning of day 43 in the desert

"It is oppression."

It's Wednesday, shopping day. I've got Mohamed lined up to drive for us. Ahmed should be here in a little over an hour. I have to remember to ask him where the skull is, and if I can get a picture of it.

Last night I met a man from Saudi Arabia, an accountant. He said he ran away from his wife and kids to meet what he hoped would be wife number two. She is meeting him in Cairo, coming from Nigeria.

"She's not Nigerian," he was quick to point out. "She's American."

"Does she mind being wife number two?" I asked.

"No," he said, surprised by the question, "she doesn't."

He showed me his Herbal Life card. I guess he deals in that as well. He was quite proud of it. He was drinking coffee. Like a good Muslim, he does not drink alcohol.

I had to go to my room to get cold beer. I went twice, brought four beers down, and damned if Moxim didn't sell one on me.

The Saudi told me a story of traveling with his aunt, wearing the veil. She was looking for drapes. The police stopped him, and he could not prove his aunt was a blood relative. The police wanted to take him to the police station, but he refused. He was eventually let go.

"If I went to the police station, I would get a ticket. But also my reputation would be ruined."

"Do the Saudi people like laws like that?" I asked him.

"No, not at all. It is oppression."

Then he leaned close to me, looked to his left, then right, then at me.

"If you say anything against the King, you will be killed," he said softly. "Not like in your country."

"It's a national past-time in my country to make fun of our leaders," I told him.

I didn't tell him the story of Billy, Darren and myself, and Ronald Reagan—Ron and Nancy McDonald.

On our way to New Orleans we blew our clutch in the Ozark Mountains. You could hear the banjos playing.

We were stuck in Springfield, Missouri, where according to our tow-truck driver, a black man who moved to Springfield was hanged in his front yard two years previous.

"What did he do?" asked Billy. "Rape a white woman?"

"Nope," said the driver. "He moved into town."

We ended up in a bar with a pile of red-necks. They were clearly quite racist, and we were glad we weren't three black guys.

"What do we do?" whispered one of my buddies after a fresh barrage of racist jokes and comments.

"Well," I said, "don't agree with them, because you don't. But don't disagree with them either." We were outnumbered a good five to one.

Later, one guy was giving us a ride back to our hotel, when I spotted a billboard with Ronald McDonald on it.

"Hey, isn't that your president?" I carelessly joked.

"Yeah, Ron and Nancy McDonald," added my friend Billy, and all three of us Canadians howled with laughter.

Screech! The car comes to a stop.

"Get out!" said the driver. "I don't care who you are. You don't make fun of our president."

Fatih and Bono were kidding me that I have cheese in my back instead of milk, because I have been away from my wife so long. Interesting analogy.

Rereading 'Bridging the Divide, Religious Dialogue and Universal Ethics' I disagree with some things, and agree with most. This book was published a year after I returned from Paris with the Universal Declaration of Human Duties and Responsibilities. Written by the Interaction Council of Former Heads of State and Government, it was edited by a fellow Canadian, Thomas Axworthy, Chairman of the Center for the Study of Democracy at Queen's University. This group, which reads like a list of who's who of former world political and spiritual leaders, prepared their own declaration they called 'A Universal Declaration of Human Responsibilities.'

Although I am a simple fisherman, I believe my declaration is superior for several reasons. Firstly, I had no egos to contend with. It was just me wrestling with it. Secondly, knowing I'm not very bright, I borrowed heavily from the Universal Declaration of Human Rights. I'm sure Eleanor Roosevelt will forgive me. Why reinvent the wheel? Remove the word 'right' and replace it with 'duty' or 'responsibility,' and it works. The vernacular in the Rights declaration has already been adopted by the United Nations, so approving my Duties and Responsibilities declaration should be a simple matter.

In their Declaration, the Inter Action Council has priorities in the wrong order, a capitulation to national sovereignty. We need new thinking, outside borders. It has to be our planet first, then our fellow humans, our offspring, and lastly ourselves. It is logical and natural.

There's some strange wording that makes their version impossible for the UN to adopt. For instance, Article 7 states: "Every person is infinitely precious and must be protected unconditionally."

Should nations beggar themselves protecting mass murderers?

I'm reading it now, and I think it's second-rate. I must e-mail Hans Kung.

Hans Kung is a Swiss Catholic priest, the president of the Foundation for a Global Ethic, and one of the high profile persons of the United Nations InterAction Council. I e-mailed him a copy of the declaration I had crafted.

"Why would I want to read a declaration when I already wrote one?" was his reply.

But like Ronald Reagan and Gord Gowie, I don't care who gets the credit. I just want to see the United Nations adopt 'a' Universal Declaration of Human Duties and Responsibilities.

Day 43 in the desert—written morning of day 44, Mohammed gets into a fight,

"I'm going to miss you."

Up early, breakfast at eight, went to check e-mails down the street, and across a small debris-filled stream. Coming back I saw about a dozen street sweepers, and a couple cop cars, with several guys talking into radios and one directing traffic. Someone important was coming by. I had heard from entrance Ali that they do that.

"When Zahi Hawass is going to see the Sphinx," said Ali, "they clean the path he will take so he thinks it is all clean."

I pulled out my camera, wanting to catch a picture of whoever it was, but hadn't the patience to wait.

Back at Siag I snuck in the back way to the office to check e-mails, then up to my room to relax and write in my journal.

The Catholic Pope is on this continent, talking about Aids.

"It cannot be overcome by the distribution of condoms," he's quoted as saying. "On the contrary, they increase the problem."

Huh?

I went out to wait for Ahmed at a quarter to eleven yesterday. There were two policemen sleeping like babies in their car outside the door, heads back, mouths open, drooling. I took out my camera, and a third police officer came out, laughing, to stop me. Mohamed, myself, and the policeman were all laughing loudly, but it still didn't wake the sleeping policemen.

Ahmed was right on time, and off we went.

Mohamed was racing through the streets, me beside him, with Ahmed in the back seat. I was getting a little concerned about his driving. We passed a small car that was badly smashed up. There were five people standing around it, apparently unhurt.

Ahmed and I started talking about car accidents. Mohamed said something to Ahmed.

"He says those people got into an accident because they drove fast," interpreted Ahmed, "but he is a professional driver, so he can drive fast."

Some comfort.

Somehow the conversation turned to road rage.

"Sometimes I yell and curse other drivers," admitted Ahmed, holding up his fist.

"That's nothing," I said, "in the US people sometimes shoot each other."

"That happens in Egypt all the time," said Ahmed.

And then I got a first hand look at Egyptian road rage.

Turning onto a freeway, Mohamed and another driver got into it. I'm not sure who cut who off. As far as I'm concerned everybody cuts everybody off, all the time. They don't seem to follow any rules, except the law of 'who gets there first.' But someone pissed someone off, and I think it was Mohamed who had the upper hand. As we were speeding up, this balding, forty-ish guy with a five o'clock shadow, (poster-boy for a terrorist) pulled up in a small blue car beside us on my side. He started hollering at Mohamed, who hollered just as loudly (and just as incomprehensibly) back at him. The two cars were inches from each other traveling at 60 miles an hour. Not that proximity was bothering either of them, hardly a car in Cairo is unscathed. The blue car was missing the driver's side door, and the madman's face was less than two feet away from mine. I was surprised I couldn't smell his breath.

I reached for my camera wanting to get a picture of this nut, but he had to slow down because he had a car in front of him. Mohamed was visibly agitated, talking rapidly to Ahmed while shrugging his shoulders, no doubt explaining his position, and his innocence. We thought it was over . . .

Blue car pulled up on Mohamed's side, hollering still, and trying to push us into the cement wall on the side of the freeway by gradually moving his car toward ours.

I had no idea what he was yelling, but I really didn't like this turn of events. We were moving closer and closer to the wall, and when I looked up ahead, I saw a woman standing in the road four feet out from the cement wall. She had nowhere to run. If something didn't change soon, the outcome would be bad. Someone would get hurt, or die.

"It's not worth it, Mohamed," I kept saying, gently, over and over. "Let it go, let it go."

Ahmed was speaking Arabic to Mohamed in the same tone, I'm sure saying something similar.

Mohamed and blue car were still screaming at each other, as we were getting closer and closer to hitting the poor woman who could see what was happening, and was moving to the wall. We could tell she was terrified.

Mohamed suddenly slowed, and blue car took off.

Mohamed was once again speaking rapidly in Arabic to Ahmed, clearly upset.

"Take a deep breath," I told him, and demonstrated such. We laughed the familiar, nervous 'that could have been bad' laugh.

"What was the guy yelling at Mohamed?" I asked Ahmed moments later.

"He was saying 'you're a donkey, you're a pig,' something about his mother, and that he was going to push his car into the wall and he would crash."

At the Khan El-Khalili bazaar police had a temporary metal detector set up because of the recent bombing. The bazaar didn't look very busy, not nearly as busy as when Jake and I were here two years ago. The vendors were obviously suffering.

We shopped all day, and Ahmed was great. At times he posed as a tour guide, so the vendors would think he was on their side and might bring future business if I was pleased. A few things stick out.

We found ourselves just outside the famous Husayn mosque as the call for prayer began singing from the loudspeaker.

Built in 1154, the Husayn mosque is named for the grandson of the prophet Mohamed, Husayn ibn Ali. It is considered to be one of the holiest Islamic sites in Cairo, and houses many sacred items, including what is believed to be the oldest complete manuscript of the Quran.

"Do you think I can go in?" I asked Ahmed.

Ahmed inquired of a local shopkeeper, and he said yes. We took our shoes off as we entered, and I saw a place to put them, a shoe check, like a coat check back home. There was a wizened old fellow there. I started to place my shoes on one of the racks.

"Don't do that," whispered Ahmed, holding his in his right hand. "Just hold onto them."

It's a beautiful mosque, the first one I entered in my life. The walls beautifully painted, but sparse. Ahmed took a picture, though I'm not sure that was allowed. The tone of the loudspeaker changed and I was worried it was because he had taken a picture. Had the camera set off an alarm?

"We must go now," said Ahmed. "Prayers are beginning."

As we left the old fellow scolded Ahmed, as he charges for checking shoes and Ahmed robbed him of a customer.

Before we had entered the mosque, I noticed a woman with a child in her lap, perhaps two years old. She was sitting beside the entrance to the mosque, begging. She used the universal beggar language of putting her thumb and first two fingers of her right hand together, and lifting them to her mouth. The message was clear—food. She was begging for food. Of course not food, but money to buy food, as it was obvious I had no food. When we left the mosque, I glanced at her and she repeated the gesture.

"I will give her some money," I told Ahmed.

"I don't think she needs money," said Ahmed, looking at her and shaking his head. To be honest, she did look well-fed, portly even. But I was thinking of the baby, and already had my money out.

I turned and gave her five pounds, which she crumpled in her hand and smiled a shy 'thank-you, though you should have given more' smile. Then, much to my surprise and amusement, the cute little curly-haired baby mimicked the mother's begging gesture 'to the T,' thumb and first two fingers together, brought up to the mouth, imploring look in the eyes. It was amazing, and I laughed out loud. The child is a prodigy.

As for gifts, I wasn't sure what I wanted but silver seemed like a good idea.

I bought a necklace and earrings for Linda for six pounds a gram, but after speaking to more silver vendors, we determined the going rate to be 5.5 pounds per gram, or roughly a dollar a gram. I bought her a bracelet, and we had tea with the vendor.

At each shop, I would get them to weigh my wedding ring, 3.2 grams, which established the trueness of their scales. They were all true.

In the car Ahmed had asked Mohamed if we could trust that the silver was silver.

"Yes, there will be a stamp."

I'm not sure why that can't be forged, but apparently it isn't done.

While drinking tea with the bracelet seller, he asked a young man to go get some knives, as I had said I wanted some for my boys. The kid came back with junk. He spoke with Ahmed.

"He says he can take us to a shop with many very good knives," said Ahmed. Reluctantly, we followed the kid. Everywhere we went, someone wanted to lead us somewhere, and I hated that.

"I don't like to be led anywhere," I said to Ahmed.

The knives all proved to be worthless, but we found an onyx dealer, and I bought some plates and two vases.

The kid kept following us, though I told him to go. When we finally were leaving he wanted money. Perhaps I should've given him some, but with my experience at the pyramids, I couldn't. I can't stand when someone takes it upon themselves to do something for you, in exchange for money. Their help is being imposed on you against your will.

There's my hypocrisy again, fine for little boys to do it, not grown men.

Our arms full of gifts, we dropped our loot off with Mohamed and returned. We once more entered the bowels of the bazaar with its many twists and turns and different levels. Almost every shopkeeper tried to get us to go upstairs where he could bargain with us away from the other vendors, many of whom sold the same things undoubtedly from the same factory. At one point I had three hands on me, trying to pull me in three different directions.

"Quit touching me!" I yelled, and they all recoiled. Rabihr's very valuable lesson.

Another vendor invited me to his shop, and we spent a good hour upstairs. I bought three stone reliefs from him, for a total of 1150 pounds. But it took a while.

"He asked me if I am with you or him," Ahmed told me later, "I told him I am with him, because we are both Egyptian."

Here I did a little Sherlock Holmes.

"Where are you from?" he asked me.

"Canada."

"My brother lives in Saskatoon," he said. "He has two daughters. I wanted to leave Egypt too, but my father would not let me."

His brother has been in Canada for 12 years. Ahmed and Samir both told me that nobody returns to Egypt once they have left, except to visit.

"You know," I said minutes later, "I live in Manitoba, right next to Saskatchewan."

I let another moment pass.

"Wait a minute, is your brother named Mohamed?" I asked. Since the brother left Egypt so long ago, and the father would not allow him to go, I assumed the brother was the eldest, and Mohamed seems to be the most common name for first-born sons in the Muslim world.

His eyes just burst out of his head.

"Yes," he said, utterly surprised.

"Does he have two little girls?" I asked, putting my hand flat at a little over waist level, hoping he had forgotten telling me that fact. I was guessing the size of the girls.

He nodded vigorously.

"A black man?" he asked, putting his hands on his face, completely amazed at this incredible coincidence.

"Yes!" I said, putting the same surprise in my own voice.

Beside himself now, he frantically pulled his wallet out, hands shaking, and began searching for a picture, which to his dismay he was unable to find. Ahmed was equally surprised by this unexpected turn of events. They were talking to each other rapidly in Arabic, and I knew I had to end it.

I 'fessed up. I was a little worried about how he would react to being fooled, but he just laughed uproariously. So did Ahmed.

"If he was Canadian," I told Ahmed back at the car, "I would've kept it up longer."

I wanted to get something for Linda's sister Marianne and her husband Joop, so as we were leaving we hopped into the first onyx shop we had visited on our way in. We went up the stairs and I found two glasses. The vendor wanted 55 pounds.

"Don't make me do this dance, just let me know the best price," I said in a weary voice. I must have been convincing because he went down to 30 pounds, and I bought them. I also bought two little carved dolphins for their girls.

"Bruce, do you remember when you were in Mohamed Cheoh's office all day?" Ahmed asked me out of the blue on the long ride back to Siag.

"Yeah."

"They kept you there to find out if you were normal, or crazy."

Back at Siag I convinced Ahmed to let me buy him supper for all his help. We had some delicious spaghetti bolognese, and then Ahmed went home.

I shook his hand, but that somehow didn't seem enough, so I gave him a hug. He's a great kid, and has been a tremendous asset to me, and a great friend. I hope he comes to Canada soon.

I went back in and had a beer at the bar. Mohamed the assistant manager of the restaurant/bar came by, and asked when I was leaving.

"A few days."

"I'm going to miss you," he said. "I love you."

"I love you too, Mohamed."

He reminded me of the Third Man in Mohamed Cheoh's office days ago.

"You'll probably be glad to see me go," I had said to him, jokingly.

He snorted, as if to say I was crazy.

"You are my lover," he said.

Day 44 in the desert

"If a man has one wife, he has one problem. If he has two wives, he has two problems."

Up at seven, breakfast at eight, can't wait to get going home. Checked my e-mails, nothing much, my cousin Wray says my Dad is worried about me.

I took a photo of the kids playing games on the computers at the internet café. Universal. Again I thought, hopefully, that maybe the next generation of humans can do a better job of getting along with each other and looking after our planet.

I started packing, and it took hours. I figured I needed more stuff for the boys so I went to get some with Ahmed the cab driver. The doorman Magdy told me to go to the Cairo Market, but there was only clothes for sale there.

As we drove, the conversation between Ahmed and I turned to women.

"Do you like the woman that look like me?" asked Ahmed.

I looked at him. "No, I like thin women," I said, smiling.

"I like many women," he said proudly. "I have known 40 women."

I was in an irritable mood, not very good. He took me to some Mr. Funky store, and it was all clothing as well. I tried explaining this to Ahmed, and we finally communicated. I was telling him no clothes, he said "I thought you meant . . ." and he opened the door to his taxi, and then suddenly slammed it shut.

"Ah-ha! You want bazaar!" he shouted, pointing at me and smiling.

"Yes."

He took me to a store that was on my walking route from Siag to the Sphinx, though I had not noticed it. Run by two brothers, you could tell business had not been brisk lately by the layer of dust on everything. I bought five silver cartouches, one for Linda, myself and our three kids.

A cartouche is like an Egyptian nameplate. Basically an oval, or a rectangle with semicircle ends, with a person's name in Egyptian hieroglyphics enclosed.

I had to go to an ABM to get more money. The younger brother drove me in his car. I was still cranky, and the traffic made me worse.

He took me to a bank machine far away.

"It is a long drive, but it always works," he said.

There was a line-up at the ATM, and to top it off an old man in a dusty dark brown suit was having problems with the machine.

I actually started walking away, thinking 'to hell with this', when I decided I better not, and went back to the brother waiting in the car. He pointed out a machine on the other side of the street and I went to that one.

The two brothers reminded me a lot of Paul and Teddy Olson, the two old fishing brothers from Gimli. This brother would laugh after making an observation, more like a snicker, or giggle, like he found the whole world and everything in it amusing. He was probably never depressed. Just like Teddy, my first skipper.

"How's business?" I asked him.

"I could lie," he said, "but I won't. It has not been good in the whole world, but soon it will pick up."

He gave me his philosophy on family.

"Few children, much happiness. Many children, no happiness. Egypt has enough people. One, two, or three children should be enough for a couple."

The Pope could learn something from this man.

"He must want people to be poor," my old skipper Teddy used to say about the Pope. "That's why he says no birth control."

Is it that, or does he need the huddled, ignorant masses to worship him?

The Egyptian also offered his views on multiple wives.

"If a man has one wife, he has one problem," he said, turning to me and smiling. "If he has two wives, he has two problems."

It's amazing what you can get from someone in a short time. The other brother was more serious, just like Paul Olson, Teddy's older brother—take care of business.

Ahmed smoked some sheesha, and was ready to go when I was done. I still haven't anything specifically for the boys. I hope Fatih can help.

I took a picture of one of the brothers, the older one. For some reason the younger one slipped out of sight when I pulled out the camera.

"I will take you to airport tomorrow," said Ahmed on the ride back to Siag.

"Hassan (Egypt-Israeli war vet) said he would get me a ride."

Ahmed said he will call Hassan to ask him for the gig.

"What, no picture for me?" asked Ahmed, in a slightly hurt tone when he dropped me off.

I took a photo right away, with him beside his cab. He wanted his number prominently displayed.

"You will not forget me," he said, smiling.

"How can I forget you? Forty women!"

He laughed, and as we were shaking hands, he pulled me close and whispered "I only know four women now, and my two wives."

"I don't like the skinny woman," he said, leaning back. "I like the big woman, strong,"

"We have sex for an hour," said Ahmed. "It only costs 50 pounds, and it's good. We remember the last time."

I took that to mean remembering all the other times. Seems old Ahmed has it goin' on.

There were many people in the lobby, Russians I thought. I was heading to go see Fatih and pick up Linda's perfume and massage oil, when Figurala came up to me.

"Mr. Bruce," he said, shaking my hand. "Tonight?"

"Yes," I said.

He was still shaking my hand, when the Russian he had been talking to put his hand on my shoulder. That was cool. Then he tried to kiss me. He put his hand behind my head and puckered up, leaning into me with his eyes closed. I pushed him away, gently.

"No kissing, buddy."

He tried to press his forehead against mine, but I held him at arms length.

"What's his problem?" I said to those around me.

"He's drunk," said Figurala.

A tour guide, appropriately, guided me away.

"He's crazy people."

I went to the elevator, glancing back to see the drunk wrestling with Figurala

It's 5:35 p.m., and I plan to go down and drink some beer soon, then go to bed really early, get up, shower, shave, finish packing, and go.

I was feeling pressure to make sure I get enough gifts for everybody, and that contributed to my grumpiness. I also have this feeling that I should be gone already.

Day 45 in the desert—Trashman goes home

"You will not forget me."

I woke at three. Outside my door Egypt-Israeli war vet Hassan had placed a baggage cart. I loaded it up with my luggage and went downstairs and out the door, where Ahmed the taxi driver was waiting. He loaded up my bags.

As I was getting in the cab, Rabbob called to me from the threshold of Siag. She ran down the steps and gave me a huge hug, and some gifts. She had gifts from Fatih as well. I will miss her, and all the others that work at Siag. It has been my home, and a great refuge from the sand of the desert. Egypt-Israeli war vet Hassan gave me a hug and a kiss on the cheek, and I climbed into Ahmed's taxi.

I gave Ahmed a hug when he dropped me off.

"You will not forget me," he said for the second time in 12 hours.

I went through security and waited for the plane to start boarding.

The Doubt was with me. Did I accomplish anything? Will the garbage start piling up again? I never did get it all anyway. Every day there was more, why would tomorrow be any different?

But that was never the point. You cannot stop the wind. It was the act of doing it that was important. Every piece of trash I picked up, I had to bend over and pick it up. Every ounce of energy given away, was left there. To what end? Did I add to the embrace? Was there some reason I felt I had to do this that I will never fathom? Again, there was no soundtrack to guide me. What genre am I playing in?

God put the idea in your head, to do this.

Why?

In the grand scheme of chaotic things, did a butterfly flap its wings?

But I do believe in the embrace. There is my rock.

Ya big dummy!

I left Egypt.

Today

It's been nearly four years since I returned to North America. Ahmed has translated the Universal Declaration of Human Duties and Responsibilities into Arabic, Yusif translated it into Russian, and both versions are on the www.thecenterforcivilization.com website.

I hired a design team out of Asheville, North Carolina, to help design the Flag of Humanity, and after four years we have Appendix C. On my return to Canada in the spring of 2012, I stopped in New York City and flew the flag in front of the United Nations building in New York City, Times Square, and other points of interest. I believe this flag, or *some* flag celebrating the commonality of being human, will be flying over all the nations of the earth someday.

Reading over my journal I can see where many times I lost my way as a Trashman, became judgmental, irritable. I'm still in need of redemption.

I try to pick garbage every day, be it an hour or two, or only a discarded can or bottle, or piece of paper found on my way walking into a store—or better yet, a pub. It's therapy for me, keeps me humble, not that I have any reason *not* to be humble.

I was walking into the Town Hall in Gimli last summer, and there on the beautifully manicured lawn was an empty can of Pepsi, contaminating the site. I scooped it up on my way in and dropped it into the trash can by the front doors. Dead easy.

"That's impressive," said a woman leaning against the side of the building, smoking.

To anyone who has waded this far through the morass that is my journal, try it. Get some gloves and some bags, and find a spot that needs a little work.

I hope I can be a Trashman all my life, build my temple to the embrace one piece of trash at a time.

I still have The Doubt. I'll never be rid of it. I can't kill it, but I have to fight it, or it could kill me. Parts of me, anyway.

Maybe I was a fool to go to Egypt, but at least I was able to stand at the foot of Khafre and sing at the top of my lungs. I did it my way.

Looking at the news, the world is bleak in so many places.

I still believe the embrace is the solution to many of the woes of this world, now more than ever. And when The Doubt is weak, and the embrace is strong in me, I have hope.

Egypt is calling me, and I have to go back. Or should I go somewhere else to be a Trashman? Moscow? Tehran? Beijing? Washington? I do take requests.

I was talking to a friend the other day, trying to convey the emotional response to my work in Egypt.

"Oh, I can see that," he said. "Somebody cares."

Appendix A

Universal Declaration of Human Duties
and Responsibilities
(Proposed by the Center for Civilization)

There are four areas of responsibility-four **Principles of Humanity**

Firstly, human beings are responsible for the Earth, for without the Earth they cannot bear any other burden, or responsibility. **Human beings are responsible for the earth.**

Secondly, each person is responsible for their fellows, that is each and all members of the human race, for if their fellows are unable to tend to the Earth, they will not be able to be responsible to the Earth, thus if human beings ignore the plight of their fellows, they are not being responsible to the Earth. **Human beings are responsible for their fellows.**

Thirdly, human beings are responsible for their offspring for if their offspring are not taught of their own responsibility to the earth and their fellows, they are not being responsible to the Earth or their fellows. **Human beings are responsible for their offspring.**

Fourthly, human beings are responsible for their own actions. **Human beings are responsible for themselves.**

Therefore,

Whereas recognition of the inherent duties and responsibilities of all members of the human family is the foundation of freedom, justice and peace in the world,

Whereas disregard and contempt for human duties and responsibilities have resulted in barbarous acts which have outraged the conscience of mankind, and the advent of a world in which human beings shall enjoy freedom of speech and belief, and freedom from fear and want has been proclaimed as the highest aspiration of the common people,

Whereas it is essential, if people are not to be compelled to have recourse, as a last resort, to rebellion against tyranny and oppression, that human duties and responsibilities be universally taught and accepted by all human beings,

Whereas it is essential to promote the development of friendly relations between nations,

Whereas the peoples of the United Nations have in the Charter reaffirmed their faith in fundamental human duties and responsibilities, in the dignity and worth of the human person, and in the equal duties and responsibilities of men and women and have determined to promote social progress and better standards of life in larger freedom,

Whereas member states have pledged themselves to achieve, in co-operation with the United Nations, the promotion of universal respect for and observance of human duties and fundamental responsibilities, Whereas a common understanding of these duties and responsibilities is of the greatest importance for the full realization of this pledge,

Now, Therefore.

The General Assembly,

Proclaims this Universal Declaration of Human Duties and Responsibilities as a common standard of achievement for all peoples and all nations, to the end that every individual and every organ of society, keeping this declaration constantly in mind, shall strive by teaching and education to promote respect for these duties and responsibilities, and by progressive measures, national and international, to secure their universal and effective recognition and observance, both among peoples of member states themselves and among the peoples of territories under their jurisdiction.

Article 1
All human beings are born equal in duties and responsibilities. They are endowed with reason and conscience and should act towards one another in a spirit of brotherhood and sisterhood.

Article 2
Everyone is accountable for all the duties and responsibilities set forth in this declaration, without distinction of any kind, such as race, color, sex, language, religion, political or other opinion, nation or social origin, property, birth or other status.

Furthermore, no distinction shall be made on the basis of the political, jurisdiction or international status to which a person belongs, whether it be independent, trust, non-self-governing or under any other limitation of sovereignty.

Article 3
Everyone is responsible to the Earth, that is our one and only planet, and has certain obligations that must be met.

Article 4
Everyone is responsible to their fellows, that is each and all members of the human race.

Article 5
Everyone is responsible for their offspring, and must teach their offspring those fundamental truths held to be self-evident, that all human beings are responsible to the Earth, their fellows, their offspring, and themselves.

Article 6
Everyone is responsible for their actions on Earth.

Article 7
Everyone is responsible to respect and embrace the four Principles of Humanity as laid out in Articles 3-6. All are equal in their responsibilities and duties to the four Principles of Humanity.

Article 8
It is the duty of everyone to stand up and speak out, and take whatever action necessary, in being responsible for their fellows, for the freedom of thought, conscience and religion; this duty includes the freedom to change their religion or belief, and freedom, either alone or in community with others and in public or private, to manifest their religion or belief, in teaching, practice, worship and observance not contrary to the Principles of Humanity.

Article 9
Everyone has the duty to stand up for freedom of peaceful assembly and association, and freedom of opinion and expression. This includes freedom to hold opinions without interference, and to seek, receive and impart information and ideas through any media and regardless of frontiers not contrary to the Principles of Humanity.

Article 10
It is everyone's duty to take part in the government of their country, in order to be responsible to the four Principles of Humanity.

Article 11
Everyone has the responsibility to work as to their capacity, in order to contribute to the four Principles of Humanity.

Article 12
Everyone must be aware of, and adhere to the four Principles of Humanity, so as to ensure continuation of human civilization.

Article 13
Everyone must use common sense when adhering to the four Principles of Humanity.

Article 14
Everyone has a duty to justice, fairness, and truthfulness in adherence to the four Principles of Humanity.

Article 15
Everyone must exercise fortitude in adherence to the four Principles of Humanity.

Appendix B

My drawing of a human flag—an adult human passing the earth to a child. I would like to see this banner flying over every nation on earth, to celebrate membership in the human race.

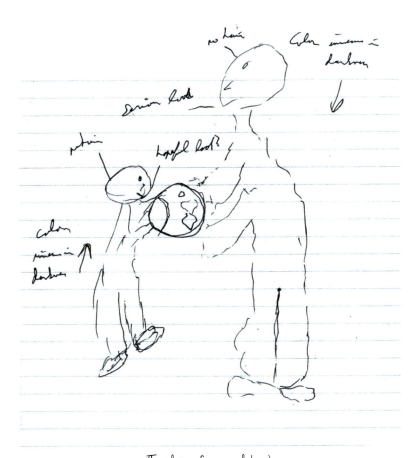

(Translation of my scrawl above)
Color increases in darkness—no hair—hopeful look—serious look—no hair—color increases in darkness

Appendix C

The flag of humanity, celebrating the commonality of being human.

"No matter a person's religion, or lack thereof; no matter a person's skin color, nationality or politics – these differences are as nothing compared to what we have in common...we are human."

Four years, and many versions later,
we have the final version of the flag of humanity.

The flag is two sets of hands, an adult and child's, both in silhouette to represent all the skin colors of the people on earth. The adult hands are passing the earth to the child. Every other flag on earth celebrates a difference - I'm Canadian, Mexican, Yugoslavian etc. This flag does not, it can be flown in all the countries of the earth, by anyone.

Appendix D

Average Daily Expenses

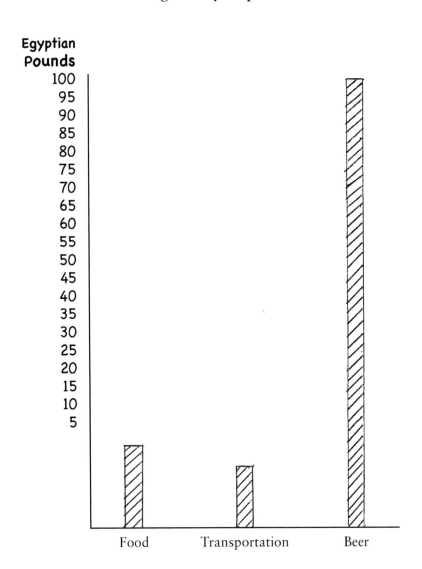

Egyptian Pounds

100
95
90
85
80
75
70
65
60
55
50
45
40
35
30
25
20
15
10
5

Food   Transportation   Beer

Epilogue

I returned to Egypt shortly after the revolution, against the advice of many friends. Once again, the Doubt was hanging over my head. Ohhh, that bitch!

It was a negotiation with my wife to get away, and I only had three weeks.

One friend of mine suggested that sometimes you can't go back, things are never the same. People I thought were nice, may prove not to be very nice at all. Friends may not be friends. Perhaps my experience was unique, and simply could not be repeated. Perhaps I would be killed. Even my local Member of Parliament, who I ran against twice, warned me to stay away.

As I approached the Sphinx Gate the first day of my return, I saw Entrance Ali, and we instantly recognized each other. What two years ago was a crowd jostling to get through the one small metal detector was just me this morning. Ali was clearly depressed. I promised him whiskey.

"Maybe instead of whiskey, you give me the money, for my family," he said, clearly uncomfortable saying it. I do not know how these people are living, with tourism nose-diving as it has.

Once inside, I stood looking at the Sphinx, and the devastation to the tourism industry in Egypt, caused by uncertainty in the wake of the revolution, was eerily apparent. There was nobody around.

Two years ago, thousands upon thousands of people came to the Giza Plateau to see the Great Pyramids and Sphinx, every day. The wind would howl 40-50 miles an hour, sand whipping through the air such that if you stood by one pyramid, you could not see another, and still they came. The mercury would rise over 40 degrees Celsius, sun beating down until you wanted to remove your skin, and still they came. Not now.

Now they are afraid.

But now is the time for people of the world to visit Egypt, for both the pleasure and fascination of seeing first-hand the antiquities of this cradle of human civilization, and to demonstrate support for the Egyptian revolution by spending money within

Egypt's borders when it is most needed. Now. Those who cheered on the near-bloodless revolution, need to keep cheering, and the best way to do that is to visit the country. Who doesn't want to go to Egypt once in their lifetime?

I walked around the right side of the Sphinx, wondering where to begin. The terrain had changed. More excavation was underway on the plateau, as the never-ending discoveries maintained their steady pace. An Egyptian archeologist once told me, if you dig in Egypt, you will find something. It does not matter where you dig.

I was awestruck by the emptiness, the solitude. It made me feel lonely, lonely for those 40 days two years ago, when every day I waded through thousands of tourists, foreign and domestic, to do my work. I thought perhaps I should just go home, what was the point? But, life has taught me to ignore myself sometimes, particularly that bad part of my brain that always thinks the worst, so I rounded the Sphinx Temple, walked through the ruins of the Valley Temple of Khafre and took off my backpack.

I looked at the profile of the Sphinx through the iron fence that surrounds the colossus. Two years ago, the fence was lined with Egyptian vendors selling their wares to the tourists inside. Not now. There was not a single vendor or tourist visible that morning.

What am I doing here? I thought once more. (Will this Doubt never end?)

Then, pragmatically, *Oh well, I'm here. I came all this way, I might as well get to work.*

I put my work gloves on and pulled a garbage bag from my pack, questioning myself again as I fluffed it open. Then, as I bent down to pick up a piece of trash, my very first piece of trash after two years, I heard the voice of an angel.

"Oh, Canada!" shouted a young Egyptian girl from inside the fence. *"You came back!"*

I looked up. She was one of hundreds of children that were selling trinkets here two years ago. I clutched my heart and looked to the sky, if ever there was a message from the heavens to obliterate the Doubt...

Much happened between that event and my last day there, and that will appear in written form later, whether anyone is interested in reading about it ... I don't know. I would like to recount an incident that occurred my last day picking trash on my return visit.

I was doing my thing near the Mena House Gate, when an Egyptian tour bus driver, sitting on the steps to his bus, asked the now familiar question.

"Why?" he asked me, shrugging his shoulders and flicking his left hand that held a cigarette palm upward, nonverbally asking the same question.

I was not in the mood for the long explanation. "I believe in the embrace...force for good...my way to show...Egypt because...cradle of civilization...yada...yada...yada..."

Instead...

"Because I love you," I said, before I even thought about it. "I love everybody." I waved my arm to indicate both literally the people in our vicinity, and figuratively everyone on earth.

"I love you too," he said, smiling.

I was drinking with a Gypsy at Hannah Flanagan's, an Irish pub in Hendersonville, and I recounted this story.

"Is that enough?" I asked her when I was done.

"Yes," was the instant and unequivocal response.

Perhaps it is.